TRAVEL AND TRANSFORMATION

Current Developments in the Geographies of Leisure and Tourism

Series Editors:

Jan Mosedale, University of Applied Sciences HTW Chur, Switzerland and **Caroline Scarles**, University of Surrey, UK in association with the Geographies of Leisure and Tourism Research Group of the Royal Geographical Society (with the Institute of British Geographers).

Tourism and leisure exist within an inherently dynamic, fluid and complex world and are therefore inherently interdisciplinary. Recognising the role of tourism and leisure in advancing debates within the social sciences, this book series, is open to contributions from cognate social science disciplines that inform geographical thought about tourism and leisure. Produced in association with the Geographies of Leisure and Tourism Research Group of the Royal Geographical Society (with the Institute of British Geographers), this series highlights and promotes cutting-edge developments and research in this field. Contributions are of a high international standard and provide theoretically-informed empirical content to facilitate the development of new research agendas in the field of tourism and leisure research. In general, the series seeks to promote academic contributions that advance contemporary debates that challenge and stimulate further discussion and research both within the fields of tourism and leisure and the wider realms of the social sciences.

Other titles in the series:

Travel and Imagination
Edited by Garth Lean, Russell Staiff and Emma Waterton

Lifestyle Mobilities
Intersections of Travel, Leisure and Migration
Edited by Tara Duncan, Scott A. Cohen and Maria Thulemark

Mediating the Tourist Experience
From Brochures to Virtual Encounters
Edited by Jo-Anne Lester and Caroline Scarles

Travel, Tourism and Art
Edited by Tijana Rakić and Jo-Anne Lester

Travel and Transformation

GARTH LEAN, RUSSELL STAIFF and EMMA WATERTON
University of Western Sydney, Australia

Routledge
Taylor & Francis Group

LONDON AND NEW YORK

First published 2014 by Ashgate Publishing

2 Park Square, Milton Park, Abingdon, Oxon OX14 4RN
711 Third Avenue, New York, NY 10017, USA

Routledge is an imprint of the Taylor & Francis Group, an informa business

First issued in paperback 2016

British Library Cataloguing in Publication Data
A catalogue record for this book is available from the British Library

The Library of Congress has cataloged the printed edition as follows:
Travel and transformation / edited by Garth Lean, Russell Staiff and Emma Waterton.
    pages cm. -- (Current developments in the geographies of leisure and tourism)
  Includes bibliographical references and index.
  ISBN 978-1-4094-6763-2 (hardback)
1. Travel--Psychological aspects. 2. Tourism--Psychological aspects.
3. Self-actualization (Psychology) I. Lean, Garth, author, editor of compilation.
II. Staiff, Russell, author, editor of compilation. III. Waterton, Emma, author, editor of compilation.

  G155.A1.T6564 2014
  910'.019--dc23

                                                                    2014003374

ISBN 978-1-4094-6763-2 (hbk)
ISBN 978-1-138-27017-6 (pbk)

Contents

List of Figures

Notes on Contributors

Fiona Allon is Australian Research Council (ARC) Future Fellow and Senior Lecturer in the Department of Gender and Cultural Studies at the University of Sydney. Her research on independent travel and travellers (backpackers and working holiday makers) has been published in the journals *Space & Culture*, *Mobilities* and *Population, Space and Place*. Her current research focuses on working holiday makers and labour within the context of global mobilities.

Jon Anderson is a senior lecturer in Human Geography in the School of Planning and Geography, Cardiff University, UK. His research focuses on the relations between culture, place and identity. He is particularly interested in the geographies, politics and practices that such relations produce. Jon has published widely in the fields of environmental action, culture and qualitative methodology. His publications include *Understanding Cultural Geography: Places and Traces* (2010) and *Water Worlds: Human Geographies of the Ocean* (with Kimberley Peters, 2014). Further information on his work can be found at www.spatialmanifesto.com.

Janice Baker is a Lecturer in the School of Media, Culture and Creative Arts at Curtin University, Western Australia. Previously an art curator, her research explores 'difference' and 'inclusion' in the theories, histories, and critiques of museology. Her book on transformation and fictional representations of cultural artefacts in cinema is forthcoming (Ashgate 2015).

David Bell is a critical human geographer. He has researched and written on sexual geographies, food and hospitality, cultural policy, and science and technology. He is currently Head of the School of Geography at the University of Leeds, UK.

Leila Dawney is a cultural geographer based at the University of Brighton, UK. Her research interests include geographies of affect and embodied practice, performance and landscape, Spinoza and new materialist theory, and the relationship between authority and community. She is a member of the Authority Research Network and is currently working to develop research on landscapes of authority and neoliberal subjectivities. She has written a number of essays and articles on space, politics and affect, and is editing a book on the idea of the commons.

Kathryn Erskine is a PhD student at the School of Planning and Geography at Cardiff University, Wales. Her research interests include identity, place formation, global travel and backpacking, with a specific focus on the mobilities of the lifestyle traveller.

Ruth Holliday is Professor of Gender and Culture at the University of Leeds. Her research centres on the social and cultural use of aesthetics, specifically as it relates to both bodies and material culture. She has published widely in the area of cosmetic surgery studies exploring social class and surgery: 'Cosmetic surgery as false beauty', *Feminist Theory* (2006) with Jacqueline Sanchez Taylor; men's experiences of surgery: 'Man made plastic', *Journal of Consumer Culture* (2007) with Allie Cairnie; and 'race' and surgery: 'Gender, globalisation and aesthetic surgery in South Korea', *Body and Society* (2012). She is also co-author with Tracey Potts of *Kitsch! Cultural Politics and Taste* (2012) published by Manchester University Press.

Meredith Jones is a media and cultural studies scholar at the University of Technology, Sydney. She has written extensively on feminism and the body, cosmetic surgery, and visual cultures. One of the pioneers of Cosmetic Surgery Studies, Meredith is the author of *Skintight: An Anatomy of Cosmetic Surgery* (Berg 2008) and *Cosmetic Surgery: A Feminist Primer* (Ashgate 2009, co-written with Cressida Heyes). She is also the co-founder (with award-winning designer Suzanne Boccalatte) of the innovative Trunk books series, comprising *Hair* (2009) and *Blood* (2013) with *Breath* planned for 2014.

Maria Koleth is a PhD candidate at the University of Sydney. Her research focuses on popular practices of third world development, such as volunteer tourism, and their implications for development ethics.

Garth Lean is a researcher and teacher in the School of Social Sciences and Psychology at the University of Western Sydney. He holds an applied science degree in environmental management and tourism, an honours degree in tourism management and an interdisciplinary PhD in travel/tourism. Garth has also worked in tourism planning and marketing with local and state governments. His research interests include: travel, tourism, mobile identities, imagination, transformation, cultural heritage, visual methods, online research, the alternative presentation of travel and tourism research and multicultural education. He has published a variety of papers on travel, along with the edited volume *Travel and Imagination* (Ashgate). He is currently developing an edited volume titled *The Poetics of Travel* (Berghahn Books) with Russell Staiff and Emma Waterton, and the sole authored book *Transformative Travel* (CABI). He is a member of the Geographies of Leisure and Tourism Research Group with the Royal Geographical Society.

Bianca Leggett is a researcher and visiting lecturer in the English and Humanities department at Birkbeck and in Media and Performing Arts at Middlesex University. Her research looks into questions of English national identity and emergent modes of cosmopolitan belonging in contemporary travel fiction. She is working on a monograph based on her doctoral research entitled *Englishness Elsewhere*. She has published on the subject of metanarrative in the fiction of Julian Barnes, self-fashioning and cosmopolitanism in Black British travel narratives and the depiction of 'Brits abroad' in *All Hail the New Puritans*. She was the co-convener of the symposium *Twenty-First Century British Fiction* and is the co-editor of a forthcoming essay collection of the same name.

Lynda Mannik is a visiting assistant professor in cultural anthropology at Trent University. Her publications include: *Canadian Indian Cowboys in Australia: Representation, Rodeo and the RCMP at the Royal Easter Show, 1939* (2006) and a co-edited volume titled, *Reclaiming Canadian Bodies: Representation and Visual Media* (2014). The chapter for this collection was inspired by memories recalled during interviews with Estonian refugees that was part of the research for her recently published book, *Photography, Memory and Refugee Identity: The Voyage of the S.S. Walnut, 1948* (2013). She has also contributed to *Visual Studies* and *Memory Studies*. One of her favourite hobbies is taking photographs while hiking and biking around Canada and afar.

Amie Matthews is a lecturer at the University of Western Sydney, Australia where she teaches in sociology and tourism and heritage studies. Amie has conducted extensive ethnographic research into the backpacking culture and her research interests include youth travel; tourism impacts; tourism, the media and the tourist imaginary; responsible tourism and tourist ethics.

Drew Ninnis is a University House Scholar at the Australian National University, and is currently completing a PhD in philosophy on the work of Michel Foucault. In particular, Drew's work focuses on recent philosophical attempts to secure a scientific foundation for psychiatry, and the core philosophical problems that this endeavour encounters. As part of this project he has written on a wide range of thinkers including controversial figures such as R.D. Laing, Thomas Szasz and Ian Hacking, as well as key figures in the philosophy of science. He has previously written on topics such as the madness and subjectivity in the writing of Robert Musil. He has also presented in international forums on radical theories of selfhood, as well as the concept of critique in Nietzsche, Deleuze and Foucault. Drew's interest in travel and transformation arises from his own desire to one day travel to the holy mountain of Mount Kailash, as well as the narratives of writers such as Colin Thubron who have made the journey.

Kimberley Peters is a lecturer in Human Geography at Aberystwyth University, UK. Her research focuses on the intersections between place, mobility, material culture and the more-than-human, most recently in the context of the sea. Kimberley's work has been published in journals including *Area, Tourism*

Geographies and *Environment and Planning A*. She is co-editor of the volume *Water Worlds: Human Geographies of the Ocean* (Ashgate).

Elspeth Probyn is Professor of Gender and Cultural Studies at the University of Sydney, as well as adjunct Professor of Cultural Geography at the University of Western Australia, and adjunct Research Professor at the University of South Australia. She has taught media, cultural studies and sociology at universities in Canada and the USA, and has held several prestigious visiting appointments around the world. Her work has helped to establish several new areas of scholarship – from embodied research methods to cultural studies of food. Professor Probyn is the author of several groundbreaking monographs and over a hundred articles and chapters across the fields of gender, media, and cultural studies, philosophy, cultural geography, anthropology and critical psychology.

Sarah Rodigari is a Sydney based artist working across mediums to create performances and installations. Her work is responsive and context specific, focusing on history, socio-political engagement, chance encounters, failure and the absurd. Her structures are varied including the lecture, duration, dialogue and improvisation. Rodigari has presented work nationally and internationally including: Museum of Contemporary Art (Sydney, Australia), Melbourne International Arts Festival, South Project (Yogyakarta), PACT Zollverein (Germany), Centre for Contemporary Art (Glasgow), The National Review of Live Art (UK), Anti-Contemporary Arts Festival (Finland), The Bell Street Project (Vienna) and Good Children (New Orleans). Sarah contributes writing to *Realtime*, *Runway Magazine*, and the *Live Art List Australia*. In 2011 Sarah presented the paper 'A calm centre in the heart of chaos' at Open Engagement, a symposium on socially engaged art, in Portland (USA). Sarah has a BA (Hons) in Sociology (University of New South Wales), Masters in Fine Art (RMIT) and is a current PhD candidate in Creative Arts (University of Wollongong).

Jacqueline Sanchez Taylor is a sociologist who has undertaken extensive international ethnographic and qualitative research on sex tourism and cosmetic surgery. Her research on the market for cosmetic surgery builds on her research on sex tourism and focuses on theoretical questions about the intersections of class, gender, race, embodiment and how economic and social structures reinforce and reproduce inequalities and social meanings attached to consuming cosmetic surgery.

Rehnuma Sazzad has recently completed her PhD on Literary and Cultural Studies at Nottingham Trent University. Her thesis was based on Edward Said, Mahmoud Darwish, and some other foremost Middle Eastern intellectuals. She has written a variety of papers on intellectuals from the region including Said, Darwish, Naguib Mahfouz, Leila Ahmed, Youssef Chahine, Mona Hatoum, Nawal El Saadawi and Lisa Suhair Majaj. She has published pieces on the Bangladeshi-

American filmmakers Tareque and Catherine Masud, and the Indian auteur Satyajit Ray. Her research interests are now moving towards South Asian history and literary creations. She aims to strengthen a cultural dialogue between the Middle Eastern and South Asian regions.

Russell Staiff holds a doctorate in art history from the University of Melbourne and is an adjunct fellow in the cultural heritage and tourism program within the School of Social Sciences, University of Western Sydney. He researches the interface between cultural heritage, tourism and communities with a special focus on Southeast Asia and is currently working on a book on heritage and the cinema. He has recently co-edited a volume on *Heritage and Tourism* for Routledge and his monograph, *Re-Imagining Heritage Interpretation: Enchanting the Past/ Future*, was published by Ashgate in early 2014.

Shannon Walsh is a filmmaker and assistant professor at the School of Creative Media, City University Hong Kong. Her first feature documentary, *H2Oil*, was recognised by the Montreal Mirror as one of the top 10 independent documentaries of 2009 for its urgent and poignant telling of the human and environmental devastation caused by Canada's tar sands. In 2011, her film *St-Henri, the 26th of August*, brought 16 filmmakers to uncover the complexity and contradictions of everyday life in a Montreal neighbourhood. *Jeppe on a Friday*, her second neighbourhood documentary co-directed with Arya Lalloo, traces the lives of five diverse people in Johannesburg's inner-city. Underlying all of her work is a focus on social justice and collaboration. Walsh received a PhD from McGill University in 2010 in Anthropology and Education, and a post-doc in the South African Research Chair in Social Change at the University of Johannesburg in 2013.

Emma Waterton is based at the University of Western Sydney, in the Institute for Culture and Society. Her interests include: unpacking the discursive constructions of 'heritage'; explorations of tourism, heritage and affect; thanatourism; visuality; and explorations of innovative methodologies. She has over 50 publications, including one authored (*Politics, Policy and the Discourses of Heritage in Britain* 2010) and two co-authored monographs (*Heritage, Communities and Archaeology*, with Laurajane Smith, 2009 and *The Semiotics of Heritage Tourism*, with Steve Watson, 2014), ten co-edited volumes and four guest edited special issues. She has served on the Editorial Board for Sociology (2008–2010), and is currently part of the Editorial Board for the *Journal of Heritage Tourism* (2012–ongoing) and the *International Journal of Heritage Studies* (2013–ongoing). She was Assistant Editor for the *International Journal of Heritage Studies* from 2009 to 2013.

Acknowledgements

It goes without saying that an edited collection is only possible with the time and effort of its contributors. Participation in such a volume invariably requires the weathering of a number of delays and editorial requests, and we are most grateful for the speed, generosity and good humour shown by our authors. We look forward to working with them again on future projects.

We would also like to name and thank, in no particular order, those who helped guide this project from its inception to its completion. In particular, we are grateful for the support provided by Jan Mosedale and Carolyn Scarles, Series Editors of the Current Developments in the Geographies of Leisure and Tourism series within which this volume finds its place. We are grateful, too, for the institutional support we have received from both the Geographies of Leisure and Tourism Research Group of the Royal Geographical Society and the School of Social Sciences and Psychology at the University of Western Sydney. Finally, we extend our appreciation to Katy Crossan, our Commissioning Editor at Ashgate, for her continuous advice and support, her prompt and patient replies to our emails, and her endless accommodation of our requests.

Any errors or omissions included within are ours alone.

Prelude

Flensed

Janice Baker

Some people smell flesh here.

I'm on a guided tour of Whale World Albany, an industrial museum at the site of a once operational whaling station. The script the guide follows is mostly one of adventure and industry, a story of progress silenced by the space itself, the last whaling station in Australia.

The site resonates with its own eloquence; however layers of human emotion mask an unsettled intensity. These emotions communicate a collective memory of whaling presented in sheds converted to photo galleries, and in texts and audio recordings that tell of male camaraderie, fortitude and skill. The memory has a tenacious hold. For when the station closed, the Albany fishermen who worked here from 1952 until whaling was banned in 1978 identified themselves as a lost race.

They built the station on flat granite rock that slopes into Frenchman Bay, part of King George Sound on the southern coast of Western Australia. It looks more tumbled up than carefully planned, a motley bunch of structures flimsy in the ancient rock landscape. Located a 20-minute drive from Albany, a port and the regional centre of an often economically depressed area, the oil from the Cheynes Beach Whaling Company's station was the region's gold.

Mostly the station rendered Sperm Whales, Humpbacks and Southern Right Whales to lubricant. Using flensing tools, men expertly peeled the skin from whales in wide and bloody blankets. The tools of their trade were crafted to perfection through generations of skinning. Today these artefacts are labelled and displayed alongside photos that reveal their purpose. The skin they flensed was precious – skin on the chest of *Balaena glacialis* alone is 40 centimetres thick and holds barrels of oil.

The grime from flensing spilled into the water and crimson waves lapped the wooden deck throughout the whaling season. Tourists and locals parked on a dirt road above the station to check out the carnage. Often a Holden or two could be seen up there – children squealing, flies swarming, Mum pouring cordial. Dad with binoculars focused on the flensing deck.

By the time the station closed there were no live whales to admire in the Bay or the Sound or along the southern coast. No living Humpbacks or Southern Rights or Pygmy Blues. No False Killer Whales. No *Balaenopteridae megaptera* swimming on their backs, flippers akimbo, singing and playing.

At the height of the whaling season about 120 men worked the station – fishermen and abattoir workers from the local meatworks but also students, bikies and drifters. It was hard-earned money particularly given the grime, the cold and the constant wet. A chill wind blows from the Antarctic. The local Noongah people call the area Kinjarling – place of rain. The worst thing was the appalling stench.

The stench was partly why the station was built outside Albany, though when the wind blew through town so did the smell. Deep, strong and fatty, gagging the throat. Workers couldn't scrub it from their skin, whale skin became their skin, and they sat in their own bar at the King George so as not to offend. Here they are, grinning at the camera huddled in a makeshift corner beside a boiler, beanies pulled down over their ears, trying to keep out the chill. They sit on wooden planks grasping enamel mugs of coffee through woollen mittens.

I'm standing in the open air on the main flensing deck. The guide points out a flat granite island in the Bay, close to shore – a convenient morgue where the station's whalers chained their daily kill. A kill that attracted sharks, an event that attracted the onlookers with binoculars. An event not unlike a scene described by Ishmael in *Moby Dick* after whale cuttings were tossed over the side of the *Pequod* – a shark massacre, a frenzy of desire with sharks snapping at each other till their own bodies end up swallowed.

Whale sightings in the region continue to increase, says the guide, though sharks are now threatened – too many fins used in soup. She follows this fact by activating an electronic device on her belt and an audio recording echoes a jolly narrative through loudspeakers – a sea shanty, chains clunking, gulls squawking, shouts of whalemen at work and a bellow from the mast-head: 'Thar she blows'!

The shore station relied on whale chasing ships to deliver them regular whales. As the whale population declined, so did the delivery, and each season the whale chasers had to hunt farther out in the Southern Ocean. One of the ships, the *Cheynes IV*, is permanently moored today at the Museum. Children clamber about the cramped vessel playing at pirates, poking faces through portholes and shimmying across the narrow catwalks that run high above the deck. An audio recording intermittently blasts out a mini-drama to delight them – a whaleman who has spotted a whale shouts to the crew and a harpooner responds ready to fire at the creature which he does with a noisy BANG.

Early each morning during the whaling season, a spotter plane would set off from Albany aerodrome to assist the whale chasers. The whales followed the deep sea channels of their traditional migration route from feeding grounds in Antarctica to breed in the waters of King George Sound. The mammals were harpooned when they surfaced for air. The harpoon grenade held explosive powder, and was attached to a line that unwound to stretch almost a kilometre. Until it died, the wounded whale pulled the ship through all kinds of seas.

From the *Pequod*'s masthead, a gigantic Sperm Whale is spotted lolling in the water ahead like the capsized hull of a frigate. The crew quietly lower rowboats and set after the beast. A harpoon is hurled by Tashtego and the vibrating line whooshes … striking the beast. All hands begin pulling the boat at the same time the boat is pulled by the stricken whale. A red tide pours from the monster and a crimson pond in the sea reflects into excited faces ... the men glow to each other. Alongside the whale now, they churn lances deep into the mammal and after cracking, agonising respirations and clotted gore spurting from its spout-hole, the creature's heart bursts.

Once the whale's outer skin was flensed on the lower deck of the Albany station, the chained whale was dragged by a mechanical winch up a ramp to a second deck. Here a sharp-toothed metal saw cut off the whale's head. The tool was see-sawed by two men, one at each end like cutting down a tree. Once 'decapitated', the beast was hung in the open on a giant hook while cut into strips that fell about the floor. The pieces of blubber were cut small enough to be pushed through holes that drop into large boiling vats below that boil the meat to pulp and liquid.

Photographs show school children and their teachers experiencing local industry in action. Standing behind a viewing rail they watch men, who were more often than not their fathers, uncles, brothers or cousins, in spiked boots drenched in blood and blubber atop a whale. They stand expert at their dangerous work by the pungent sea; proud astride their whale, rubber boots above their knees, black stubby footy shorts, chopping tools in their hands. How come more were not injured? Perhaps they were but no one told.

Aboard the *Pequod*, Tashtego loses his footing and topples into a whale corpse slung to the side of the ship. He nearly drowns; which in the end happens anyway. The crew succumb to Captain Ahab's madness, and in a collective oath of revenge his feud becomes theirs. Seeking vengeance, Moby Dick the great white whale repeatedly rams the vessel and all the crew perish. All except Ishmael who is sucked, round and round, by the sinking ship's whirlpool, but the whirl subsides to a creamy pool and he manages to cling to a coffin that bobs to the surface.

So too, Albany fishermen and tourists are regularly lost. Washed out to sea by king waves or sucked into wave-worn blowholes.

Ishmael dwells on the manifold mistakes made throughout history in representing whales; an error arising because the living whale has never floated himself for his portrait. As he puts it: 'Though elephants have stood for their full lengths, the living Leviathan has never yet done so.' He concludes that the only way precisely to see a whale is to go a-whaling, an adventure with merit apart from the considerable risk of being 'eternally stove and sunk' (Melville 1992: 288–9).

Today, a shop at the entrance to the Museum sells books, maps, t-shirts and piles of cheap trinkets including staplers with whales glued into transparent plastic. I buy a water dome for my collection, the miniature whale see-saws up and down as I jiggle the souvenir. Much of the merchandise boasts the Museum's logo – a whale grimacing through sharp teeth, poised to fire a harpoon. Next to the shop is the Whaler's Galley Café Restaurant with a spectacular view of the Bay. Between the shop/cafe and the industrial site there's a picnic area and a playground with fibreglass whales that kids can swing from, or slide down the inside of (so says the Museum brochure). No one seems to be utilising the BBQ facilities or conveniently positioned 'whale tables'.

The tour ends and I wander the site alone. I'm in a large engineering workshop with a massive skeleton that has been trussed and glued; its enormous old bones are bleached and yellowed. The label says this whale died on 20 November 1978, the last whale killed on the last day of whaling in Australia. Its oil was pumped into one of several oil silos and then piped to a sea tanker in the Bay. And so the whale was returned to the ocean as lubricant, stored in an iron hulk that churned through the water with a chugging sensed below in the sea channels where once it swam. Such was the fate of over 16,000 whales.

The oil silos today are converted to cinemas. In one silo, I climb metal steps that wind around the inner wall to a raised viewing platform. Though scrubbed clean the brownish tin walls exude a patent oiliness that I sense through my skin. I am inside the whale; this silo was filled with whale oil for decades. In this disembodied space, once I would have drowned. The lighting is dimmed, and a screen flickers below on the floor. A film about whales begins. The images floating on the ground draw me into a deep sea channel, and I slip into the undulation with the living sea creatures ... undrowned, I am a fish ...

As I bus with the tour group back to town I glimpse the island morgue in the Bay. I suppose today it's more accurately a memorial rather than a mortuary. I dwell on my time at Whale World not in terms of an imaginary identification with whales but something else, some other re-composition that has to do with the idea of the indomitable human being disgraced. This is the eloquence of the nonhuman things we gather in our museums. No matter the stories and emotions we give to the things we collect, they reassemble us with their own expression, they hold the potential to undo us by revealing that the way to become more human is to become less so.

* * *

I'm in Berlin for three days. It's warm and there's a vague odour from the sewers that I find oddly intoxicating. I turn into Ebertstrasse. In front of me stretch thousands of concrete stelai lined into geometric rows, each artefact smooth and unmarked. The Memorial to the Murdered Jews of Europe encompasses an entire street block of the city.

I enter between two rows that descend gradually. The artefacts become taller until dense and close around me. Not a labyrinth or maze because I can see outside, but I'm unsure where to turn in the new terrain; a space out of time. Other people are passing through, they're wending their way to the other side and I'm glad not to be alone.

Beneath the Kubrick-like blocks an underground memorial has been carefully engineered; a consecrated bunker, part of the vast underworld beneath Berlin. I read the policies of Nazi extermination and move on. The walls have long friezes listing numbers of dead, and maps that outline sites of persecution, deportation routes and death marches, places of mass executions and camps. All displayed in crepuscular lighting.

Adolf Hitler's bunker is near here; where he ordered his generals to raze what was left of Berlin, where he ate his last vegan meal, where Frau Goebbels fed her six children cyanide. The site of the Führerbunker is unmarked for its fascination would be hard to contain and this city of excesses is careful now, mindful of careless desires.

From the memorial I walk through the city to the Reichstag. The glass dome encasing the three-levelled roof terrace provides an exhilarating view across the sky above Berlin. A permanent display of photos circles the first level. The images reflect the collective memory that measures everything in this city. The Third Reich is presented as a chronological history across the photos while below, in the building's Chambers, sits the reunified German Bundestag. The pictures show grim-faced members of the doomed Weimer Government, Goering as a gloating Reichstag President, SA Brownshirts occupying a large block of the Chamber. And so a tyranny was legislated beneath my feet. I stand in a fractured moment in the sky, in a re-democratised space; in a cupola of glass where the fragility of peace is tangible.

Across the sky, defiant and tall, is the Siegessäule; Berlin's Victory Column with the Greek Goddess Viktoria strident at the top. In my Berlin snow dome, she's lost some of her glitter, a minuscule figure. Actually she looks more like a devil than a God, the helmety crown on her head resembles a set of horns. I set her by the computer next to my Albany whale. I like to configure my snow domes into my thinking; they shrink huge notions to a more manageable size (see Figure P.1).

Figure P.1 A cleansed distance. My souvenirs from Berlin and Whale World Albany

Source: Photograph Simon Peter Fox, Deakin University.

Walter Benjamin declared the Victory Column a funerary emblem of history, a celebration of Prussian militarism. As a child he watched Berliners high on the viewing platform, silhouettes against the sky. There are striking images in Wim Wender's film *Wings of Desire* of two angels, Damiel and Cassiel, resting against the monument's golden wings. They are tuned to the incessant babble of the mortal and watch as lives fade … a dying motorcyclist, mothers searching bombed rubble, a falling man. What would Benjamin make of the pair up there observing Cold War Berlin with its Wall and no-way streets? Adults are too blinded by desire to see angels but Benjamin would have seen; it was his way to avoid the common sense of history.

He would have been unsurprised by Sachsenhausen, the Nazi death camp close to Berlin. Sachsenhausen was a blueprint for other Nazi death camps. It was initially devised to take the overflow from Berlin's prisons which were crowded with 'political' prisoners but soon became a model death camp, overseen by Heinrich Himmler. Today the Camp is a memorial and museum.

To reach Sachsenhausen I catch a train from central Berlin to Oranienburg Station and from there it's a short walk. This is the same route taken by perhaps 200,000 prisoners; the precise number remains unknown. The Camp is at the edge of an unremarkable residential district. There's an air of neglect; houses with peeling paint, broken fences and careless gardens though once the area flourished by servicing the Camp as well as the SS and constant visitors who came to observe Himmler's achievement.

My walk from the station collapses time; I'm neither here now nor there then. These streets don't conform to Spielbergian emotions qua *Schindler's List* that I almost expect, perhaps even desire, to feel from memorials to the Holocaust. Here, in this place, is a different intensity. Not the emotional impact of Auschwitz – horror at the vast pile of human hair continuing to grey behind glass, all those names and addresses written by the dead on emptied suitcases, the endless lists and signs of pinpoint organisation. These are impacts I recognise through films, documentaries and literature; a collective memorialisation processed as images already thought. Here in the street, my unsettling has to do with something felt in the present; I only realise later that what I felt was the everydayness of it all.

Sachsenhausen is a cultural artefact – a vast stretch of flat earth with neat rows of low wooden barracks surrounded by brick walls regularly dotted with guard towers. Few of the Camp's smaller items remain, apart from some battered tin mugs, spoons and bottles. Within the inner wall there are tumbles of barbed wire, the remains of a gas chamber and crematorium. Although I expect these objects, I don't expect the incongruities. For on this piece of earth the Nazis strung up lights on the gallows pole to make a Christmas tree. And following the war, Soviet soldiers used the crematorium as a BBQ, stomping in ash.

The Camp guards resided in an outer zone and the buildings where they lived have been converted into exhibition spaces. The exhibits trace community life in the district, there are school photos, sporting trophies, wedding albums, newspaper articles, brochures of cultural events and photos of grinning Hitler youth. Collective desires communicated through families, clubs, congregations and institutions. Without declamation, what is conveyed is that fascism evolves somewhere.

The Camp extends in a triangular configuration; a lonely expanse without the tourist crowds to merge into at Auschwitz or Dachau. It is coloured a desolate European summer brown. The area the Camp covers was once forest at the edge of the district; it was clear-felled by prisoners overseen by the Camp's drunken commandant. There are photos of his marriage to a guard held in the forest in a strange Teutonic ritual. Apparently he was quite mad, even by Nazi standards, and Himmler had him executed for embezzlement.

To augment the pure Aryan, experiments were performed in one of the barracks that served as a pathology 'ward'. Jewish children were brought here from other camps and injected with diseases. Eight-year-old Joseph Liebermann was pumped with hepatitis and observed until he died. He lay on this white tiled slab. The slab with its drainage hole is thoroughly practical. The square tiles that cover it are white and antiseptic. Upon the slab an earlier visitor has placed a red rose that has just begun to wilt.

Beneath the building is a mortuary. A large, cold space, low with wooden arches, reminiscent of a medieval wine cellar. Bodies were trundled down on a simple, hand-pushed wooded cart. Here is the cart; carefully crafted. Perhaps made by a prisoner; or perhaps a replica? Either way I'm bombarded by images of plague victims piled in such carts, of rats and of people taken to be guillotined. All these images lurking somewhere coalesce. I realise quite suddenly that my stoicism is gone and I leave. Nothing will be quite the same again; not that I feel sorrow or fear. These affects are too softly named.

* * *

The first thing I notice about Berlin's Jewish Museum is the zinc-clad façade and windows that recall the slits of a bunker. The second is that the building has no street entrance. It is located on Lindenstrasse but accessed by a staircase from within a stately baroque building. The area was bombed heavily, but somehow the baroque façade survived and in the 1960s was restored to become the Berlin Museum. Daniel Libeskind designed the new Jewish Museum to attach to the nineteenth-century building like a concrete fold. It's actually hard to get a sense of the configuration between the two buildings, where one begins and the other ends, but this seems apt. Neatly framing anything in Berlin involves a host of complexities, part of the weight of memorialisation.

I'm through the electronic security screening and downstairs in a space of underground corridors. Two of the corridors end at oversized concrete voids, the third ascends gradually to culminate in a garden at street level. The corridors are sparse; a vascular system that has been emptied.

The corridors are named Exile, Holocaust and Continuity. At the end of the corridor of Exile a door opens onto a slanting grid of concrete pillars. The tall pillars lean in unison like a windswept grove. Each contains a willow tree; the central tree grows in soil brought from Jerusalem. The site slopes uncomfortably and I walk with a dragging gait; the most familiar of movements has become uncomfortable. This surprises me, and then I'm surprised at being surprised. I'm affected by the weight of my movement, at steps that are outside my usual rhythm, at a movement that requires a new attentiveness.

Along the corridor of Continuity I'm moved by the tenacity of the few items on display – a book, a teapot, a suitcase. These simple items are far from simple. I wonder what they have seen. Their silent eloquence is the witness that I can never be. They have a duration and durability that unsettles my own solidity.

The Holocaust Tower has an unnatural dimension. An attendant opens the heavy steel door and with a small group of strangers I enter the Tower; a dim, narrow space four stories high. The door closes. Someone whispers. The light cannot be discerned clearly. It's not entirely unpleasant, rather it is part of a drama and we are waiting in the wings.

Of course, all along I know we will be released. There is something liturgical about being in this hollow with its too far away light and about sharing its manufacture of intense feeling with strangers. There is a requirement to labour at empathy; the responsibility for memorialisation that weighs this city. But it is not real even if I fully embrace the pretence of being captive. I am captivated. Not forced here by deportation and selected at some bleak industrial railway siding. As I write, much later, the moment remains connected; one of those feelings that linger long after an event is supposedly done.

A second void in the building is occupied by an installation that the artist has intended to be walked across by visitors. Menashe Kadishman has cut 10,000 faces from flat steel and layered the faces to form a carpet between high concrete walls. Each welded face has holes for eyes and a mouth. All these eyes and mouths are open wide in a collective scream that is given expression in the metallic crunch beneath my feet. It is impossible to cross the space quietly; my footsteps grate as a loud, ostentatious movement.

A crossing that takes away my curatorial complacency, wraps it in acid-proof paper, packs it in a solander box and stores it upon a high shelf. Not that the scream is somehow transferred to me, rather the space that is opened is some other connection. The act of walking upon the vulnerable is an act of stopping our ears, of closing our eyes, of avoidance. Here though, right now in the moment I cannot hide. I am watched, by visitors, museum surveillance, by ghosts underfoot. Of course, these are silent witnesses and no one remarks at my loud tread. The whole encounter goes entirely unremarked. But I still recall the grating metal beneath my boots: the sound reassembled me, guarding my words against false witness and complacency.

I leave the underground section of the Museum and venture up a wide staircase to the part of the building that can be seen from the street. As I climb, light flickers through the glass slit windows in the outer wall.

Upstairs is different. Here artefacts of Jewish culture are the main exhibits whereas downstairs the architecture is the object of attention. There's a warmer mood and quite a few people milling around. There are screens and TV monitors and the various technologies sit comfortably amongst the artefacts. I sit down, don headphones and listen to a long interview with a lawyer at the Nuremberg trials who reveals the impact that the unrepentant bombast of Hermann Goering had upon him. Fear is the most important injury, the prosecutor says, and you can tell from his old-man eyes.

Vinyl footsteps are strategically placed on the floor to guide visitors through rooms of exhibits. But I don't feel the need for a clear itinerary. At random I open drawers that contain items pertaining to German Jewish culture and history. Around me are images, maps and portraits. There's quite a lot of text which I scan rather than closely read, though in the process I find myself formulating a chronology. It begins with Jewish people entering Germany with the Roman legions. They become travelling merchants, and flourish in communities along the Rhine, at Speyer, Worms and Mainz. Many communities were wiped out by the Crusaders and the Black Death; they were blamed for the latter. Few survived the Holocaust to remain in Germany, but following the Cold War, the Jewish population started to increase and today there are 200,000 Jewish people living in Germany, mostly from the former USSR and refugees from Africa and the Middle East.

* * *

Walking back to my hotel, I'm struck by the beautiful day, and the warmth on my skin. I'm struck by how thinking bends as we travel, and that encounters with cultural objects have their own intensity to rupture the emotional expectations that keep us circling in the past. In the materiality of places and artefacts so different to our own brief moment in time, the aesthetic and ethical possibilities of new relations, human and nonhuman, can be thought and hence, perhaps, realised.

Reference

Melville, H. 1992. *Moby-Dick or, the Whale*. Penguin Classics.

Chapter 1

Exploring Travel and Transformation

Garth Lean, Russell Staiff and Emma Waterton

Travel has a long association with the idea of transformation, both in terms of the self and social collectives. Some of the earliest surviving works of literature, such as *The Epic of Gilgamesh* ([eighteenth–tenth century BCE] 1972) and Homer's *The Odyssey* ([eighth century BCE] 2004), tell tales of individuals heading off on 'heroic' quests that would strip them of their worldly possessions, status and relationships, bringing them to the bare essentials of being and, consequently, transforming their thinking and behaviours. One need only scan the back-cover blurbs of the travel books at their local book store to see that this trope is still alive and well. Even if we consider pre-recorded history, archaeology and genetic science locate the origin of the human species in East Africa, our ancestors rising to their feet, spreading across the globe and forming diverse social structures and cultures in relationship with the unique contexts in which they found themselves. Physical mobility enabled these social groups to move, and interact, in various ways around the world – to varying degrees of distance, through different modes of travel and with divergent intentions – exploring, 'salvaging', 'saving', invading, pillaging, exploiting, conscripting, conquering, colonising, converting, forming alliances with, studying, learning from, 'educating', 're-educating', 'enlightening', and spreading diseases, languages, beliefs, flora, fauna, genes, cultures, practices, objects (to name only a few limited and vague labels) across, and between, continents in processes that were undeniably transformative for both 'visitor' and 'visited'. Beyond individuals, these collective movements acted to alter and mark spaces, places, landscapes and ecosystems. And of course these places, in all their various stages of alteration, acted upon the individuals, collectives, minds, bodies, life-forms and objects moving through, engaging with and relocating to them, along with those inhabiting (whether 'temporarily' or 'permanently'), in varying ways. As such, our present selves, and social, cultural and ecological landscapes, are indelibly marked by, and entwined in, this complex history of human mobility.

Transformation in the context of contemporary corporeal travel is arguably even more complex. Some commentaries have argued that the world in which we travel offers few of the opportunities for novelty and discovery that were available in past travels; the world has been 'discovered' – it is 'known' and does not afford the same possibility for transformation. It has been contended that people no longer need to travel corporeally and can experience places through literature, visual and Internet media. For others, this itself is a problematic argument because it detracts from the richness of the physical travel experience; the embodied, sensual performances that take place, the unique psychological and physiological reactions triggered by physical, carnal encounter, the altered performances that travel away from familiarity seems to permit and the effects of the plethora of random happenings that may unfold – varying degrees of encounter with mobile, fluid and transforming spaces, places, landscapes, people/s and objects at unique moments in time.

Recent research by one of the editors supports this, arguing that anyone can be transformed by corporeal travel, a phenomenon influenced by a complex array of processes taking place 'before', 'during' and 'after' any given physical travel experience (see Lean 2012a, forthcoming). Drawing upon a movement to position geographical, sociological and cultural thinking within a mobilities paradigm (see Bauman 2000, 2005, Urry 2000, 2007), this work argues that one does not simply move from one physical location to another, varying in discernible degrees of difference to their own, with an eventual return to the place of origin. Instead, one travels as an emotional and sensual *being* that has been travelling (albeit to varying degrees) physically, virtually, imaginatively and communicatively since, before any particular corporeal travel experience. These travels endue an individual with unique, and complex, subjectivities that may be triggered (or not) in all manner of ways throughout a journey. What is more, a traveller is not a static body moving through space. Just as 'before' a journey, they continue to travel in ways that stretch well beyond physical movement, and all of these mobilities feed into a continually changing 'self', shifting in different moments and spaces.

Unprecedented physical mobility, and a greater diversity of cultures on the move than ever before (not to mention non-physical mobilities), has not only increased the likelihood of familiarity, but also the possibility of the 'exotic', both at 'home' and abroad. The ways in which individuals encounter and interact (or do not) with these elements, and the manner in which these various individuals and collectives mark and shape – and are marked and shaped by – the environments and places through which they move, vary *ad infinitum*. Thus, we would argue that an increasingly mobile and fluid world does not limit the potential for transformation through physical travel; rather, it makes it a far more complex, multifaceted and intricate phenomenon to explore.

Given the common association of transformation with travel, it is somewhat surprising that it has remained relatively underexplored and unchallenged, with little in the way of a balanced corpus of academic material surrounding such themes. Instead, much of the literature remains focused upon describing and categorising travel and tourism experiences from a supply-side perspective, and taxonomising travellers on the basis of their level of involvement and interest, often using problematic, and uncritical, assumptions. Occasional forays into theory have generated some important milestone contributions (see Bruner 1991 for example), but there have been few new attempts at a rigorous re-theorisation of the issues. Thus, while threads of research have emerged that take 'transformation' seriously, these have tended to focus upon particular niches – study abroad (see for example: Creamer 2004, Fordham 2005, Stephenson 1999), backpacking (see for example: Matthews 2007, Noy 2004a, 2004b), volunteer tourism (see for example: Broad 2003, Matthews 2008, Wearing et al. 2008), nature-based recreation (see for example: Beaumont 2001, Charters 1996, Ross and Wall 1999) and so forth. Among many other things, research looking at these themes has argued that travel can promote learning (for example, of languages, cultures, history, religions and places; see for example: Forgues 2005, Immetman and Schneider 1998, Roberson 2002, 2003), cross-cultural understanding and peace (see for example: Blanchard and Higgins-Desbiolles 2013, D'Amore 1988a, 1988b, Litvin 1998, 2003, Moufakkir and Kelly 2010, Pizam 1996, Pizam et al. 1991, Var and Ap 2001), an awareness of various global issues (for example, poverty, conflicts, migration, trade and power imbalances; see for example: Butcher and Smith 2010, Palacios 2010, Salazar 2002, 2004), environmental consciousness and sustainability ideals (see for example: Beaumont 2001, Charters 1996, Lean 2009, Ross and Wall 1999) and wellness (see for example: Kottler 1997, 2002, 2003, Kottler and Montgomery 2000). It is also argued that these momentary insights can have long-term attitudinal and behavioural implications (Kottler 1997, Lean 2009, 2012b).

Much of the scholarship conducted on this topic to date presents tourism and travel in an overly positive light. In fact, Pritchard et al. (2011: 941–2) write that the position taken by scholars purporting to the transformative benefits of tourism, which 'combines co-transformative learning and action', represents the emergence of an 'academy of hope' (this article was subsequently reworked as the introduction for Reisinger (2013)). It is important to acknowledge, however, that this 'positive vision' is contested. Some argue that travel simply reinforces an existing way of seeing and acting in (and on) the world, supporting prejudices, misguided/'false' representations and, in the case of travel from developed to less developed nations, the continuation of colonial relations (Bruner 1991, 2005, Hall and Tucker 2004, Tucker and Akama 2009). Research and anecdotes also suggest that any 'positive' effects that may be delivered by tourism and travel are often only temporary, falling by the wayside as more pertinent concerns capture one's attention upon return (Lean 2009, Salazar 2002, 2004). This overemphasis on the benefits of tourism/travel arises from a failure to adequately acknowledge the negative impacts, the power imbalances between those who benefit, and those who do not, including other facets like who has the right to access tourism/travel and who determines what constitutes a 'positive' transformation. There is also a reluctance to look at the broader landscape of non-leisurely physical mobilities (working abroad, migration, refugees, forced migration) and their intersections and commonalities with tourism. There is a significant risk that comes with framing tourism as a panacea – and this has been explored extensively over the last two decades, and should not be forgotten.

Given the arguments presented above, this volume calls for an extensive reinvigoration of the scholarship examining transformation through physical travel, with the aim of developing a new, wide ranging canon of work investigating travel and transformation. This is a key theme in the conceptualisation of tourism, travel and mobilities, and it is important that a body of scholarship is developed that explores it in its full complexity. We know that travel can be transformative: as highlighted above, the belief that it can act as an agent of change which broadens the mind, among other transformative qualities, stretches back to the earliest recorded stories and literature (Leed 1991). Yet, there seems to be a number of problematic assumptions embedded within that belief, especially those concerning who can be transformed, the circumstances in which transformation/change can, or cannot, occur, the types of transformation that can, and cannot, be brought about and what constitutes the very nature of travel itself. Many of these assumptions abide by an out-dated paradigm of tourism/travel research that has a modernist fascination with developing typologies and conceptualising travel as movement between static, unchanging locations in a formulaic and predictable manner. In addition, it often frames tourism and travel as a process that is the antithesis to one's 'everyday existence' (see Lean 2012a: 153; see also Mavrič and Urry 2009).

With this in mind, we see it as important that the academy begins to draw upon new and emerging debates not only within tourism studies, but cognate fields such as geography, heritage studies and cultural studies, to name but a few, in order to adequately explore not only travel and transformation but travel and tourism more broadly (see Franklin 2007, Franklin and Crang 2001, Robinson and Jamal 2009). For example, the importation of a Mobilities paradigm into the field has helped to highlight the redundancy of many earlier attempts at touristic enquiry. Now, more than ever, we are aware of the richness and complexity of such a state of continual travel – the ways in which people move and do not move, separate from and continue connections, the ways in which travel and transformation are represented and storied, and subsequently distributed, the ways in which spaces, places, individuals, minds and bodies are marked and transformed, and continue to be shifted through ongoing mobilities, and the relationship of the transformations brought by physical travel to other mobilities. It is the intention of this volume to build upon emerging work looking at transformative travel in order to provide a catalyst for a multi- and interdisciplinary cohort of scholars to explore travel and transformation in a contemporary context. While the volume itself is not a comprehensive exploration of these issues (this would be impossible to achieve), we hope it whets the appetite and provides a springboard for exciting, colourful and creative new avenues of enquiry under the banner of travel and transformation.

The Gravitational Pull of Modernity and (Late/Post) Modernism in a Mobile World

All movement transforms: spaces, places, people and environments. All movement is transformative whether we move from our bed to the garden, from our abode to the local market, from remote village to bustling town or city, from New York to Phnom Penh, from Kabul to Sydney. Movement is what we are; movement is what makes everything – the universe, planets, galaxies and all life forms. Movement is everywhere and everything. No movement, because of time and the endless fluidity of place, is repeated and so each movement through time/place transforms, changes, creates and destroys. Movement defines things, gives them shape, identities, chronologies and trajectories. And conversely, there is no stasis, ever.

Thus, in the widest sense, this 'truth' of the universe, of the nature of all things, visible and invisible, animates the chapters in this volume. Unsurprisingly, given the rubric of the book when we called for contributions, a theme that permeates the chapters is movement/mobility/travel, all of which are inextricably interconnected with transformation/change/identities. Not cause and effect, but interchangeable because all movement changes. A second theme is an analytic that we would want to describe as an ongoing dance between modernity and modernism but perhaps with a re-imagined choreography, a culturally inscribed analytic born of particular history/ies and particular knowledge practices (that are, in these chapters, Western ways of seeing, knowing and representing). How do we *think* movement and transformation?

Most of the writers occupy a potent space that exists in, around and between coexisting nodes (that are themselves never stable or static): social analysis and poetics; Western modernities and advanced/post modernisms; observing/feeling/ being and recording these; understanding/rationality and affect/aesthetics. What is remarkable is that the writers not only investigate movement/transformation, but also create writings that themselves are full of dynamism, fissures, loops, portals, speculations, open-endedness as though resolutions, destinations and certainties would deny the *subject being thought*. For the writers in this volume transformation is never complete and never entirely fulfilled, teleology is denied; destinations are provisional, just temporary moorings at most. Significantly, in these writings, the horizon is always receding, always being re-calibrated even when the subjects/ travellers set out to purposely change their lives in some way, whether through walking, migrating to a new country, backpacking, cosmetic surgery, as exiles, as pilgrims and so on.

On one level, despite the common subject matter – travel and transformation – quite tenuous threads hold these chapters together. Both 'travel and 'transformation' are simultaneously nebulous, elastic and porous concepts that are co-produced by particular circumstances and, when put together, they become even more so for most of the contributors. But this lack of any easy idea of consensus or commonality gives way, on another level, to something that is symptomatic of the collection. Born of modernity and modernism, travel and transformation as a description is beholden to the historical conditions that make it visible and intelligible and the post- (or late-) modern circumstances that enable the investigation of travel and transformation to be a form of critical engagement that reverberates beyond the 'travel and transformation' tag.

Despite historical antecedents (St Paul, the Buddha, Lao-Tsu), transformative travel is a modern post-Enlightenment conception (as are almost all ideas about contemporary travel), a phenomenon grounded in modernity and therefore propelled by the traits associated with 'modern life': disenchantment, alienation, migration, the urban condition, industrialisation and commodification, fractured identities, liberation, notions of the 'individual' and of 'freedom', loss, displacement, exile, memory, powerlessness, marginalisation, survival, struggle, escape, creativity, post-colonialism, existential angst, secularism, globalisation, cosmopolitanism, sectarianism and so forth. The reign of Western modernity has produced both the phenomenon and our understanding of that phenomenon, both the means to be ever more mobile and the deep ambivalence about a life of perpetual motion, the desire and the willingness to move with our faces turned, almost by compulsion, towards tomorrow, or the future (however conceived) and yet with a deep-rooted critique of the conditions that enable travel and transformation with its implicit (partial) denial of the past, of previous states of being except in memory, as a measure of our movement, as a marker of pre- and post-travel/transformation, perhaps as nostalgia, as a scar, an imprint of loss.

How is it that we are alert to the pain of the exile, the yearnings of the dispossessed, the liminal experiences of backpackers and overseas volunteers, the anguish of forced migration, the desire to change our bodies, the quest for self-knowledge, the journeys of outsiders, artists and poets, the need for transcendence, the search for 'wholeness' in places/worlds deemed fractured, splintered and empty of meaning? The visibility, the *understanding* and the emotional resonances – often powerfully evoked and felt – by *individual* subjects that we meet in this collection are, in turn, dependent on our ability as readers to not just empathise but recognise and know. What makes this possible? Modernity and modernism haunt this collection. They are the twin enablers that provide the crucial portal into our seeing, knowing and feeling. Travel and transformation, as explored, interrogated, ruminated upon, thought and written in the forthcoming chapters vibrates and gains traction within us as readers through the language and the analytic we have come to associate with modernism.

Modernism is, of course, a difficult word but in its many manifestations across time and space it reveals itself by the many who profess on its behalf and who produce its oeuvre. This collection of chapters reminds us of the genealogy of Western modernism and asks us to consider travel and transformation as its love child. We encounter in these studies self-definition and loneliness; the life of an exile or a migrant, or life as constant mobility; there is perpetual loss and a perpetual search; denied or fractured identities and created (or recreated) identities; subjects always en route rather than being rooted (and if the latter, how tenuous and ambiguous rootedness is); dispossession in various guises, the question of belonging, of 'out of placeness', displacement and, simultaneously, the continuous transformation of place; the attempts to connect to others on whatever journey is being considered and the joy and relief such connection (real or imagined) brings; alienation, tearing apart and remaking; consumer capitalism as enabler and destroyer with its 'dark realities' of inequality, conflict, poverty, ecological disaster and the spectre of apocalyptic or dystopian futures; the radical rupture with the past and the hope of a reconfigured 'new' self and even, perhaps, 'new' futures; the ambiguities of technology and 'progress', technology as a resource and a source of empowerment, as an embodied reality, but simultaneously the creator of menace, conformity, surveillance and entrapment, both perspectives symptomatic of 'modern life'; the primacy of experience self-knowledge and 'freedom' and its complex and difficult, sometimes cryptic, relationship to belief, transcendence, spirituality and religion; the question of what it is to be 'modern' in a perpetually mobile world. The landscape of modernity/modernism conjured and explored in the chapters in this volume is expansive and multi-directional, a restless and critical evocation of some of Western modernism's most famous epithets, 'all that is solid melts into air' (Karl Marx); 'things fall apart, the centre cannot hold' (William Butler Yeats) and 'we shall not cease from exploration /and the end of all our exploring /will be to arrive where we started /and know the place for the first time' (T.S. Eliot).

The literature about modernism is vast (for recent overviews see Butler 2010, Levenson 2011, Tew and Murray 2009). However, if we suggest, as we do, that the chapters are subject to the gravitational pull of modernism and are couched in a recognisable language of modernism (whether late- or post- is not the point), what are we referring to? We are certainly not suggesting that the chapters are reinhabiting the modernism of the twentieth century in some sort of recuperative project. Rather, the chapters indicate that despite the significance and the lasting achievements of post-modernity in the last 40 years, modernism has not been entirely left behind, something indicated, of course, by the 'post' in postmodernism.

The powerful impact of modernism continues to influence how we think and how we consider our thoughts and actions, even subliminally, given the deep cultural resonances modernist discourse and modernist work has had since the early decades of the twentieth century (and earlier). As Levenson (2011: 2) has put it so well, 'we are still learning how not to be Modernists'. The ongoing impacts and effects of modernism should not, therefore, be a surprise. There is much from the modernist project that arouses in us a way of being and an intellectual charge. We remain discontents. The vast landscape of modernism (now incorporating perspectives from across all continents and regions of the world) with all its contrary motions and paradoxes still produces expressiveness, still animates the profound issues of our times, still informs us, for better or ill, we are estranged from the past, from tradition, from convention, from continuity (even as these are newly asserted by so many). The 'new', the 'immediate', the 'creative act', the 'unconscious', the 'disturbing', the 'irrational', the 'sceptical', the 'innovative' still enthral. And so too the critique we mount when modernism tackles and harshly confronts 'the modern' or 'being modern' by exposing the many permutations that forge modernity whether economic, political, social, cultural or personal. We still perceive ourselves as living in a world in crisis. We still face scenarios of human-engineered apocalypse. We still believe in the ingenuity of the individual and the creative will of the self. And, at the same time, we still despair and feel alienated, disempowered and absurd. The *idea* of being transformed by travel resides in this messy amalgam of modernist thinking.

Chapter Summaries

Before reaching our own Introduction, readers of the volume will have encountered the powerful narrative composed by Janice Baker, 'flensed' – our prelude –, which evocatively charts the creativity and emergence of travel. In a manner reminiscent of Eve Sedgwick's (1997) 'weak theory' or the ethnographic writings of Kathleen Stewart (2007), this is a narrative that points to the rhythms, imaginings, nuances, differences and ruptures of travel. Though distinct in genre to other contributions to the volume – it is no hard analytical piece, after all – it nonetheless has teeth, impact: and it pulls at our senses. We see in it transformations which erupt, forcefully, out of the textual residues of Baker's recollections of far more bodily experiences at Whale World, Albany (an industrial museum in Australia) and her wanderings through Berlin. And through those recollections, we are invited to participate *with* her as she pieces together new modes of understanding her movements, right there in the cut and thrust of everyday life. There, we see and feel her transformations. In allowing us such, Baker is simultaneously offering an important entry point into the volume itself; an entry point that manages to pick up *more* textures and densities as the volume moves from her own reflections, into and across each part and subsequent chapters.

In order to provide some semblance of an organisational structure, we have divided the volume into four parts: 'Transformation Speculations' (Part I), 'Transformation, Representation, Story' (Part II), 'Transformation in Motion' (Part III) and 'Marking Transformation' (Part IV). The first part commences with a contribution by Jon Anderson and Kathyrn Erskine (Chapter 2), which explores the relationship between identity, place and travel as articulated through the experiences of 'lifestyle travellers'. Much of the chapter revolves around identity realisation, pursued through that contact zone that emerges in the tensions between external mobility and internal reconciliation, prompted here by a love or quest for change, to be *moved* and emerge with a new 'selfhood' that has been thrown together in experience. This is a narrative of hope and possibility, movement rather than stillness, almost as if our identities could only really be snapped into place whilst in motion. The participant voices at the heart of the chapter are motivated by a hopefulness that emerges out of the unexpected: being *in* something different allowing them to *feel* more coherent, less comfortable, yet more comforted. In stark distinction, Drew Ninnis commences his evocative and powerful contribution (Chapter 3) by questioning what he sees as the potentially illusory nature of transformation through travel. Here, travel becomes 'a disappointed promise', borne of the need to return, to stop, to draw back and retreat into the structures of our everyday lives. These are not the hopeful lines of escape we are used to finding in the tourism literature. Yet though his commentary is far less forgiving of the notion of 'change' than others in the volume, he nonetheless traces moments of transformation, or 'forms of being otherwise', through reflections on the writings of Colin Thubron and his journey into the Tibetan mountains using the analytical import of Foucauldian logic, particularly Foucault's notion of heterotopia. Kailas, Tibet, provides the backdrop for much of the chapter. There, he traces acute realisations of travel as opening up the 'very possibility of critique', leading to transformations that might affect not only the constitution of an individual 'self', but of space, too. The final chapter (Chapter 4) making up Part I, offered by Fiona Allon and Maria Koleth, emerges out of the intellectual itinerary provided by contemporary philosopher Rosi Braidotti, particularly her concept of 'transpositions' and her attempts to capture and represent the conditions of being human. Like Anderson and Erskine in Chapter 2, this is an analysis that targets a specific segment of the tourism economy, volunteer tourism, and draws on interview material gathered from Australian volunteer tourists in a bid to examine processes of self-transformation through what the authors call 'instrumentalised travel'. Like other contributions to the volume, Allon and Koleth draw upon notions of liminality, posthumanism and the mobilities paradigm, but what sets their analysis apart is their attention to the newly emerging experience economy, which is viewed through the concept of transposition, or that 'in-between space', which allows for a moving away from what Braidotti (2005: 269) refers to as the 'fantasy of unity, totality and one-ness'.

Part II, 'Transformation, Representation, Story', begins with a chapter authored by Bianca Leggett (Chapter 5), who provides an exploration of pilgrimage literature and the attendant possibilities for a form of travel that might have the capacity to realise dreams of transcendence. To make her case, Leggett draws on the excruciating tensions and charged desires that characterise the work of Geoff Dyer and his *Jeff in Venice/Death in Varanasi* (2009). This is a narrative that is full of tales about the efforts of life, foregrounding the effects of a breakdown, estrangement and existing on the periphery, all of which amount to a strident articulation of transformation. Much is made of the paradoxes of travel in Leggett's exposition, borne no doubt from the playfulness of Dyer's own text, which provides a series of moments or accrued layers through which Leggett is able to explore issues of power, authenticity, injustice, poverty and that stalwart of tourism conundrums, the apparent contradiction between 'the real' and 'the fake'. No clearer illustration of the complexity of these concepts is offered than by her reflections on the sale of a coke can. Leggett's chapter is followed by a contribution by Rehnuma Sazzad (Chapter 6), who takes as her focus the Palestinian author Mahmond Darwish – who is at once an exile, traveller and poet – and his narratives of dispossession, myth, longing and history. In some ways, this is a chapter that harks back to Allon and Koleth's attempts to get at the human condition, though Sazzad's is an illustration of transformation as achieved through the lens of exile. The touch point of this contribution is its singular attention to the *ongoing* as opposed to those transformations that emerge, almost in regimental fashion, from an epiphany, a particular experience, person or place. Instead, what distinguishes this chapter is that Sazzad's reflections are perceived in retrospect and by a third party – never are they personal. Yet, her reflections on political exile, cut with extracts from the poetry of Darwish, also offer a sort of homecoming that is not in a different register to those expressions of an immigrant's journey articulated in Mannik's chapter (Chapter 9). Part II is closed with a contribution from Shannon Walsh (Chapter 7), who introduces us to four distinct voices less often associated with the literature explicitly focused on travel and transformation: the nomad, the refugee, the developer and the migrant. This is a contribution that takes the reader to Johannesburg, South Africa and, like Ninnis, pushes us to think differently about the spaces of a city, particularly those spaces unsettled by the constancy of reminders of political disruption. Based on the project *Jeppe on a Friday*, a documentary film shot over one day in March 2012, this chapter speaks about physical movement through a city newly marked with mobility after a recent history of almost precisely the opposite. Walsh's reporting on the ways in which each protagonist moves through the city is again reminiscent of the work of Kathleen Stewart (2008: 71) and her attention to the 'textures, rhythms, trajectories, and nodes of attunement, attachment and composition' that afford affective potency to any space as we move through it.

Our third part, 'Transformation in Motion', begins with a chapter by Leila Dawney (Chapter 8) who returns us to themes already familiar, such as pilgrimage, selfhood and movement, which she addresses with the aid of Michel Foucault's concept of hypomnemata, or self-writing. In terms of geographical space, this contribution whisks us to the walking trails of the South West Coast Path National Trail in England, where the perfectly ordinary practice of walking is rearticulated as a way of working on, and attending to, the self – re-knowing, re-relating – through physical movement. The 'self', here, is far from essentialised, however, as Dawney is entirely cognisant of the possibility for those half-knowns that emerge and solidify into ways of *knowing* within the spaces of leisure to work on double or multiple 'selves' simultaneously. Though continuing with a theme of physical movement, the following chapter (Chapter 9) provided by Lynda Mannik focuses upon a specific vehicle of transformation by relating events of the forced transformation of a small group of Estonian refugees in 1948 as they crossed the Atlantic from Sweden to Canada aboard the HMS *Walnut*, an old British minesweeper. We see in this analysis, again, the presence and influence of Michel Foucault and his concept of heterotopia. Here, it is used to make sense of the recollections of 30 passengers, whose narratives are used to represent so vividly – and with considerable analytical aplomb – a series of physical and symbolic transformations, all of which are pieced together through the concept of liminal space. These are experiences of transformation by boat, as refugee, which inevitably sew together a rich tapestry of memory, emotion and trauma, along with the constructions of self-identity that erupt within the spaces in between. The net result is a complex weaving together of both individual and collective memories of transformation that are, in essence, about positive change in spite of adversity.

The third chapter in Part III, written by Amie Matthews (Chapter 10), offers a reinvigorated sociological perspective on ritual and transformation. Like Ninnis in Chapter 3, Matthews' contribution offers an acute interrogation of the possibilities for transformation, though this time through a focus on the often cited trope of 'rites of passage', particularly as articulated by Victor Turner. Once again, we as readers are returned to the concept of liminality, though this time it is the liminoid spaces of travel – encountered and experienced by Australian backpacker tourists – that are the focus of attention. For Matthews, while it may be the individual backpacker that stands up as the quintessential traveller in search of that endlessly fascinating rite of passage, it is simultaneously those spaces of commonality, or communitias, forged in and *between* backpackers, that are transformative, especially when you really lean into them. It is in *those* spaces, for example, that permission is granted – in the absence of home and the structures of behaviour that ordinarily monitor our behaviour – for newly changed identities, directions, aspirations, forms, behaviours, attitudes and opinions to emerge. Sarah Rodigari's contribution (Chapter 11), which draws Part III to a close, continues the analytical work of Matthews by offering another layer of attention to both physical and metaphorical movement. Returning, too, to the concept of 'walking', Rodigari explores the potential for transformation through a six-week performative walk between Melbourne and Sydney. Analytically, Rodigari introduces the concept of 'sympathetic magic', coined by James Frazer, as well as the concepts of empathy and affective contagion. Drawing on a sense of empathy as afforded by the affective spaces of performative art, Rodigari is able to speak not only to her own sense of transformation, but to those participants who engaged with her performance alongside her.

Our final part of the volume, Part IV, 'Marking Transformation', commences with a chapter (Chapter 12) written by Meredith Jones, David Bell, Ruth Holliday, Elspeth Probyn and Jacqueline Sanchez Taylor, detailing their explorations of cosmetic surgery and medical tourism. Nowhere in the volume is 'transformation' more starkly and radically understood as the *literal* changing of a body through surgery. As with other contributions, the chapter is unflinching in its adoption of a post-essentialist approach to the female body and insists upon an acceptance of the inter-subjectivity of such practices. This is an image of an everyday life *charged* with the need to change – and to plan for it – brought into assemblage with the many networks of a particular cultural practice, including other patients, surgeons, hospitals, procedures, insurance, family members and so forth. In addition to narrating literal, physical transformation, the chapter also points to practices of transformation that occur in tandem, online, where a sense of community is drawn upon to facilitate that physical transformation with an emotional journey that is both validated and supported by a community of others who have 'been there, done that', united almost entirely by their shared desire to change their bodies. The final chapter in Part IV, contributed by Kimberley Peters (Chapter 13), focuses on 'home' spaces, but without recourse to any rigid separation implied between 'home' and 'away'. Instead, Peter's reflections are far more fluid, processual and relational, and articulate what she refers to as a 'third space', another *in between*, within which the lives of souvenirs, amongst other things, can be better understood as nuanced and changing. Adopting a biographical approach, Peter's explores the ways in which those things we bring home from travel, our souvenirs, reminders, are also seen to transform and take on new meanings/new roles once relocated in the home. Finally, we draw the volume to a close with some of our reflections: things we have gleaned along the way, from our own experiences of travel and, indeed, working on this volume. Much of what we have to say in these closing pages is infused with our everyday lives, though punctuated by certain moments that, for us at least, have worked to crack open *something* to transformation – our 'selves', our routines, our knowledge, our friends, our families, our homes, our jobs. Perspectives that we hope will stir further exploration of the topic.

References

Bauman, Z. 2000. *Liquid Modernity*. Cambridge: Polity Press.

Bauman, Z. 2005. *Liquid Life*. Cambridge: Polity Press.

Beaumont, N.K. 2001. Ecotourism and the conservation ethic: Recruiting the uninitiated or preaching to the converted? *Journal of Sustainable Tourism*, 9(4), 317–41.

Blanchard, L. and Higgins-Desbiolles, F. (eds) 2013. *Peace Through Tourism: Promoting Human Security Through International Citizenship*. London: Routledge.

Braidotti, R.M. 2005. *Transpositions: On Nomadic Ethics*. London and New York: Polity Press.

Broad, S. 2003. Living the Thai life: A case study of volunteer tourism at the Gibbon Rehabilitation Project, Thailand. *Tourism Recreation Research*, 28(3), 63–72.

Bruner, E.M. 1991. Transformation of self in tourism. *Annals of Tourism Research*, 18(2), 238–50.

Bruner, E.M. 2005. *Culture on Tour: Ethnographies of Travel*. Chicago: The University of Chicago Press.

Butcher, J. and Smith, P. 2010. 'Making a difference': Volunteer tourism and development. *Tourism Recreation Research*, 35(1), 27–36.

Butler, C. 2010. *Modernism: A Very Short Introduction*. Oxford: Oxford University Press.

Charters, T. 1996. Ecotourism: A tool for conservation, in *National Parks: Private Sector's Role*, edited by T. Charters, M. Gabriel and S. Prasser. Toowoomba: University of Southern Queensland Press, 77–84.

Creamer, J.M. 2004. Facing Japan while living in the United States: The study abroad experiences and expectations of Japanese women. PhD thesis, University of Illinois at Urbana-Champaign, USA. Retrieved from ProQuest Dissertations and Theses Database (Publication No: AAT 3153280).

D'Amore, L.J. 1988a. Tourism: A vital force for peace. *Annals of Tourism Research*, 15(1), 269–70.

D'Amore, L.J. 1988b. Tourism: The world's peace industry. *Journal of Travel Research*, 27(1), 35–40.

The Epic of Gilgamesh [eighteenth–tenth century BCE] 1972. Translated by N.K Sanders. Harmondsworth: Penguin.

Fordham, T.A. 2005. Pedagogies of cultural change: The Rotary International Youth Exchange Program and narratives of travel and transformation. *Journal of Tourism and Cultural Change*, 3(3), 143–59.

Forgues, D.M. 2005. A study of the relationship of study abroad and students' attitudes toward diversity and culture. PhD thesis, State University of New York at Buffalo, USA. Retrieved from ProQuest Dissertations and Theses Database (Publication No: AAT 3174147).

Franklin, A. 2007. The problem with tourism theory, in *The Critical Turn in Tourism Studies: Innovative Research Methodologies*, edited by I. Ateljevic, A. Pritchard and N. Morgan. Oxford: Elsevier, 131–48.

Franklin, A. and Crang, M. 2001. The trouble with tourism and travel theory. *Tourist Studies*, 1(1), 5–22.

Hall, C.M. and Tucker, H. (eds) 2004. *Tourism and Postcolonialism: Contested Discourses, Identities and Representations*. London: Routledge.

Homer [eighth century BCE] 2004. *The Odyssey*. Translated by R. Eagles. London: Penguin Books.

Immetman, A. and Schneider, P. 1998. Assessing student learning in study-abroad programs: A conceptual framework and methodology for assessing student learning in study-abroad programs. *Journal of Studies in International Education*, 2(2), 59–80.

Kottler, J.A. 1997. *Travel That Can Change Your Life: How to Create a Transformative Experience*. San Francisco: Jossey-Bass.

Kottler, J.A. 2002. Transformative travel: International counselling in action. *International Journal for the Advancement of Counseling*, 24(4), 207–10.

Kottler, J.A. 2003. Transformative travel as the antidote for acute burnout and professional despair. *International Journal for the Advancement of Counseling*, 25(2/3), 137–44.

Kottler, J.A. and Montgomery, M. 2000. Perspective travel and adventure-based activities as adjuncts to counselling. *Guidance and Counselling*, 15(2), 8–11.

Lean, G.L. 2009. Transformative travel: Inspiring sustainability, in *Wellness and Tourism: Mind, Body, Spirit, Place*, edited by R. Bushell and P.J. Sheldon. Elmsford: Cognizant Communication, 191–205.

Lean, G.L. 2012a. Transformative travel: A mobilities perspective. *Tourist Studies*, 12(2), 151–72.

Lean, G. 2012b. The lingering moment, in *The Cultural Moment in Tourism*, edited by L. Smith, E. Waterton and S. Watson. Abingdon: Routledge, 274–91.

Lean, G. forthcoming. *Transformative Travel in a Mobile World*. Wallingford: CABI.

Leed, E.J. 1991. *The Mind of the Traveller: From Gilgamesh to Global Tourism*. New York: Basic Books.

Levenson, M. (ed.) 2011. *The Cambridge Companion to Modernism*, 2nd edition. Cambridge: Cambridge University Press.

Litvin, S.W. 1998. Tourism: The world's peace industry? *Journal of Travel Research*, 37(1), 63–6.

Litvin, S.W. 2003. Tourism and understanding. *Annals of Tourism Research*, 30(1), 77–93.

Matthews, A. 2007. 'Becoming a citizen of the world': Understanding the experiential significance of young people's journeys through liminoidity. PhD thesis, University of Newcastle, Newcastle, Australia.

Matthews, A. 2008. Negotiated selves: Exploring the impact of local-global interactions on young volunteer travellers, in *Journeys of Discovery in Volunteer Tourism: International Case Study Perspectives*, edited by K.D. Lyons and S. Wearing. Wallingford: CABI, 101–17.

Mavrič, M. and Urry, J. 2009. Tourism studies and the New Mobilities Paradigm (NMP), in *The Sage Handbook of Tourism Studies*, edited by T. Jamal and M. Robinson. London: SAGE.

Moufakkir, O. and Kelly, I. (eds) 2010. *Tourism, Progress and Peace*. Wallingford: CABI.

Noy, C. 2004a. Performing identity: Touristic narratives of self-change. *Text and Performance Quarterly*, 24(2), 115–38.

Noy, C. 2004b. This trip really changed me: Backpackers' narratives of self-change. *Annals of Tourism Research*, 31(1), 78–102.

Palacios, C.M. 2010. Volunteer tourism, development and education in a postcolonial world: Conceiving global connections beyond aid. *Journal of Sustainable Tourism*, 18(7), 861–78.

Pizam, A. 1996. Does tourism promote peace and understanding between unfriendly nations?, in *Tourism, Crime and International Security Issues*, edited by A. Pizam and Y. Mansfeld. Chichester: Wiley, 203–14.

Pizam, A., Jafari, J. and Milman, A. 1991. Influences of tourism on attitudes: US students visiting USSR. *Tourism Management*, 12(1), 47–54.

Pritchard, A., Morgan, N. and Ateljevic, I. 2011. Hopeful tourism: A new transformative perspective. *Annals of Tourism Research*, 38(3), 941–63.

Reisinger, Y. (ed.) 2013. *Transformational Tourism: Tourist Perspectives*. Wallingford: CABI.

Roberson, D.N. 2002. *School of Travel: An Exploration of The Convergence of Andragogy and Travel*. ERIC (Education Resources Information Center). Retrieved from http://www.eric.ed.gov/PDFS/ED465075.pdf.

Roberson, D.N. 2003. Learning experiences of senior travelers. *Studies in Continuing Education*, 25(1), 125–44.

Robinson, M. and Jamal, T. 2009. Conclusions: Tourism studies – past omissions, emergent challenges, in *The SAGE Handbook of Tourism Studies*, edited by T. Jamal and M. Robinson. London: SAGE, 693–701.

Ross, S. and Wall, G. 1999. Ecotourism: Towards congruence between theory and practice. *Tourism Management*, 20(1), 123–32.

Salazar, N.B. 2002. Seeing the 'other' tourist consumption in 'development(al)' tourism'. MA thesis, Katholieke Universiteit Leuven, Belgium.

Salazar, N.B. 2004. Developmental tourists vs. development tourism: A case study, in *Tourist Behaviour: A Psychological Perspective*, edited by A. Raj. New Delhi: Kanishka Publishers, 85–107.

Sedgwick, E.K. 1997. Paranoid reading and reparative reading: Or, you're so paranoid, you probably think this introduction is about you, in *Novel Gazing: Queer Readings in Fiction*, edited by E. Sedgwick. Durham, NC: Duke University Press, 1–40.

Stephenson, S. 1999. Study abroad as a transformational experience and its effect upon study abroad students and host nationals in Santiago, Chile. *Frontiers: The Interdisciplinary Journal of Study Abroad*, 5(2), 1–38.

Stewart, K. 2007. *Ordinary Affects*. Durham, NC: Duke University Press.

Stewart, K. 2008. Weak theory in an unfinished world. *Journal of Folklore Research*, 45(1), 71–82.

Tew, P. and Murray, A. (eds) 2009. *The Modernism Handbook*. London and New York: Continuum Books.

Tucker, H. and Akama, J. 2009. Tourism as postcolonialism, in *The SAGE Handbook of Tourism Studies*, edited by T. Jamal and M. Robinson. London: SAGE, 504–20.

Urry, J. 2000. *Sociology Beyond Societies*. London: Routledge.

Urry, J. 2007. *Mobilities*. Cambridge: Polity Press.

Var, T. and Ap, J. 2001. Tourism and world peace, in *Global Tourism*, 2nd edition, edited by W.F. Theobald. Oxford: Butterworth-Heinemann, 44–57.

Wearing, S., DeVille, A. and Lyons, K.D. 2008. The volunteer's journey through leisure into the self, in *Journeys of Discovery in Volunteer Tourism: International Case Study Perspectives*, edited by K.D. Lyons and S. Wearing. Wallingford: CABI, 63–71.

PART I
Transformation Speculations

Chapter 2

Lifestyle Travel, Tropophila and Identity Transformation

Jon Anderson and Kathryn Erskine

Introduction

In recent years it has been argued that the traditional relations between people and place are being dismantled through processes of globalisation and mobility. As a result, the relations between people and place are now being reframed as constantly changing and provisional. As we have argued (Anderson and Erskine 2012), this reframing raises a number of questions concerning the nature of place (in terms of its variety and multiplicity), the pace of place (in terms of its trajectory, direction and speed of change/mobility), alongside the nature of the individual and their own pace of change. In this chapter these questions are interrogated further through the case of lifestyle travel.

As Cohen (2010: 64) outlines, the lifestyle traveller is one who actively pursues travel indefinitely, rather than as a temporal or 'cyclical break' from normality. Such a preferred lifestyle choice exemplifies the alternative and 'networked patterns of social life' (Duffy 2004: 32) that characterise the twenty-first century, with such individuals serving as a corporeal example of increasing global mobility and the subsequent destabilisation of existing lifestyles and understandings of place attachment, constancy and topophilia (or love of stable relations between people and place).

Drawing on Rojek (1993) and O'Reilly (2005), we argue that a key motivation for lifestyle travel is not the active pursuit of mobility for its own sake (that is, simply to keep moving from one random place to another), rather it is to realise identity challenge and transformation. External (or geographical) mobility is thus undertaken in order to realise an internal (or identity-related) mobility – to invoke change and challenge to aspects of selfhood. Similarly, lifestyle travellers are happy to remain 'moored', or temporally located in one place, if that location allows that individual to be challenged and changed. Once an individual's need for internal 'mobility' is exhausted within one location, then the lifestyle traveller moves on. This chapter will demonstrate how mobilities and moorings intersect to promote forms of self-transformation in lifestyle travellers. Mobilities occurring within place (such as immersion, integration and learning), as well as mobilities between places, are shown to be equally vital to the self-progression that is essential to the lifestyle travel phenomenon.

From Constant to Changing Places

As argued elsewhere (Anderson 2010), people are tied into places through
everyday activities, cultures, belief systems and aspirations. Places themselves
are formed by, and through, our literal and metaphoric constructions and co-
constituted by our lived experiences, emotions and cultural attachments. People
and place are intimately connected; as Said suggests, no human is ever 'outside
or beyond geography' (Said 1993: 7, also cited in Moore 1997 and Soja 2010).
Such intimate interconnection has tended to encourage a particular framing of
geographical place – specifically, geographical sites have been framed as fixed
and static in nature. According to Cresswell (2004) such static configurations are
part of a 'sedentary metaphysics' (after Malkki 1992) which seeks to 'divide the
world up into clearly bounded territorial units' (Cresswell 2004: 109). From this
perspective, our geographies are established in: 'things like nations, states, counties
and places. Thinking of the world as rooted and bounded actively territorialises
identities in property, in region, in nation – in place' (Cresswell 2004: 110).

    Due to the intimate interconnection between people and place, such a
sedentary and static approach to the latter category has implications for senses
of selfhood (be it individual or collective). In a world that is framed by closed,
bounded and stabilised places, not only are place identities deemed to be coherent
and stable, but so too are the cultures that are created within and through them. As
'intrinsically spatial beings' (Soja 2010: 18), this coherence and constancy of place
gives a platform from which human identities and cultures can be formed. People
can root themselves in the constancy of place, become 'attached' to place, and
enjoy a sense of belonging to a geographical hearth and home (see, for example,
Relph 1976, Seamon and Mugerauer 1985). As Tuan (1977: 179) argues, place has
to be consistent and unchanging in order for these senses of belonging and home
to be rooted; in his words, place has to be: 'a static concept. If we see the world as
process, constantly changing, we would not be able to develop any sense of place.'

    As we have noted elsewhere (Anderson and Erskine 2012), Tuan (1974)
emphasises the affective capacity of the rooted relations between people and place
through the neologism *topophilia*. Topophilia refers to the affective bond – or
relational sensibility as Anderson (2009) has argued – that is registered in a person,
but created by their co-constitution with a particular place. A positive relation
between people and place (for example in a home setting) would be termed
topophilia, whilst a negative feeling (perhaps in a strange or unwelcoming place)
would be its counterpoint – topophobia. Such affective connections between people
and place have the implication that any changes to the nature of place can be easily
felt by those rooted in that location. Generally speaking, due to the positive nature
of topophilia, it is common for narratives of change to become pejoratively framed
as a threat. Much research in environmental psychology and geography documents
the expressions of mourning, grief and loss felt by individuals and groups as a
consequence of place changes (see, for example, Manzo 2003, Twigger-Ross

and Uzzell 1996). Such phenomena provoke protectionist and conservationist discourses which seek to preserve the constancy of place in the face of change.

Due to the affective relation between people and place, the constancy of place is deemed a common good; as Tuan (2004: 49) tells us:

> by remaining the same, they [constant places] tell us that, for all the loss of hair and accretion of weight that make us almost unrecognisable to ourselves in the mirror, our basic values and selves remain more or less intact.

Topophilia is thus nurtured in these conditions and transmits a sense of security, longevity and belonging to people through a place's constancy. However, with the rise of globalisation, and the associated mobilities of commodities, ideas and people, many scholars have challenged static concepts of place and the topophilic affects such concepts suggest (see: Adey 2009, Cresswell 2010a, 2010b, 2011, Gustafson 2001, Hannam et al. 2006, Massey 2005, 2006, Sheller and Urry 2004, 2006). As humans are inherently spatial beings, the mobility of people on one hand, and of place on the other, have inevitable effects on the geographical self (for a concise overview see Price 2013). These dynamic interrelations raise questions concerning the continued relevance of static accounts of the relations between people and place. In a world where rootedness is displaced, or at least combined with routedness, home and belonging can no longer be simply understood in terms of how attached an individual is to an unchanging geographical place. In a world of mobilities, a sense of home and well-being may also come to be defined by how complementary and synergistic the dynamics of place are to the dynamics of an individual's selfhood. As we have stated elsewhere (Anderson and Erskine 2012), from this view, the stability of place may actually *impede* personal growth; change and mobility (of both a personal and geographical nature) is something that is desired rather than discouraged. In other words, a love of change and mobility – that is, *tropophilia* – may be more appropriate. Tropophilia refers to an individual's need *to move* and *be moved*, to be stimulated and challenged in terms of their relations to place. Due to an individual's co-ingredience with place, this challenge comes from a new geographical location, how one place's diversity and dynamism stimulate an individual, or through the ways in which humans interact with a particular place (for example, through changing their job, their identity, or their habitual practices, as we will discuss below). After a brief discussion of methodology, the chapter goes on to investigate these issues through the case of lifestyle travel. In this discussion we will demonstrate how tropophilia is experienced in relation to mobilities, both within and between places.

Mobilising Method for the Lifestyle Traveller

In order to investigate how lifestyle travellers see, know and consume the world (Germann Molz 2010), this chapter draws on a research project that adopted a qualitative methodology encompassing ethnographic travel and open-ended interviews.[1] One of the authors spent 18 months researching lifestyle travel(lers) in Australia, Malaysia, Indonesia and Thailand, and this chapter is based on extensive interviews with 23 self-defined lifestyle travellers moving through this part of the world. Recruitment occurred through the opportune meeting of lifestyle travellers 'on the road', but was also facilitated through the social networking site 'Couch Surfing'. Here messages could be posted on various location 'walls' requesting respondents. Interviewees sourced through both strategies were educated in, and originated from, developed nations (seven were from Australia, seven from Europe, eight from North America and one from Asia). The vast majority of respondents were travelling on their own. Thirteen were male, ten female, and respondents ranged in age from 21 to 34. All were voluntary travellers, rather than forcibly exiled from home locations, and in terms of duration had been travelling from 14 months (minimum) to 156 months (with the average of time travelled being 43 months per person). Despite their developed world origins, and their privileged position in being able to choose when and where to travel, it was nevertheless difficult to categorise respondents into a straightforward socioeconomic class; the vast majority of travellers worked to travel, and due to their temporal and physical dislocation from the norms of their original location, could no longer be straightforwardly allocated into stable class or socioeconomic categories (cf. hobos, see Cresswell 2001, or neo-nomads, D'Andrea 2006).

Mobilities Between Places: Tropophilia in Lifestyle Travel

Motivations for lifestyle travel are manifold in nature and it is often difficult to strictly categorise or limit the definition of the lifestyle traveller. However, what all lifestyle travellers have in common is the tropophilia they require; in other words, the need *to move* and *be moved* in terms of their relationships to place. As we will see in this section, geographical mobility is one means through which this mobilisation and identity transformation can be enabled, but in certain circumstances, moorings can also facilitate this change. 'I wasn't changing at home, just kind of stifling myself so getting away was good' (Enzo). For lifestyle travellers like Enzo, tropophilia was realised through external relocation, with geographical mobility central to instigating exploration of both themselves and the world. As Felicity describes: 'I'm a really curious person and I really like to

---

1   This chapter is part of a larger project which interviewed 50 lifestyle travellers in Asia, Australasia, Europe and India between 2010 and 2012. The age range of respondents in Australasia and Asia is not wholly representative of lifestyle travellers in other parts of the world; in other locations, many continue to participate in this phenomenon well into their middle age. This situation raises questions related to types of places that lifestyle travellers 'feel the urge' (see Sheller and Urry 2004: 1) to be constituted by at different stages of the lifecourse. Unfortunately these questions are beyond the scope of this chapter.

constantly be discovering and ... have my mind stimulated, I have this curiosity about elsewhere.'

For these lifestyle travellers, personal growth and transformation could be satisfied through movement to new person–place relations. Travel did not simply offer a 'way out', but a 'way to grow' (see Desforges 1998, 2000, O'Reilly 2006). The notion of 'finding oneself' through transformative travel was widely discussed by these lifestyle travellers:

> I don't think you find yourself, I think you make yourself but yes there's a certain confidence that comes from putting yourself against the world and throwing yourself in the deep end and discovering that you can actually swim. (Nicola)

> ... the point is not to find yourself, the point is to create yourself ... I don't know if there was anything there pre-existing that I was supposed to find but I definitely created myself along the way. (Mark)

The possibility of 'finding oneself' through mobility was widely discussed, but often disputed by lifestyle travellers; the implied finality and singularity in the notion conflicted with their desire for constant change and transformation. Instead, ideas relating to fragmented and malleable identities were preferred (see: Anderson 2004, Bauman 1996, 2001, Beck and Beck-Gernsheim 2002, Featherstone 1995, Maxey 1999). These notions emphasised lifestyle travellers' need for perpetual creation and construction of the different selves that they would encounter in and through different places. For Nicola, this challenge came from 'pitting' one's self against the world and requiring the former to expand and grow (a challenge that would be unnecessary, or unlikely, if she remained in her home place). In this way, Nicola suggests that continual exposure to new places induced a heightened 'testing' or questioning of selves. Mark corroborates this in suggesting that travel somehow encourages a more creative and dynamic path for identity formation. In this way, physical relocation may not simply be synonymous with personal growth and the ongoing transformation of identity, but also the disposal and shedding of unwanted identity roles. This idea is emphasised by the following lifestyle travellers:

> ... the life I'd lived up until I was 21 years old I was always known as Ben and I was always expected to live in a certain way because it was living with and around the people that had always known me: my family and my friends I'd had for a very long time. They all knew me as a certain type of person and they all knew me as Ben. The people I met in Oman knew a totally different person, I could in effect reinvent myself and I effectively did because of the confidence I gained through travel. (Ben)

> When you go to a new place, basically you can be whoever you want to be and
> no-one knows you, no-one knows anything about you. (Gem)

> ... people say you travel to 'find yourself' but I know myself and I don't want to
> find myself, I wanna lose myself if anything. (Nigel)

For these lifestyle travellers, physical mobility enabled a new set of person–place relations to be constructed that facilitated the structuring parameters of home places to be discarded, and new versions of identity to be lived. Geographical relocation thus enabled tropophilia, with new contexts and situations facilitating personal growth, reinvention and transformation. For Nigel, travel provides the opportunity to un-know (him)self and, like Ben, he no longer has to be concerned with who he is or what is expected of him. Travel in this manner offers the blanket of anonymity; travellers can give themselves up to new places and new situations and perhaps test new identities without being 'expected to live a certain way' (see also Golden-Gelman 2011). Furthermore, for these lifestyle travellers, geographical relocation also removes the pressure to 'know oneself' through concentrating on the novelty of new cultures and countries. When travelling, Nigel no longer needs to be conscious about who he is or what he should do as new identities can be tested implicitly through being exposed to novelty. In essence, Nigel seeks to become lost in the external changing world rather than being concerned with some inward voyage, expectant that this inward transformation will happen in due course as an inevitable product of travelling.

In slight contrast, Gem explicitly uses new situations to change her identity; for her, identity is a more considered and 'freely chosen game' (Bauman 1996: 18). For Gem, travel offers the freedom to be who she wants, becoming liberated to explore or test new identities by being a stranger in new places (Golden-Gelman 2011). Lifestyle travel encourages this autonomy and as her 'stranger status' is prolonged through continual relocation, she is liberated to test many versions of herself over time:

> ... so when you go to a new place ... no-one knows anything about you. I could
> tell them that I grew up in California they'd have no idea, you know ... you can
> kinda just make stuff up and just be who you wanna be. (Gem)

The capacity for self-invention is thus heightened for Gem when she is freed from the sense of obligation or inertia to acquire and maintain a static, rooted relationship with place. Vacating social roles and expectations allows her to construct new and freer identities, divorcing herself/ves from pre-established 'home' identities, in a similar manner to the way to Ben did in Oman, and therefore allowing the creation of new selves that are potentially unrecognisable from past ones. Geographical freedom thus produces internal transformation in lifestyle travellers. The freedom to move between places, and to be unfettered by static person–place relations, enhances a sense of autonomy and encourages lifestyle travellers to test and transform their identity.

Mobilities Within Places: Tropophilia in Lifestyle Travel

Despite the significance of physical movement and relocation in the delivery of tropophilia, all participants in this project nevertheless had 'pauses' within their mobility (Ingold 2005). For lifestyle travellers, therefore, geographical movement went hand-in-hand with relative *im*mobility. Although this 'mooring' was often anathema to identity change, for some individuals this immobility provided the opportunity to continue personal transformation. In these cases, mobilities within places could engender tropophilia for lifestyle travellers.

> I don't want to wander non-stop. (Anna)

> ... within about 2 months I wanted to stop somewhere just because I was exhausted, continuous travel exhausts me, emotionally and physically ... so we found this town in China ... (and stayed) for like a month or more. (Kai)

> I started thinking about going to Laos ... so I went there, loved it (and) stayed for a month and a half. (Johanna)

As Urry (2002) suggests, it is important to examine mobility as more than simply the passive relocation between places; it is vital to study not only mobility, but also temporary moorings. In the case of lifestyle travel, it is crucial, therefore, to explore not only how often individuals travel, but also how long they stop in particular locations and what effect this has on their personal transformation. As we will see below, in many cases lifestyle travellers use their relative immobility in a new location to get their fix of tropophilia.

One method which many participants used to help them temporarily 'moor' in a location was the online social networking site 'Couch Surfing'. For lifestyle travellers, Couch Surfing functions as a way to experiment with new forms of person–place relations by connecting with local home stays in a range of places across the globe (see Zuev 2011). The use of Couch Surfing gave lifestyle travellers 'access', not only to less traversed geographical routes, but also to the possibility of obtaining a deeper relationship to place that would test and transform their identity. In these ways, Couch Surfing enabled travellers to transcend the passive 'tourist' experience (see: Cohen 2004, Coleman and Crang 2002, Edensor 2000) and move them out of their comfort zone. As Alice states, using Couch Surfing allowed her to develop from being a 'stupid Australian that goes everywhere', into a more independent, and multi-phrenic (see Anderson 2004) traveller. By seeking alternative routes off the beaten track most participants viewed Couch Surfing as an effective way to surpass the glossy and sanitised version of a place and get behind the scenes through engaging with the routines and everyday practices of local people (Urry 2002). Practising Couch Surfing was therefore a way to 'achieve' (after Jones 2009) an alternative and 'local' impression of place; as the following lifestyle travellers put it:

> I really wanted to connect with locals, have that experience outside the normal stuff in tourist brochures. (Mark)

> I like to have the local contact as well and Couch Surfing is awesome for that, to put you in touch with local people. (Laura)

As OJ explains further, the virtual connections made through Couch Surfing enabled him to practice the 'everyday' mobilities within place by giving him the opportunity to live like a local:

> I stayed with two different people in Egypt, one guy in Cairo, which was really nice, we hung out, [had] shisha and played dominoes, met his family. That was really cool to see that side of Cairo ... Then I stayed with another guy in a tiny town ... where no tourists go 'cos there was nothing there, so I hung out with him, went to his doctor's surgery, and sat in with all his consults so I really got to learn a lot from them [the patients] 'cos I was asking them questions and having conversations, it was a really bizarre experience ... That's what made Egypt bearable for me because before that I was just travelling round with my parents, it's horrible just as a tourist, but when you're with an Egyptian guy its completely different. (OJ)

Here, OJ was able to do everyday things – playing games, smoking shisha, 'hanging out', spending time at the doctors – and to meet 'everyday' people. In this manner his routes bypassed the undesired tourist circuit and tapped into a local's life in order to achieve a 'real' and completely different sense of place. 'Following' the routes of a local, traversing their daily life and seeing Cairo through their eyes gave OJ a more rewarding and transformative experience.

Similarly for Kristen, Couch Surfing created the opportunity for her to have a transformative experience whilst being moored within a local place. Her host's 'insider knowledge' and enthusiasm for their place meant she was able to mobilise versions of her self that surpassed those that she could 'achieve' on her own:

> every person that I met was so willing to share their home, willing to take you out and show you what their town is about and give you tips and it's so much better ... from that first night in Switzerland I spent three nights in a hostel in two months. (Kristen)

For these participants, Couch Surfing afforded a way to have new experiences within place through tapping into the regular rhythms and routines of individuals.

Felicity stressed the value of Couch Surfing for transforming the self in this way. Rather than merely spectating from the peripheries, Couch Surfing allowed her to participate and engage with place, to temporarily become a part of it through activity. Participation meant lifestyle travellers reciprocally acted within place and proactively tested themselves in a new environment:

> It's easier to go to a place and look at it from the eyes of a tourist you know, wander round and you're almost just consuming the place, visually and passively, you're not really participating. But if you spend a week there, or a month there or you stay with local families, which is why I love Couch Surfing, you get this other aspect of the place. (Felicity)

Felicity confirms how Couch Surfing functions as a way to 'achieve' an alternative 'aspect' of place and self. Couch Surfing offers her a 'path' to participate when moored in a place, allowing her to actively carve out new person–place relations. For Felicity, identity transformation is about becoming absorbed into a place and putting down 'temporary roots', a goal that she can realise through the facilitating function of Couch Surfing.

As a facilitator, Couch Surfing further expands lifestyle travellers' access to different kinds of people, as well as accelerating the time at which relationships with people and place develop. This is particularly useful for lifestyle travellers who only wish to be *temporarily* moored in one location, as Henry states:

> It's like you can drop into someone's life and live it for a day or two days, you get to see what it's like … And … especially when you're there for a week or so, it kind of encourages you to live out the entirety of the relationship in that confined amount of time …
>
> I Couch Surfed with a guy, ended up staying with him for two weeks and kind of dabbled in his life.

Here Henry demonstrates that, like OJ, he enjoys the opportunity to live like a local and test out that lifestyle through 'dropping in' on people, using Couch Surfing as a permissible tool to do so. This almost infers a kind of 'game playing' (Bauman 1996) where one can 'dabble in … ' different lives before moving on and testing out others. Rather than forming routes *alongside* people like OJ, it also infers a specific insight into the person as well as the place in which they reside. Couch Surfing therefore functions as an intense method to accelerate relationships with people and place, as well as forming deep connections through heightened personal contact and exposure. In this manner, despite their temporality, new selves, friendships and experiences are formed and lives are learnt at a rapid pace. In this manner, to be moored was to become a part of place, if only temporarily. Carving one's way in the world through lifestyle travel ensured that alternative senses of place, belonging and community could be acquired despite the preference for a life 'on the move'.

Conclusion

This chapter has sought to look afresh at relations between people and place. Once codified as static and stable entities, the relations between people and place were commonly argued to give rise to feelings of topophilia, or love of place. Over recent years, however, these notions have been transformed into dynamic, multiple and provisional processes, and these transformations raise questions concerning how the relations between them should be understood. This chapter has explored these questions through the example of lifestyle travel. It has suggested how notions of *topophilia* can be supplemented by *tropophilia* – or the love of mobility, change and transformation in the person–place relation. The chapter has demonstrated how the geographical (or external) mobility of lifestyle travellers is undertaken in order to realise identity-related (or internal) mobility – mobility is adopted to invoke a challenge to and prompt a change in aspects of selfhood. As we have seen, lifestyle travel extends the wanderlust of tourism into a lifestyle choice, re-defining geographical mobility as delivering 'the expectation of pleasure from novelty and change experienced' (Cohen 2004: 29).

However, for lifestyle travellers the transformation of self occurs not only through moving to novel geographic surroundings, but also through engaging in new lives and experiences when they temporarily moor in a place. To understand lifestyle travel, therefore, it is as important to understand relative immobility, as well as movement. For lifestyle travellers, to be 'moored' does not represent an 'exit' from travel (Cohen 2011), rather it means that different types of mobility are practised. Through mechanisms such as Couch Surfing, moorings enable individuals to get under the skin of a place in a short amount of time, bypassing tourist trails and living like a local off the beaten track. Through becoming temporary participants within a place, rather than simple spectators of it, lifestyle travellers are able to continue their identity transformation – their internal mobility – even when their travel is temporarily paused. In this way, lifestyle travellers obtain the best of both worlds; they are able to lay down routes without becoming rooted, to be mobile but not passively moving, and to become a part of place without anchoring there. For lifestyle travellers, just as being mobile does not erode the importance of person–place relations, being immobile does not undermine their desire for tropophilia. For them, maintaining a balance between mobility and mooring is crucial. Once the desired state of place immersion or integration is complete, physical mobility becomes imperative in order to initiate identity transformation elsewhere. By diagnosing these ongoing relations between mobility and mooring, lifestyle travel offers a unique insight into how mobility between and within places combines to characterise the processual relations between place and identity.

References

Adey, P. 2009. *Mobility*. London: Routledge.

Anderson, J. 2004. The ties that bind? Self- and place-identity in environmental direct action. *Ethics, Place and Environment*, 7(1–2), 45–58.

Anderson, J. 2009. Transient convergence and relational sensibility: Beyond the modern constitution of nature. *Emotion, Space, & Society*, 2(2), 120–27.

Anderson, J. 2010. *Understanding Cultural Geography: Places and Traces*. London: Routledge.

Anderson, J. and Erskine, K. 2012. Tropophilia: A study of people, place and lifestyle travel. *Mobilities* [Online], 1–16. Available at: http://dx.doi.org/10.10 80/17450101.2012.743702 [accessed: 20 June 2012].

Bauman, Z. 1996. From pilgrim to tourist – or a short history of identity, in *Questions of Cultural Identity*, edited by S. Hall and P. du Gay. London: SAGE, 1–17.

Bauman, Z. 2001. On mass, individuals, and peg communities, in *The Consumption of Mass*, edited by N. Lee and R. Munro. Blackwell: Oxford, 102–13.

Beck, U. and Beck-Gernsheim, E. 2002. *Individualization*. London: SAGE.

Cohen, E. 2004. *Contemporary Tourism: Diversity and Change*. Oxford: Elsevier.

Cohen, S. 2010. Chasing a myth? Searching for 'self' through lifestyle travel. *Tourist Studies*, 10(2), 117–33.

Cohen, S. 2011. Lifestyle travellers: Backpacking as a way of life. *Annals of Tourism Research*, 38(4), 1535–55.

Coleman, S. and Crang, M. 2002. Grounded tourists, travelling theory, in *Tourism: Between Place and Performance*, edited by S. Coleman and M. Crang. New York: Berghahn Books, 1–17.

Cresswell, T. 2001. *The Tramp in America*. London: Reaktion.

Cresswell, T. 2004. *Place: A Short Introduction*. Oxford: Blackwell.

Cresswell, T. 2010a. Mobilities I: Catching up. *Progress in Human Geography*, 35(4), 550–58.

Cresswell, T. 2010b. Towards a politics of mobility. *Environment & Planning D, Society & Space*, 28(1), 17–31.

Cresswell, T. 2011. Mobilities II: Still. *Progress in Human Geography*, 36(5), 645–53.

D'Andrea, A. 2006. Neo-nomadism: A theory of post-identitarian mobility in the global age. *Mobilities*, 1(1), 95–119.

Desforges, L. 1998. Checking out the planet: Global representations/local identities and youth travel, in *Cool Places: Geographies of Youth Cultures*, edited by T. Skelton and G. Valentine. London: Routledge, 175–94.

Desforges, L. 2000. Travelling the world, identity and travel biography. *Annals of Tourism Research*, 27(4), 926–45.

Duffy, R. 2004. Ecotourists on the beach, in *Tourism Mobilities: Places to Play, Places in Play*, edited by M. Sheller and J. Urry. London: Routledge, 32–43.

Edensor, T. 2000. Staging tourism: Tourists as performers. *Annals of Tourism Research*, 27(2), 322–44.

Featherstone, M. 1995. *Undoing Culture*. London: SAGE.

Germann Molz, J. 2010. Performing global geographies: Time, space, place and pace in narratives of round-the-world travel. *Tourism Geographies: An International Journal of Tourism Space, Place and Environment*, 12(3), 329–48.

Golden-Gelman, R. 2011. *Tales of a Female Nomad: Living at Large in the World*. New York: Random House.

Gustafson, P. 2001. Place attachment and mobility, in *Multiple Dwelling and Tourism: Negotiating Place, Home and Identity*, edited by N. McIntyre, D. Williams and K. McHugh. Oxfordshire: CABI, 17–31.

Hannam, K. Sheller, M. and Urry, J. 2006. Editorial: Mobilities, immobilities and moorings. *Mobilities*, 1(1), 1–22.

Ingold, T. 2005. Up, across and along. *Delft Universirty of Technology* [Online], 45–54 Available at: http://www.spacesyntax.tudelft.nl/media/Long%20papers%20I/tim%20ingold.pdf [accessed: 20 July 2009].

Jones, M. 2009. Phase space: Geography, relational thinking, and beyond. *Progress in Human Geography*, 33(4), 487–506.

Malkki, L. 1992. National geographic: The rooting of peoples and the territorialisation of national identity among scholars and refugees. *Cultural Anthropology*, 7(1), 24–44.

Manzo, L. 2003. Beyond house and haven: Toward a revisioning of emotional relationships with places. *Journal of Environmental Psychology*, 23(1), 47–61.

Massey, D. 2005. *For Space*. London: SAGE.

Massey, D. 2006. Landscape as a provocation: Reflections on moving mountains. *Journal of Material Culture*, 11(1–2), 33–48.

Maxey, I. 1999. Beyond boundaries? Activism, academia, reflexivity and research. *Area*, 31, 199–208.

Moore, D. 1997. Remapping resistance: Ground for struggle and the politics of place, in *Geographies of Resistance*, edited by S. Pile and M. Keith. London: Routledge, 87–106.

O'Reilly, C. 2005. Tourist or traveller? Narrating backpacker identity, in *Discourse Communication and Tourism*, edited by A. Jaworski and A. Pritchard. Clevedon: Channel View Publications, 150–70.

O'Reilly, C. 2006. From drifter to gap year tourist: Mainstreaming backpacker travel. *Annals of Tourism Research*, 33(4), 998–1017.

Price, P. 2013. Place, in *The Wiley-Blackwell Companion to Cultural Geography*, edited by N.C. Johnson, R.H. Schein and J. Winders. Oxford: Wiley Blackwell, 118–29.

Relph, E. 1976. *Place and Placelessness*. London: Pion.

Rojek, C. 1993. *Ways of Escape: Modern Transformations in Leisure and Travel*. London: Macmillan.

Said, E. 1993. *Culture and Imperialism*. London: Vintage.

Seamon, D. and Mugerauer, R. (eds) 1985. *Dwelling, Place and Environment: Toward a Phenomenology of Person and World*. Malabar: Kluwer.

Sheller, M. and Urry, J. 2004. Places to play, places in play, in *Tourism Mobilities: Places to Play, Places in Play*, edited by M. Sheller and J. Urry. London: Routledge, 1–10.

Sheller, M. and Urry, J. 2006. The new mobilities paradigm. *Environment and Planning A*, 38(2), 207–26.

Soja, E. 2010. *Postmodern Geographies: The Reassertion of Space in Critical Social Theory*. London: Verso.

Tuan, Y.-F. 1974. *Topophilia: A Study of Environmental Perception, Attitudes and Values*. London: Prentice Hall.

Tuan, Y.-F. 1977. *Space and Place: The Perspective of Experience*. Minneapolis: University of Minnesota Press.

Tuan, Y.-F. 2004. Sense of place: Its relationship to self and time, in *Reanimating Places*, edited by T. Mels. Aldershot: Ashgate, 45–56.

Twigger-Ross, C.L. and Uzzell, D. 1996. Place and identity processes. *Journal of Environmental Psychology*, 16(3), 205–20.

Urry, J. 2002. *The Tourist Gaze*, 2nd edition. London: Sage Publications.

Zuev, D. 2011. CouchSurfing as a spatial practice: Accessing and producing xenotopos. *Hospitality & Society*, 1(3), 227–44.

Chapter 3
Travel as Critique and Transgression in Michel Foucault and Colin Thubron

Drew Ninnis

The slopes of Mt. Kailas have never been scaled. It rises in miraculous independence from a chain of lesser mountains, and has been worshiped for centuries as a place holy to a fifth of humankind. It is to here that Colin Thubron journeys, in his narrative *To a Mountain in Tibet*, in order to come to terms with the death of his mother. He writes that:

> You cannot walk out your grief, I know, or absolve yourself of your survival, or bring anyone back. You are left with the desire only that things not be as they are. So you choose somewhere meaningful on the earth's surface, as if planning a secular pilgrimage. Yet the meaning is not your own. Then you go on a journey (it's my profession, after all), walking to a place beyond your own history, to the sound of the river flowing the other way. In the end you come to rest at a mountain that is holy to others. The reason for this is beyond articulation. (Thubron 2011: 9–10)

He allows himself the forethought that 'a journey is not a cure. It brings an illusion, only, of change, and becomes at best a spartan comfort' and a Tibetan monk responds 'the soul has no memory ... [t]he dead do not feel their past' (Thubron 2011: 10). In beginning his journey, Thubron identifies his desire for transformation, but forecloses any opportunity of realising it. Why, then, take the journey?

I will argue below that certain forms of travel offer limited but powerful avenues for individual transformation; and that they do so through opening up opportunities for critique within our everyday modes of being, and for transgression. My argument is influenced by an unusual combination of two diverse writers and thinkers – Colin Thubron and Michel Foucault. From Foucault I derive a philosophical methodology which allows us to engage in what he calls a 'critical ontology of the present' in order to appreciate the fragility of the hidden structures that channel our experiences, and to identify opportunities to bring these structures into question and experiment with their transgression (Foucault 1998: 74). From Thubron I derive the raw experience of confronting other modes of being within a context heavily loaded with both everyday and metaphysical significance, which is not only alien to certain traditions of experience but also inadvertently brings the foundations of those experiences into question. What also makes Foucault's analyses significant and popular is the manner in which he links the historical development of these institutions to the forms of power they develop and exercise, and the kinds of subjectivities they are able to produce within the individuals that are subject to them. Read together, these two thinkers offer an interesting perspective on travel as a form of transformation and a series of important confrontations with forms of being otherwise; making travel simultaneously the most radical and accessible form of critique and transgression available to us.

Epistemic Transformations

When we travel for pleasure, we travel in order to experience new things and as a form of escape. Both are intimately bound up with each other; as we attempt to escape the demands that structure our everyday modes of being and in order to commune with experiences that are either beyond our existential horizons or which exceed our lived pasts.

Yet the paradox is that our contemporary notion of travel also contains the notion of return; the realisation that our period of leave will end, and we will be drawn back to the modes of being that we have left behind. Just like Thubron, we might ask: what do we gain when we travel? In this sense, travel is inevitably a disappointed promise – a promise of escape, tinged with the inexorability of return. How can travel ever promise transformation if it is beholden to the larger calendar of our lives and the geography of our homes? Something else seems to be at work here, a subtler form of transformation, and one that I would relate to a famous anecdote from the Zen teacher, D.T. Suzuki:

> Before studying Zen, men are men and mountains are mountains. While studying Zen, things become confused. After studying Zen, men are men and mountains are mountains. After telling this, Dr. Suzuki was asked, 'What is the difference between before and after'? He said, 'No difference, only the feet are a little bit off the ground'. (Cited in Larson 2012: xiv)

The transformation described here is difficult to conceptualise, as it seems to rest either on some frustratingly obscure mystical realisation or an intellectual refinement that the mind is not quick to grasp. I would argue that it is the latter; that when we travel, and experience other modes of being, the fragility and contingency of the facets of our own existence at home suddenly comes to the fore. What seemed an inevitable and inescapable way of being – of thinking about the world, or relating to it, or experiencing it – is suddenly confronted by completely different and equally possible modes of being. When we return we carry the realisation of this fragility with us; while we may reoccupy our old routines and lives, we are suddenly aware of the tiny details that could be otherwise and through this realisation, as Suzuki remarks, 'the feet are a little bit off the ground' (Larson 2012: xiv).

On a philosophical level, this is an apprehension of the contingency of the structures that govern our existence – and this is the first step towards a critique and then transgression of them. In his much-cited article, 'What is enlightenment?', Foucault (1999: 319) describes the project of critique as building a 'critical ontology of the present'. By this he means that we add a historical dimension to the structures that we regularly encounter, and temper their inevitability with an appreciation of the historical accidents that led to their emergence and their seeming dominance. Foucault employs history to illustrate how some of the predominating logics of our age – such as certain forms of political rationality – are the product of unique circumstances, and are not as universal as they might first seem. Indeed, Foucault's histories seek to show how often it has been otherwise, and how different modes of being have coexisted and been transformed. The closest we can come to experiencing these other modes and transformations for ourselves is to travel. Therefore, travel opens up the very possibility of critique.

The first shock within these forms of travel and critique can be said to be epistemic; and does not require much physical travel at all. In his preface to *The Order of Things*, Foucault is shocked into laughter by 'the impossibility of thinking *that*' (Foucault 1989: xvi, emphasis in original). The '*that*' in question is a supposed ancient Chinese system for ordering the objects of the universe, found in Borges' (2000: 231) description of the 'Celestial Empire of Benevolent Knowledge':

> In its remote pages it is written that the animals are divided into: (a) belonging to the emperor, (b) embalmed, (c) tame, (d) sucking pigs, (e) sirens, (f) fabulous, (g) stray dogs, (h) included in the present classification, (i) frenzied, (j) innumerable, (k) drawn with a very fine camelhair brush, (l) et cetera, (m) having just broken the water pitcher, (n) that from a long way off look like flies.

Foucault writes that upon reading this, he experienced 'all the familiar landmarks of my thought – our thought, the thought that bears the stamp of our age and our geography – breaking up all the ordered surfaces and all the planes with which we are accustomed to tame the wild profusion of existing things' (Foucault 1989: xvi). The article itself is likely to have been fabricated by Borges; however, this does not lessen its force and, indeed, seems to open up other possibilities that are even more troubling. What is the source of this disruption? And why does the doubt it creates not resolve, even when we discover that it was a cunning, amusing phantasm? It does not detract from the force of the shock that the realisation brings; particularly to the individual attempting to rearrange the structures within their mind to accommodate this new way of looking at the world. On the contrary, it seems to illustrate that even our imaginations are tempered by the structures of certain actualities, and that one of the most potent means of liberating them and of transforming our conceptions of the world is to encounter other wonders through travel. In *The Order of Things*, Foucault uses this particular shock for the specific purpose of critiquing the current structure of knowledge within the human sciences, particularly the way in which it constitutes the individual as an object of knowledge and the manner in which this has transformed over the centuries. Likewise, travel can force us to navigate a foreign culture's means of conceptualising the world, as well as the numerous relationships between its objects and their various significances.

This is the exact situation that Colin Thubron encounters in his travels to Mt. Kailas. He undertakes the traditional pilgrimage around the base of Mt. Kailas, which is sacred to four religions – Hindu, Buddhist, Bön and Jainism – and 'one fifth of humankind' (Thubron 2011: 4). Thubron writes that 'for all its mass, the mountain is light' and that:

> [i]n Tibetan folklore it flew here from another, unknown country – many of
> Tibet's mountains fly – and was staked in place by prayer-banners and chains
> before devils could pull it underground. Then, to prevent the celestial gods
> from lifting it up and returning it to where it came from, the Buddha nailed it
> down with four of his footprints. But now, they say, it is the age of Kaliyuga, of
> degeneration, and at any moment the mountain could fly away again. (2011: 163)

The belief that mountains 'could fly away' is a cousin to the Western metaphysical anxiety that an object may disappear when it is unseen, or that our individual experiences of reality might prove to be a solipsistic illusion. The epistemic shock of trying to understand the belief brings us to contemplate the foundations of our own thinking about the mountain; that it might be a distinct object, separable and able to be weighed, and by virtue of this possessing a great weight which would make its flight impossible. Within our thinking and Thubron's writing on Kailas there is the weighing of an object, a consciousness of individual objects (even of *a* mountain, separated) against a background space, and in the moment of Foucault's laughter this is shattered by the Buddhist conception of Kailas as a part of the holy sky.

This moment is one among many in Thubron's journey around the mountain, all of which lead to the experience, similar to studying Zen, where 'things become confused' (Larson 2012: xiv). Our common vision of representation and poetics is challenged; instead of seeing the heavy earth stretching up towards the sky, we are encouraged to experience the mountain as part of the holy sky stretching down to touch the ground, a connection kept open through the passage of the devout's footsteps. The moment is also philosophical in its critique, and it would be tempting to cast it as the challenge of a lost Heraclitean conception of impermanence confronting a long dominant Platonic doctrine of intransigence. Yet even this ancient Western debate fails to capture the radical difference between two modes of thought that Thubron must gradually adjust to. In any case, contemplating other modes of conceptualising these epistemic relationships makes us sensitive to the contradictions at the foundations of our own thinking. It invites a slow transformation of epistemic perspective, which begins with a critical appreciation of the contingency of our own conceptualisations and the possibility of thinking otherwise. One may read about it in literature on Buddhist thought; but as Thubron highlights, the experience of that thought only becomes possible when travelling through the exceptional place occupied by Mt. Kailas.

This makes travel a kind of epistemic transformation; and one that complements Foucault's own epistemic critiques of certain predominant Western structures. If Foucault highlights the epistemic contingency of certain forms of knowledge through genealogy and history, then journeys such as Thubron's highlight this epistemic contingency geographically. Both juxtapose the experience of a different mode of thinking in order to reactivate our ability to imagine other modes of thought outside of the framework we have acclimatised to; and it is the pleasure of this opening up of thought that draws us back to travel and to the experience of a different cultural horizon.

Ontological Transformations

When we travel, an essential transformation that we undergo is that of our conceptualisation of space. Suddenly, confronted with an experience of certain spaces and their different relationships to other spaces, we are forced to revisit the manner in which we conceptualise and give meaning to these spaces. Early on in his journey, Thubron confronts the stark realisation that his current location – in Nepal, attempting to cross into Tibet – bears a direct and close relationship to many of the place names that he read on a map as a child, places where his father had hunted game and of which he had heard stories (Thubron 2011: 30). He suddenly stands mere kilometres from not only a literal place, but also from the experiences of his father and his child's interpretation of the stories of those experiences, which shifts his own history and relationship with them. As he comes closer to his goal, the land seems to 'shed its strangeness' as he encounters the everyday lives of the individuals who populate these spaces and maintain very different relationships to them (Thubron 2011: 31–2). I would argue that there are three levels on which we relate to a given space within the context of a journey or of travel: the literal, which concerns how we navigate the terrain of a space; the ontological, which concerns the way in which a space engenders certain ways of living and modes of being; and the aesthetic, which directly impacts how we experience a space and how we continue to represent it or imagine its relationship with us. Thubron radically changes his conception on all of these levels, through navigating this one space: experiencing it as a physical phenomenon, of tiredness, fatigue and challenge; participating in the lives of locals, and experiencing the alterations in behaviour that his presence in this space brings; and in waking to a new reality of a space that he previously pictured differently. All of these transformations concern the traveller's changing relationship with particular spaces, and the manner in which they are changed from the experience of a journey through them.

Foucault (1999), in a little known article entitled 'Different spaces', posits the idea of a *heterotopia*, which is an exceptional space in which transformations of the individual's mode of being occur. He writes that contemporary philosophy, particularly phenomenology, has given credibility to the idea that 'we are living not in a homogeneous and empty space but, on the contrary, in a space that is laden with qualities, a space that may also be haunted by fantasy' (Foucault 1999: 177). This is certainly the experience that Thubron has of Kailas, an area that is not just a rugged mountain terrain, but is populated by demons and the imaginary, as well as with penitents actively seeking to transform their existences or gain something from forces beyond mere physical geography. For Foucault, the 'present age may be the age of space instead' and he argues that we are 'in an era of the simultaneous, of juxtaposition, of the near and the far, of the side-by-side, of the scattered' (Foucault 1999: 175). What he means by this is that the very mobility that the modern age has brought to these places, the very core of our ability to travel, has also brought the juxtapositioning of experiences of diverse, contradictory and exceptional spaces. Thubron brings with him relationships to spaces that, for us, are reasonably conventional; and yet the exceptional meanings that load down Kailas form a challenge to those relationships at every turn. Travelling to Kailas is not just experiencing another mountain landscape, but also to become immersed in and transformed by the forms that give Kailas its diverse significances – the rituals, the shifting explanations and narratives of the place, and the ontological relationship that one enters in joining others in a pilgrimage around a mountain. It is a 'space haunted by fantasy' (Foucault 1999: 177) more than any other, in that four religions share it and narrate it; doubly so for Thubron, who must accommodate the narrative of his childhood alongside the experiences and accounts of his fellow pilgrims.

To return to Foucault (1999), in conceptualising these exceptional spaces – which are a series of experiences as much as they are places – he posits six loose principles of heterotopias. The first is 'that there is probably not a single culture in the world that does not establish heterotopias', but they 'obviously take forms that are very diverse' (Foucault 1999: 179). What all heterotopias share is their purpose, which is affecting a change in the state of the individual passing through them. Secondly, he notes that heterotopias are historical focal points in that their functions and purposes can be slowly transformed to take on new meanings or to produce different states within the individual. As an example Foucault mentions cemeteries, which have undergone many transformations in the constitution of their meaning and relationship to broader societies (and Kailas, as Thubron observes, also functions as a place of the dead). Thirdly, Foucault observes that the 'heterotopia has the ability to juxtapose in a single real place several emplacements that are incompatible in themselves' (Foucault 1999: 180), meaning that heterotopias are not just physical places but also places of representation that stand in for other places throughout the process of transformation. At Kailas, millennia-old battles are played out and the location itself serves as a theatre to four faiths and narratives of the individual's relation to the divine.

Fourthly, heterotopias also break with external conceptions of time and substitute their own, often in the form of a crisis. Foucault remarks that the 'heterotopia begins to function fully when men are in a kind of absolute break with their traditional time' and again offers the example of a cemetery, which contrasts the divide between 'that strange heterochronia that loss of life constitutes for an individual, and that quasi eternity in which he perpetually dissolves and fades away' (Foucault 1999: 182). Fifthly, Foucault highlights that heterotopias 'always presuppose a system of opening and closing that isolates them and makes them penetrable at the same time' (Foucault 1999: 183). By this, Foucault means that the uniqueness of the place always involves a journey and it is not simply like entering one's living room; rather, the individual must undergo a series of preparations and small transformations within themselves in order to enter. Travel is a conscious undertaking to experience difference and attempt to enter the spaces or heterotopias of others. We uproot our way of living, and prepare to experience others, in preparation for our journey into these heterotopias. Finally, Foucault writes that despite their isolation heterotopias 'have a function in relation to the remaining space' (Foucault 1999: 184).

Foucault's six principles for the operation of heterotopias attempt to disclose how it is that certain exceptional spaces gain meaning and attempt to transform the individual in specific ways. While being culturally unique, they share the quality of transforming the manner in which we live our lives – at least within that space – and also aim to reform or impact our modes of being once we return from our journey. They do this by creating a space loaded with representations and haunted by fantasy that is played out in the physical relationship that the individual has to the space. Just as European cathedrals attempt to inspire awe at the thought of a Christian God (and often illustrate the acts of faith on their surfaces), so too is Kailas a place where demons inhabit certain boulders and the myths of the holy sky are made doubly present by the aesthetic experience of sacred Lake Mansarovar and Mt. Kailas; the space is expanded and elaborated by the many narratives that occupy it. The space breaks with traditional conceptions of time, and forces the individual to attune to its own unique rhythms and means of measuring existence. The heterotopia regulates entrance, and it operates in specific relation to the other everyday spaces that we may occupy. Heterotopias are machines for transformation; and in their journey to Mt. Kailas, pilgrims hope to be transformed through establishing a relationship with the heavens and the holy places through which they ritually travel.

This is the experience that Thubron relates on his way to Mt. Kailas – and it accounts for both the detail that he puts into describing the transformation of the landscapes and the conversations that he has, but also explains the important silences in his work where he is unable to relate what he seeks there, what he finds, or what follows within his inner life afterwards. On passing a group of monks he identifies the inexplicable transformation the place works on these pilgrims that he is unable to articulate within his own experience, writing:

> As they walk on, I wonder at them, their lightness, their lack of need. They
> might already have passed through a painless, premature death. They have shed
> what others shed in dying. They will leave nothing material behind them to be
> divided, claimed or loved. Their dispossession strikes me as at once freedom,
> and a poignant depletion. Their buoyant laughter follows me up the valley, but I
> do not quite envy them. I only wonder with a muffled pang what it would be in
> the West to step outside the chain of bequeathal and inheritance, as they do, until
> human artefacts mean nothing at all. (Thubron 2011: 54)

Certainly, this has a lot to do with their training and their religious order. Yet this
too is a preparation for their travel to the exceptional space that Kailas constitutes.
The place, and the journey to this place, has an essential role in effecting the
transformation that Thubron seeks; wishing to glimpse some of the experience of
liberation and relation to death that he observes in the monks. The hidden rhythm
of the space carries him part way there, and he writes:

> You look back down the valley and wonder: how did I come so far? A few
> minutes ago, or perhaps an hour, you passed a trader's shelter – a sheepskin
> draped between rocks – and now it has dwindled to a fleck below you. Perhaps,
> after all, you have walked this path unawares, drugged by the rhythm of
> your boots, as if dreaming, and only a passage of startling beauty or hardship
> wrenched you awake. (Thubron 2011: 72)

When confronted with meeting a group of fellow European trekkers, bearers
of his shared culture, Thubron recoils at the possible shattering of the fragile
transformation he has unknowingly undergone, as he explains he has 'felt a
stressless self-diffusion, as if my own culture were growing lighter on my
shoulders' (Thubron 2011: 95).

In reading this, the transformative elements of Foucault's analysis of
heterotopias fall into place. On entering and travelling through the heterotopia
we break with our conceptions of time and space ('how did I come so far'); we
break with our everyday experience of certain cultures ('as if my own culture were
growing lighter'); we constitute our relationship to the space as something more
than physical ('imagined these mountains as mine'); and we are awakened to a
different relationship to the space and its representation ('a passage of startling
beauty or hardship wrenched you awake').

Thubron illustrates how the experience of a different space is strongly linked to
complimentary aesthetic, epistemic and ontological transformations that are only
made possible by travelling through this exceptional space. On concluding his
pilgrimage he writes that 'as the last pilgrim drops from sight under the gleam of
Kailas, the beliefs of many peoples – from ancient Egypt to aboriginal Australia –
seem starkly natural' (Thubron 2011: 184). His experiences and conceptualisations
have been transformed from a mythical imagining of his fathers' hunting grounds
into an experience of a series of beliefs foundational to another mode of being – a

'world turned crimson' where it is 'easy to imagine this an apocalyptic fracture in the order of things' (Thubron 2011: 132). Foucault, equally as attuned to the fragility in the order of things, fleshes out the different levels on which these transformations take place and invites us to consider the relationship of these heterotopias to our everyday experiences of space.

Metaphysical Transformations

Underpinning our relationship to space and to discourse is a fundamental question concerning the manner in which we constitute ourselves as selves, and our relationship to truth. This question is central to all of Foucault's work. In one of his lectures to the *Collège de France* he categorises this constitution of the self as 'techniques of the self' and 'technologies of selfhood' (Foucault 1998: 87–8). Travel is one such technique of transforming one's subjectivity, or at least attempting to experiment with different modes of being in order to see how it is possible to live otherwise. As I have attempted to argue above, Kailas represents one of these unique sites where a journey is undertaken in order to transform one's relationship to oneself and to truth. Part of this transformation is tied up in space, narrative and representation; but what is at stake in the pilgrimage to Kailas is also the hope for a direct participation in certain forms of truth, and a transformation of the individual's relation to truth. Thubron explains the significance of the pilgrimage to Kailas for the faithful, and writes:

> A single mountain circuit, it is said, if walked in piety, will dispel the defilement of a lifetime, and bring requital for the murder of even a lama or a parent, while 108 such koras lift the pilgrim into Buddhahood ... even now, if a pilgrim rides a yak or a pony, half the merit goes to the beast. (Thubron 2011: 158–9)

What is at stake in this journey is not just any experience, but an experience of certain forms of truth and the remaking of the self involved in those experiences.

Thubron is initially dubious that the myth of Kailas could possibly have force in the world, let alone have the power to change his own understanding of the world, and expresses this doubt to an abbot in Kathmandu (Thubron 2011: 45). However, at key points Thubron is confronted by his own realisation that his conceptualisation of transformation through certain forms of religious practice is utterly inadequate; and trapped within a Western conception of the nature of faith and divinity – the abbot, mentioned above, 'who had studied tantra for three years now, refused to call it a philosophy, still less a faith' (Thubron 2011: 135). Rather, the abbot conceives of his religious practices as a series of exercises in self-making and consciousness, claiming that the 'gods were only guides to the enlightenment that would erase them' and saying 'I think it is a science, anyone can do it – I think you can do it' (Thubron 2011: 135). What is at stake in such practices is not so much an assertion of or belief in a claim to truth, as it may be in other religions, but a series of exercises through which one attempts to enter into a relationship with a certain sort of truth. Concluding his discussion with the abbot, Thubron (2011: 135–6) writes: '[b]ut tantrism was a way to be lived, Tashi said, not a doctrine to be learnt. You could not know it until you experienced it. Though by then, perhaps, it would be too late to return'.

There are two points to be made here. The first is a question of exposure. Without his travel to Kathmandu, Thubron would have been unaware of the approach that the abbot takes to transforming himself and his relationship to truth. Encounters with others through travel, at the very least, allow us to appreciate a differing perspective of truth and realise that there is possibly a different relationship that we could have with the truth or with certain forms of thought. But the second point goes to the necessity of *experiencing* this difference, rather than simply hearing about it. Thubron recollects these conversations as he marches towards Kailas, reflecting that the relationship of space and the shapes of thought that he has been exposed to somehow gives truth to these different forms of relationships and possible modes of being. As I quoted above, he comes to feel that 'the beliefs of many peoples seem starkly natural' (Thubron 2011: 184).

In short, the transformation that travel effects is not just an exposure to new ideas or ways of life or senses of space, but also a transformation that occurs through allowing the traveller brief glimpses of a different relationship to truth and a different mode of being. Thubron is unlikely to convert to Buddhism; but by passing through this exceptional space, he is suddenly brought closer to the reality that animates the teachings and experiences of this once alien system of thought. Similarly, this realisation offers Thubron the ability to distance himself from the experiences and modes of being that previously grounded him; allowing him to reflect on the death of his family members, his life upon return, and critically engage not only with the experience that he has of the monks or pilgrims that he encounters at Kailas but also the experience of himself that he will have when he returns from travel. In this manner, travel is a form of self-making, or at least self-examination, and in this way very close to what Foucault conceptualises as critique.

Foucault labels this critical experience as 'problematization', by which he means 'the development of a domain of acts, practices, and thoughts that seem to me to pose problems for politics' (Foucault 1998: 114). What Thubron's travels problematise is 'a complex experience ... constituted from and around certain forms of behaviour' that is common within our own societies, and which we constitute ourselves or are constituted as subjectivities – we are objects of a 'field of knowledge' (consumers, patients, legal subjects); we are subject to 'a collection of rules' (laws, regulations, codes of conduct); and we occupy 'a mode of relation between the individual and himself' (as desirers, consumers, plaintiffs) (Foucault 1998: 200). Throughout his work, Foucault argues that these methods of constituting subjects and their subjectivities are the product of contingent historical forces, structures and institutions – as well as indicating that they could be otherwise. Therefore, for Foucault, critique is:

an awareness that criticism – understood as an analysis of the historical conditions that bear on the creation of links to truth, to rules, and to the self – does not mark out impassable boundaries or describe closed systems; it brings to light transformable singularities. (Foucault 1998: 201)

This is exactly what Thubron's experience of other modes of being provides; an awareness that certain ways of constituting oneself and one's relationship to truth are not absolute, but highly contingent and open to transformation or transgression. Difference does not necessarily mean more desirable, it simply marks that difference and indicates that where one difference can exist many more may be possible. Thubron's most poignant encounter comes towards the end of his travels, where he encounters a fellow traveller:

Another man is walking behind me: a pilgrim, with his wife and child and beast. Recent centuries have not touched him. He has his own. He sees with a bright, focused intensity. He has come from the lake country to the north, or perhaps from farther, and the distance brings merit. He prostrates often to the god mountain, and the earth feels hot under him. The prayer's words are strong, although he does not understand them, and the gods breathe back from the summits. He has remembered everything the village shaman spoke of, and placated the *klu* in the stream, in case they are there. The water's coldness comes cleansing to the touch. He puts it in a phial for his sick mother. That is what he has come for, and for the black earth-lords to spare his barley crop, and for the calving of the third yak. These are the great things. His wife, whom he shares with his brother, has other thoughts. Women's. He knows what they are, he thinks. (Thubron 2011: 206)

There is so much in this figure that is familiar, yet unfathomable, and we cannot help but be conscious of the existential chasm that separates us from him. Yet there is something that is gained within the experience of this encounter; not so much a wish to occupy his shoes, but a desire to be brought closer to this other mode of relating to the world. To Thubron he seems to come from a different time, he struggles to survive and support his family, he shares his wife with his brother – yet, in reading the account, Thubron's respect for the man's integrity comes through clearly. Again, like the encounter with the monks, there is a partial envy in Thubron's voice even as he would not wish to take their place. This is, I believe, the very form of problematisation that Foucault highlights within critique; we do not wish to adopt this mode of being, but it cannot help indicating the fragility and missing elements of our own relationship to ourselves and to certain forms of truth.

The conclusion to Thubron's journey is ambiguous, its consequences left hidden by the author. He writes that 'it is the custom to leave some object on Drolma's pass, and to take something else away', yet he does not tell us what he takes or what he leaves (Thubron 2011: 210). On one level that which he leaves and takes is obvious – in that he leaves behind the imaginary strangeness and mysticism of his childhood Tibet, and takes away the potential for a new relationship to truth. This, rather like the existential impact of the experiences of his travel, would be impossible to describe. Travel is unlike any other form of transformation because it is an experience and an encounter with difference that can only be weakly conveyed in any other form. Foucault, too, recognises this weakness in his own work; recognising that his writing is but one form of an encounter with critique, and a futile one if one does not then engage in the existential work of transgression and transformation. Travel to these exceptional places is a form of critique, transgression and transformation because it forces us to engage with different modes of being and ways of living – different systems of thought, experiences of space, and relationships with truth. As Foucault remarks, 'thus, contestation shapes an experience ... and in its most essential form, "the immediacy of being"' (Foucault 1999: 75).

Ethical Confrontations

And yet it is too easy to fetishise cultures as rich as Buddhism, Jainism, Bön or Hinduism which occupy the steps of Mt. Kailas. Thubron's travel is not without troubling signs, which are generally sorted into two categories – either the influence of the West or the influence of China. Tibet is not a magical place where its people are preserved from outside influence, but the contrary: an area that has a long history of contestation, and one which continues to struggle with its identity and the future of its people. Thubron, when speaking with a monk in Nepal, is reminded that 'it is you who can go to Kailas', while the monk cannot due to the political situation at the border (Thubron 2011: 47). Sometimes the situation is humorous – as when 'all morning a helmeted Chinese fire officer stands alone and rigid, fulfilling some regulation, with a canister on either side of him and nothing flammable in sight' – but more often than not it represents the ongoing transformation of a place to fit within a larger political and cultural order (Thubron 2011: 158).

This is not to say that the problem is merely one political regime's claims over another, but is more broadly representative of the growing influence of the West and the international order, which this place must now navigate. When speaking of his cherished practices, the abbot from Kathmandu remarks that 'we live in an age of decline. I think before the Chinese invaded Tibet, and our Buddhist people were dispersed, that our faith was much purer. Now we're exposed to Western ways, and of course to women' (Thubron 2011: 70). It is also difficult to discern how one should respond to these elements; on the one hand, Tibet is opening up to the world, but on the other, certain historical forms and practices are being lost. Thubron's guide remarks that 'in the city, we are like you in the West now' (Thubron 2011: 39) When interrogated further about this the guide remarks:

'Love?' I ask. 'How can you know?'

'I've read magazines. I've seen the films. I'll have two children, a boy and a girl, and I'll make sure they're educated'. He glances at Dhabu, who is grinning to himself, uneducated, on a rock. 'I've read about it all'. (Thubron 2011: 43)

The account is touching precisely because we recognise within it our own idealisations of the West, just as Thubron recognises his own fantasies of Tibet, while also knowing the aching complexities and differences within our own lives that give lie to such a picture. Thubron is also brutally honest not only about the hardship that he encounters on his travels, but also the naïve hope that the locals he encounters place in his own way of life. He writes:

Then a man joins us on the path. He is vivid with troubles. His jacket is patched, his trainers split. He fires a volley of questions at the sherpa. How can he get out of this place? There's nothing for anybody here. His family can't support itself on its patch of rice field ... it isn't enough ... His eyes spear us out of a sun-blackened face. He follows us for miles. He cannot bear to let us go: we, who carry the aura of a wider world. (Thubron 2011: 3)

My own reaction to Thubron's account is complicated by a series of conflicting desires. On the one hand I mourn for the loss of traditional ways of life, and the possibility for others to experience this exceptional space as it is; but on the other hand, I recognise the fundamental selfishness that rests at the base of this traveller's desire. It represents the loss of a site of experience; a cost that is hard to justify in the face of other considerations such as poverty, and the right of these individuals to experiment with their own means of living otherwise. While travel may offer the opportunity of critique, transgression, and transformation it is hard not to recognise the *Brave New World* inequality it can be founded on.

So why, then, travel? What do we gain when we travel? The individual that passes through the experience of one mode of being into another takes with them the remnants of their experience rather than the strictures of their frameworks. Perhaps this is the core of the transformation that we undergo when we travel, beyond critique or transgression; the memory of a participation in something significantly different, which is only able to be grasped in those fleeting moments, unable to be elaborated according to a different framework of expression but only through thoughtscape and dream. In this way travel is critique, in that it does not exactly open up that mode of existence for us – the tourist, the foreigner – to take up, but rather finds spaces within our own modes of being as yet unarticulated and able to be cultivated into something else. It opens up the space to perceive certain structures as otherwise, to transform our existing modes of being, and through those transformations allow us to pass from critique to transgression and beyond. Then, we must return; and upon emerging from the shadow of Kailas

Thubron writes 'in minutes before sleep, a shadowy melancholy descends: the bewilderment when something long awaited has gone' (Thubron 2011: 214).

As poetic or radical as that may sound, I would argue that the reality is much more modest and that these realisations are not new. When we travel as a means of participating in difference, self or societal critique, and eventually transformation we participate in a form of journey as old as human experience itself. Travel as transformation – be it to a mountain in Tibet or elsewhere – is ultimately the ancient act of pilgrimage. After the transformation and return that travel offers us, there is '*no difference, only the feet are a little bit off the ground*'.

References

Borges, J.L. 2000. The analytical language of John Wilkins, in *Borges: Selected Non-Fictions*. Translated by E. Weinberger. London: Penguin, 229–32.

Foucault, M. 1989. *The Order of Things: An Archaeology of the Human Sciences*. London: Routledge.

Foucault, M. 1998. *Ethics: Subjectivity and Truth (Essential Works of Foucault, 1954–1984, Vol. 1)*, edited by J. Faubion, R. Hurley and P. Rabinow. New York: The New Press.

Foucault, M. 1999. *Aesthetics, Method, and Epistemology (Essential Works of Foucault, 1954–1984, Vol. 2)*, edited by J. Faubion, R. Hurley and P. Rabinow. New York: The New Press.

Larson, K. 2012. *Where the Heart Beats: John Cage, Zen Buddhism, and the Inner Life of Artists*. London: Penguin.

Thubron, C. 2011. *To a Mountain in Tibet*. London: Chatto & Windus.

Chapter 4

Doing Good: Transforming the Self by Transforming the World

Fiona Allon and Maria Koleth

It was pretty amazing ... building this house. At the moment they are in tarps and next week they'll be in a brick house and the other family that we were also working with were going to get kicked out of their rental accommodation house so there was a real sense ... that we can, as individuals, make a difference. (Jessica, 2 June 2012)

Jessica is recalling building two houses for Cambodian families with Habitat for Humanity. At the time, the trip was transformative for everyone involved and more so because it appeared to be tangibly improving the lives of the families who Jessica and her college friends came to know well. Undertaking volunteer travel, in Jessica's words, 'makes a difference', 'helps to give perspective' and occasions a change in decisions about study and life purpose among those who go on the trip. Moreover, the narrative of transformation that Jessica recounted was itself a catalyst for further transformation, mobilised in her professional work context during 'strengths-based exercises' to demonstrate initiative and resilience. Exercises of this type ask employees to reflect on experiences in which they demonstrated particular strength and effectiveness, which can then be used to inform and inspire ordinary work patterns. The narrative also extended well beyond the event from which it originated, and was constantly being added to by other stories and travels, creating a reserve of experience, insight and knowledge that could be tapped into when necessary. The trip constituted evidence of the making of a well-rounded person, furnished with a broader understanding of the world.

Transformation at a personal, social and global level is a key trope of the contemporary era. The imperative today is to use every experience as a terrain for personal transformation that can be harnessed for broader social and cultural change. Calls to 'make a difference' and 'do something good' have proliferated in many different settings but nowhere more so than in relation to contemporary practices of travel and tourism. The consequent instrumentalisation of travel, evident in the explosion of working holidays and forms of ethical, volunteer and eco-tourism, extends travel in terms of the potential contributions it can make to more equitable forms of global transformation. While travel has traditionally been construed as a means for individual discovery and actualisation, there is considerable evidence that such newer forms of travel have led to a change in the nature of the transformations occasioned by travel today (Duffy and Moore 2010, Ingram 2011, Lyons et al. 2012, McGehee and Santos 2005, Mostafanezhad 2012, Palacios 2010, Scheyvens 2002, Spencer 2010, Vrasti 2013).

This chapter considers the role that travel plays in collapsing boundaries between personal and global transformation by drawing on the ethical framework provided by Rosi Braidotti's (2006) concept of 'transpositions'. Braidotti uses this concept to reconfigure traditional conceptualisations of transformation in a way that is more attuned to the dynamism and endless mobility of the neoliberal economy. Following Braidotti's lead, the chapter takes up the concept of 'transpositions' to recast the personal and global transformations of contemporary travel, not in terms of an absolute revolution, but rather in terms of an 'intertextual, cross-boundary or transversal transfer ... playing the positivity of difference as a specific theme of its own' (Braidotti 2006: 5). The chapter uses the concept of transpositions to consider one increasingly popular form of travel – volunteer tourism – and draws on research interviews conducted with Australian volunteer tourists. Volunteer tourism is receiving increasing amounts of critical attention, in terms of both its impact and motivations (Benson and Siebert 2009, Brown 2005, Coghlan and Fennell 2009, Gray and Campbell 2007, Guttentag 2009, McGehee and Santos 2005, Matthews 2008, Mostafanezhad 2012, Mustonen 2007, Palacios 2010, Simpson 2005, Spencer 2010, Stoddart and Rogerson 2004, Tomazos and Butler 2012, Vrasti 2013). However, the transformations wrought by volunteer and related forms of travel are not only still under-theorised (Benson 2011, McGehee 2012), but are also more incomplete and ambivalent in their becoming than popular understandings credit. In addition, the transformations/transpositions that are of interest here feature not only in the journeys of First World tourists across dynamic 'Third World' spaces, but are also implicated in the fraught journeys of multiple, human and non-human agents.

Data and Methods

This chapter is based on data drawn from ongoing PhD research at the University of Sydney on volunteering and 'Third World' development. The purpose of this research is to explore the impact of volunteer tourism on Third World development ethics. This chapter cites material from 30 semi-structured interviews carried out with returned volunteer tourists in Sydney and through Skype to other capital cities in Australia during 2012. These volunteer tourists each took part in two interviews and participated in programmes run between 2010 and 2012 by a range of different organisations including Habitat for Humanity Australia, Australian company Antipodeans Abroad, UK based companies Projects Abroad and i-to-i Volunteers. Research participants were recruited through emails sent to the Australian volunteer mailing lists of the organisations and companies listed, with the cooperation of the respective companies and organisations. The volunteer tourists who participated in interviews had travelled to many different 'Third

World' destinations including the Maldives, Cambodia, Vietnam, Malaysia, Peru and Ecuador. All their trips involved a payment from volunteers to the organisations with which they travelled. The volunteering programmes they had taken part in ranged from two-week placements to gap year odysseys that involved teaching, construction work or health work. The participants were aged between 20 to 45 years and, while most of the participants were in their early twenties, they brought many different life experiences to the subject of volunteering and development. While the data is not designed to be representative, it provides an insight into specific experiences of transposition as transformation.

From Travel as Self-Transformation to the Altruistic Transfer

The links between travel and a modern narrative of self-transformation are long and extensive. Stories abound of the individual that finds autonomy and modern selfhood by leaving home and tradition behind and stepping out into an unfamiliar world. Travel is the privileged conduit for the process of self-actualisation, enabling a journey of discovery of both the Self and potentially many different Others. MacCannell (1999) provides one of the most memorable explorations of this relationship between travel and transformation in *The Tourist*, where the search for self-development through travel is construed as a central civilisational trope. For MacCannell, the venerable theme of 'self-discovery through a complex and sometimes arduous search for an Absolute Other' is, within modernity, 'a universal experience' (MacCannell 1999: 5). The tourist searches for the Other as a result of a longing for authenticity in modern society: 'condemned to look elsewhere, everywhere, for his authenticity, to see if he can catch a glimpse of it reflected in the simplicity, poverty, chastity or purity of others' (MacCannell 1999: 91). In other words, both modernity and travel propel the same kind of transformative movement – one long trip in search of an authenticity assumed to exist elsewhere (Allon 2004, Frow 1997). MacCannell's tourist collects and accumulates experiences, and struggles to impose coherence and totality in order to eventually find 'his' place in society. This linear narrative of the self is not only implicitly gendered as masculine (Jokinen and Veijola 2004), but also in turn constructs the world as chaotic and fragmented and in need of individual mastery through an equally linear view of progress. Self-transformation through travel is thus conceived as a voyage from stasis and the familiar into a world of complexity and difference that can then be tamed and domesticated (Allon 2000, Morris 1988).

The cultural imaginary that depicts the tourist as a subject of modernity, playing out a drama of departure, transcendence and, ultimately, transformation, reflects a particular conceptualisation of experience and encounter. Implicitly structured by an economy of sameness and identity, this social and symbolic order articulates a system of distinct, self-enclosed and mutually exclusive forms that divides subjects from objects, centres from margins, here from there, and inscribes a presence always marked by the cloying of absence. Such an imaginary organises rational subjects in a transparent field of relations between fixed and separate points, with space translated as distance to be overcome, while time represents the passage to a final destination. This is 'reflexive modernity' conceptualised as a systemic dissatisfaction with the here and now, as a pilgrimage for meaning, truth and identity, and a search for authentic purpose and gratification that only results in its infinite deferral (Beck et al. 1994). The tourist/subject is compelled to seek out individualisation, and to engage in the self-reflexive development of a biography that properly reflects a life that has been lived authentically and to the full, yet remaining condemned to feeling inauthentic and unfulfilled and hence forever on the journey to enlightenment.

In many respects the growth in volunteer tourism is grounded in, and extends, this notion of an authentic self, seeking exalted individualisation. Yet what we are calling here 'instrumentalised travel' has, we argue, fundamentally changed the nature of the tourist experience and dominant understandings of travel and the travelling self. Volunteer tourism, like eco-tourism and other ethical travel products, aims to have a positive impact on host communities and involves tourists volunteering with community development and service organisations in disadvantaged communities (Wearing 2001). This kind of altruistic transfer into disadvantaged communities is part of the economic shift towards the productive use of travel experiences (Ingram 2011).

The value placed on 'personal experience' today, not just in tourism but also in contemporary society more widely, demonstrates how pervasive the idea of an experience economy has become. For Pine and Gilmore (1999), the 'Experience Economy' provided a framework for business to harness the affective dimensions of meaningful experience as a way of avoiding the modern fate of 'commoditisation' – the flattening, depersonalised effects that follow from consumerism conforming to the logic of the business transaction. Yet this functional deployment of experience also gives rise to a new process of valuation and commodification – the 'experiential commodity' whose value is not contained in the form of a thing but, rather, in social relationships, ways of life, and kinds of personhood. Indeed, MacCannell (1999: 23) prefigured many of the debates on the experience economy, as well as on 'immaterial' and 'symbolic' labour, with his analysis of tourism as an exemplar of the social condition in general:

> [the] value of such things as programs, trips, courses, reports, articles, shows, conferences, parades, opinions, events, sights, spectacles, scenes and situations of modernity is not determined by the amount of labour required for their production. Their value is a function of the quality and quantity of *experience* they promise.

However, what MacCannell did not foresee is the broader process of transvaluation that could potentially take place when such experiential commodities began to multiply. The category of the 'volunteer tourist', for example, is one who is not just singularly interested in accruing personal experience and value in the present, but also in changing social relationships and creating future long-term benefits throughout social life, for others primarily, but also hopefully, and simultaneously, for herself. While volunteer tourism therefore provides a strong grounding for forms of self-transformation through travel, the transformation of the self is contingent on the immersive experience of contributing to positive global change within specific communities overseas and on more multiply-defined, open-ended benefits for multiple agents. Wearing (2001), in one of the first studies of volunteer tourism, highlights that because volunteers spend longer periods of time interacting with local communities they are able to engage in a more profound form of self-development. Ingram (2011: 211), in her study of volunteer tourism, suggests that it is more likely that a longing for global change rather than personal change is paramount in the motivations of the increasing numbers of people that choose to undertake volunteer tourism, particularly in developing countries. Any personal growth achieved by volunteers is schematised as a part of mutual exchange with the community with whom they are volunteering (Matthews 2008, Scheyvens 2002, Spencer 2010).

Due to the claim of simultaneously transforming self and world, there is a difficulty in defining and drawing the limits of the kinds of transformation that occur in volunteer travel. The experiences of volunteer tourists differ significantly from traditional portrayals of the traveller as being on a quest for personal transformation. Traditional tropes of transformation in travel were usually animated by a belief that formative travel was a once-in-a-lifetime experience, in which travellers were irrevocably changed and in which they typically returned home better able to perform their prescribed role in their own society. This is what van den Abbeele (1980: 13) calls the 'metaphorics of the voyage', a discursive mode that implicitly presupposes a 'fixed position' or 'home' from which the voyage begins, and to which, in the end, it returns. Within this model, the voyage itself is explicitly conceived as a life strategy preoccupied with self-realisation, identity-building, and a quest for truth and enlightenment.

This view of travel also frequently references the journey through liminality to communitas narrated by Turner (1982), whereby an individual or social group passes from one status or category to another more 'whole' or complete stage of development. Transformation is often an integral, indeed highly characteristic, feature of the rituals and rites of passage that are enacted at the moment of liminality or 'inbetweenness', when one state of being is left behind and a new identity is about to be taken up (Matthews 2008). Liminal experiences of passage and transformation take place in, and are constitutive of, liminal spaces, the thresholds between clearly defined states of life and sites of social interaction (see Chapter 10, this volume). The resolution of liminal states secures the proper alignment of the relations between centres and boundaries, and ensures the stability and homogeneity of the spaces in which the values of home community are maintained. Through rites of passage, the transformed 'foreign body' is incorporated into the domestic realm and vice versa. Within this anthropological model there are clearly defined boundaries between the home community and foreignness, and the transformative experience of liminality is necessary only inasmuch as it reinforces this division and the stability of each state and domain; this is its primary function. There are obvious parallels here between modern industrial leisure and the religious practice of pilgrimage, with both offering liminal experiences that are often 'fragmentary ... experimental, idiosyncratic, quirky, subversive, utopian' (Turner and Turner 1978: 253), but which, again, ultimately result in the reinscription of the 'normal' values of hearth and home upon return.

The 'mobilities paradigm' has done much within tourism research to decentre the dominant trope of travellers being transformed by static places or singular journeys. The mobilities approach emphasises the constantly changing nature of the places that travellers visit as a result of the changing technologies of travel themselves, the impact of external influences such as new diseases, and ongoing receptivity to tourists. As Sheller and Urry argue, 'tourism activities are not so separate from the places that are visited. Those places are moreover not fixed and unchanging but depend in part upon what happens to be practised within them' (Sheller and Urry 2004: 5). The mobilities approach also draws attention to the simultaneous mobilities of various human and non-human actors alongside tourist journeys. Decentring the modern self-made and self-actualised individual that is at the heart of many traditional narratives of *travel as transformation* enables one to recognise the many different kinds of mobilities that constitute tourism and shape the places and destinations where tourism is performed. As Sheller and Urry (2004: 1) further argue, the 'mobilities of people and objects, airplanes and suitcases, plants and animals, images and brands, data systems and satellites, all go into doing tourism'. Increasingly tourism research is becoming more responsive to the interactions between human and non-human agents and their importance for tourists' movements through various landscapes and the complexity of the networks and processes in tourism (Haldrup and Larson 2006, Pons 2003, Ren 2011, Rodger et al. 2009). The recognition of this ubiquitous mobility has in turn rendered the transformations that the travellers themselves undergo more variable, contingent and ambivalent than either the initiate's journey into liminality or the tourist's search for an Other.

Transposing Others: Travel as Transposition

Reflecting trends in the broader instrumentalisation of travel, the convergence of self and global transformation in volunteer tourism has become institutionalised as a part of the educational and vocational training in the neoliberal economy. In her study of the increasing professionalisation of volunteer-tourism and gap year programmes, Simpson (2005) argues that the kinds of self-development enabled by volunteering programmes, mostly in the Third World, are increasingly being seen as important for educational and corporate training programmes. The kind of self that volunteer tourism develops exhibits qualities that can only be developed when taking part in the simultaneous global transformation implicated in this kind of travel. Volunteer tourism agencies are explicit about this educational/ training dimension, and publicise their programmes as opportunities that enable the development of important skills such as leadership and teamwork. One of the many advantages of volunteer tourism, it is frequently suggested in promotional materials, is that such transferable skills are both honed and heightened by the demands of the far-off, disadvantaged communities where volunteers work, providing volunteers with a competitive advantage over other potential employees in future workplaces (Simpson 2005, Vrasti 2013).

In this sense, the professionalisation of individual travel is contributing to the global transformations of the neoliberal economy in which economic subjects are driven by the requirements of a down-sizing, competitive neoliberal market to render even their leisure time verifiably useful. This development represents a considerable reconceptualisation of the very meaning and purpose of travel and, in particular, conventional understandings of leisure time as 'free time'. Leisure has traditionally been understood in opposition to the world of work and labour, as representing a space of *freedom* from the push and pull of everyday obligation, duty and responsibility. It has been overwhelmingly viewed as a term describing activities that are conducted in the 'time off' from regular routines such as paid employment. When we engage in leisure, therefore, we are automatically assumed to be using periods of 'free time' to pursue interests that are not associated with direct economic necessity or calculation. In this equation, leisure – as a practice involving the deployment of free will in free time – is freedom *from* the demands of the marketplace. Indeed, as Rojek (2010: 1) states, 'for over two centuries, leisure has become almost irretrievably fused with the concept of freedom'.

The types of volunteer tourism that we are focusing on here, however, disrupt this conventional leisure/labour distinction. Instead, they represent forms of leisure and recreation that now involve practices of labour that are explicitly connected to the formation of socially and economically productive individuals, and which feed directly into the concerns of government, lifestyle services and the market. For Rojek (2010), leisure and tourism are increasingly harnessed to the project of building personal *competence*, an attribute that is prized in all kinds of settings, from the demands of workplaces to everyday life-worlds. 'By placing competence as the means and end of activity', Rojek (2010: 27) argues, labour not only becomes a seemingly constant process, incorporating new forms of emotional labour such as life-coaching and volunteering, but clear demarcations between leisure and work, pleasure and discipline, cease to exist.

From this perspective, volunteer tourism is just one component of the substantial amount of 'emotional labour' involved in the production of the emotionally intelligent, competent, personable, confident and well-rounded individual – the most desirable worker around today. As such, the performance of emotional labour and the accumulation of emotional intelligence and competence – practices which are indispensable to the ideal neoliberal workplace – turn conventional definitions of leisure on their head. When we are continually exhorted to engage in self-monitoring and reconnaissance, to constantly 'work' on the formation and development of our character, self-presentation and employability, both for the economic market and interpersonal relations, emotional labour is frequently a round-the-clock undertaking in which there is no 'free time' or 'time off' (Rojek 2010: 147).

In these terms, travel, as one of the most quintessential forms of leisure, ceases to be the reward for work. It becomes instead recast as a form of 'immaterial' or 'affective' labour (Hardt and Negri 2009), enmeshed in the cultivation of emotional intelligence and the accumulation of social capital, experience and other valuable life-skills that are required for the programmatic development of a particular kind of person. Moreover, the primary purpose of such new forms and configurations of labour is not necessarily to produce physical commodities but rather ways of being, relationships and forms of social life. In other words, labour merges with leisure and life, production merges with consumption, and value is generated unpredictably at multiple points within affective encounters. Yet while this seems like a radically new development, it is in a certain sense quite old. As Rojek (2010) points out, the etymology of the Ancient Greek word for leisure is 'schole', and the root of our word for 'school': 'leisure is a school for life. The end of schooling is to maintain and enhance competence, relevance and credibility' (Rojek 2010: 189). From this perspective, it is perhaps not so surprising to find that today, volunteer tourism is one of the most popular and fashionable paths to demonstrate cultural competence and the values of good global citizenship (Lyons et al. 2012). Volunteer tourism successfully combines the immaterial, emotional labour of self-actualisation with the very material, physical labour of community development and global change.

Indeed, the global dimension to this neoliberal citizenship frequently represents the apotheosis of desirable forms of self-development in contemporary travel. Lyons et al. (2012: 363), in a recent exploration of discourses of global citizenship in volunteer tourism, outline that taking part in this form of travel appears to provide 'the best way for individuals to outwardly demonstrate their claims to global citizenship'. The generation that is currently taking on the task of global transformation in volunteer tourism as a part of their formative experiences of self-development have also been crucially shaped by the expansion of Internet access in the last 20 years and the increased availability of global media. While volunteer tourists still cite self-development as a strong motivation for their travels, there is an attendant increase in their awareness of how their travels are contextualised within wider global issues and problems (Lyons et al. 2012). The collapse of self-transformation in travel into global transformation has then been a product of substantial, global shifts in the grounds on which personal self-development occurs (Koleth 2014). But does this simply represent the neoliberal colonisation of travel and leisure? Or is there more at stake? Jessica's narration of her travels highlights that her perceptions of the transformations she enabled were troubled by ambivalence, slippages and transfers that seemed to overwhelm the good that she and other travellers had meant to do in the communities that they were in. As she reflected, 'in some cases a lot of international projects have the opportunity to create more detrimental effects than positive effects because we can't really quantify them'.

Contrary to both the idea of the complete transformation occasioned by a prescribed journey outside a given community and the idea of a search for an absolute Other, the transformations occasioned by contemporary travel appear to be much more fractured and more ambiguous. In these terms, for example, Jessica's troubling reference to detrimental effects that '*we can't really quantify*', represents a qualitatively different kind of transformation. As Duffy and Moore (2010) recognise in a recent study of nature tourism, the way in which these newer forms of travel fit into a neoliberal society, renders an analysis attuned to the lived complexities and multiplicities of neoliberalism ever more necessary. Braidotti (2006) attempts to reconfigure change and transformation in a neoliberal society as a response to precisely the kinds of changes that Jessica refers to, and which volunteer tourism in general, reflects. Braidotti (2006) argues that in a world driven by the schizophrenia of neoliberalism, new hybrid human/non-human collaborations multiply but in a seemingly dematerialised and paralysing celebration of the political status quo. As an attempt to materialise and vivify the hybrid entities of a neoliberal economy, Braidotti's concept of the transposition is a form of travel, a 'leap from one code, field or axis into another ... in the qualitative sense of complex multiplicities' (Braidotti 2006: 5). To the traditional conception of transformation in travel as a journey into liminality and back again, the concept of transpositions recognises a destabilising materiality, which reappropriates the liminal space from stability, homogeneity and the status quo and transforms it into an unpredictable and diverse contestation of fixed states of being. As Braidotti (2006: 6) posits, the interconnection between two different fields that becomes a transposition is a 'creative leap that produces a prolific in-between space'. Rather than being structured as a closed individual, the human organism is a product of such a leap as an 'in-between that is plugged into and connected to a variety of possible sources and forces' (Braidotti 2006: 267). These forces are testament to the strength of *zoe* or non-human life and help situate 'individual' transformations within the multiply connected livingness of the world (Braidotti 2006).

Instead of a search for, or mutual exchange with, a defined Other, the concept of transpositions imposes a process of becoming the diverse others that animate a patriarchal, white and neoliberal hegemony (Braidotti 2006). Braidotti (2006: 269) argues that what 'needs to be broken is the fantasy of unity, totality and one-ness'. To make room for this multiplicity, she draws attention to the othered multiplicities of racialised differences and non-human others in a way that recalls the mobilities approach in theories of travel but grants that approach the strength of a political agenda. Transpositions are movements that are 'non-linear but not chaotic; nomadic, yet accountable and committed' (Braidotti 2006: 5). The transpositions that mark the process of becoming-other in volunteer travel can be traced in the complex flows of volunteers' transfers of money and data. The radically changed dimensions of this form of travel are ultimately evident in the ongoing nature of its transformations.

The Stakes: On Multi-scalar Transformations

The financial assistance provided to worthwhile projects and organisations through tourists' payments to volunteering organisations constitute an important part of the good that they attempt to do. A contemporary transfer of money as a transposition easily becomes a complex multiplicity in its own right. Starting off as a bank transfer or a cheque from a personal account and going into the accounts or subsidiaries of the company or organisation that the volunteer is doing their placement with in multiple countries, the money is then distributed as that organisation, and those that it partners with in host countries, see fit. The self-transformation occasioned by the transfer of money between various locations should not be underestimated as there is a certain capability and power exercised by the traveller in making this instantaneous and substantial transfer of money. Katie, a 20-year-old teacher who did a volunteer teaching trip when she was a student, expressed her pride in being able to afford the volunteering trip because she had worked to raise the money for it, as she reflected:

> I had money, that was the other thing, I'd worked all my way through uni ... flights were two and half thousand dollars and there was two and a half thousand dollars for everything else we did for a month so when you think about it that way, that's rent and our ... food, everything like that, transport ... I think if I didn't have the money I wouldn't have gone ... but I had the money so because $5000 is a lot of money ... for a uni student as well particularly.

In addition to the expression of power, Katie's transfer attests to a deeper transformation, of that part of herself that worked for the money, which then goes into the material financial transactions with the volunteering organisations, and is further transposed into various spaces, agents and processes within the volunteer tourism industry more widely.

Few volunteers in the study had knowledge of, or expressed a curiosity about, where the money they transfer goes, which implies that the transpositions multiplying from their transaction are largely unknown and ignored. Studies of volunteer organisations have emphasised that most organisations, which identify as non-profit, state that they take the minimum from volunteers' payments to cover operating costs and salaries (Tomazos and Cooper 2012). However, few organisations explicitly detail where their money goes leading to a considerable variability and ambiguity in the information about pricing and accounting that is provided to volunteer tourists (Tomazos and Cooper 2012). For those volunteers in the study who did wonder where their money had gone, they felt that their questions were not important enough for them to take effective action to have them answered. For example, Mary, a 46-year-old volunteer who went to an animal sanctuary for her placement with i-to-i Volunteers, expressed questions about where her money was going. As Mary queried:

> I think it was $1900 to participate as a volunteer and I was just wondering how much of that money went to the actual Sanctuary and whether, you know apart from my in-kind volunteering how much of the money that I had paid went towards you know feeding the animals or continuing construction of the project.

The concern expressed here is important when Mary's own self-transformation into the processes to which the money contributes is taken into account. Mary's question could well have been 'am I being transformed into and transforming the feed for the animals or the materials that house them, or am I being put into a corporate logo or an administrative process?' Although she questioned where the money went, Mary went on to delegitimise her own question by reflecting that she did not ask the organisation, stating 'I didn't, you know, quibble too much about where the money goes … they have to make a profit out of it somehow but yeah probably wondered where the money was going'. Such a devaluing of critical attention to the details of money transfers arguably contributes to the acceptance of the status quo that Braidotti (2006) posits. The obfuscation over the destination of the money transfers made by volunteers raises questions about the positive nature of the global transformations being facilitated by volunteer and other forms of ethical travel (Ingram 2011).

For many volunteers, at a time when travel is increasingly informed by contributions to various forms of social media, the good that volunteer tourists do both for themselves and the world is immediately amplified through their transformation into data. As a personal transformation, parts of the self, such as memories, affinities and actions, are transposed into popular forms of data, making for larger and sometimes unpredictable subsequent transformations. As a global transformation, the amplification of the individual acts of volunteers contributes to more people being inspired to volunteer and the greater legitimation of this form of travel as a way of doing good and transforming the world. Teresa, a 21-year-old volunteer on a nursing placement with Projects Abroad, started a blog and was dedicated in posting her lengthy and detailed recounts of what happened on the placement. Teresa reflected that, 'the main reason I started it was so I didn't have to email like ten people I could just do the blog … I posted them up on Facebook so anyone can read it that way as well'. Teresa was reminded of the unpredictable nature of the blog as well as its transformative impact in recalling that:

> my mum, she's a nurse and so when she'd go to work she was giving the blog to people to read and well it was kind of nice one of the nurses has an 11 year old daughter and she read it and she was commenting on the blogs and stuff and said how amazing and I want to do this.

The easily replicated nature of Teresa's transposition into data, within various sites of engagement, demonstrates the unpredictability of this form of transformation. While she sees the inspiration given to the girl who read her blog as a positive outcome, she did not necessarily target her blog's material to such a wide audience.

Despite Teresa's intentions, the blog acted as a wider promotion for volunteer tourism, ensuring further self and global transformation.

The increasing mobility of contemporary travellers is contributing to the greater unpredictability of their transformations. The leaps that volunteers, like other travellers, make from place to place do not necessarily represent a lack of commitment, but rather reflect changing perceptions of the individual's capacity to enact transformation on many places in the world. Jemma, a volunteer in her early thirties, was transformed by her volunteer teaching trip at a school in Cambodia to such an extent that she decided to return to the community that she had been volunteering with for a couple of months every year. She decided to set up a training and mentoring programme for the children who graduate from the school where she had been volunteering. It was her transposition into Cambodia as a volunteer that allowed her to make a creative leap in building a community project of her own. As Jemma described it, she had to move from Australia to Cambodia to transform herself and her capacity to transform the world for the better. However, this would by no means be the last transformative journey she would make, as Jemma observed before she went to Cambodia:

> I was feeling frustrated and I was feeling less of myself here because I felt like I wasn't achieving what I was meant to be achieving. I guess a part of me thinks yeah maybe I'll feel like that at some point over there you know when I've done what I need to do there and that's all up and running maybe I'll start to get that feeling again. Now, though, it's time to move.

That there is no mention in Jemma's account of finding an absolute Other in Cambodia, and that there is no mention of *looking* for an ultimate Other in either her account or the accounts of other volunteer tourists within the study, cannot be mere coincidence. In fact, the only 'Other' conjured up in Jemma's account are the variously connected selves that she has not yet been transformed into, but that remain a siren-like possibility in the future.

Jemma appears not to be alone in feeling that achieving the next transformation as a temporary, if committed, transposition means that it is time to move on (see Chapter 2, this volume). The sentiment is daily repeated by countless contemporary travellers and their fixation on the future seems appropriate in an era in which the excesses of a neoliberal capitalist hegemony, within an environmentally and politically fragile universe, have made that future questionable. As Braidotti (2006: 137) argues, recasting transformations within the multiple techno-scientific complexities of our current age is important because 'what is at stake is the very possibility of a future'. The transformations of volunteers and their travels into data and money, as well as the cumulative changes that these then inspire, raises the question of whether the growth of volunteering travel can initiate the substantive shifts necessary to ensure more liveable futures.

The recent studies of volunteer tourism continuously seek to address the realities of the commodification of volunteer tourism and the question of whether it is doing good on a global scale. For example, Simpson (2005) highlights that the financial and moral power exercised by volunteers like Katie takes power away from those in the Third World who are not free to move in the way that they are. Gray and Campbell (2007) show that there are elements of both commodified and decommodified experiences within the phenomenon. Tomazos and Butler demonstrate that in order to be effective, volunteer tourism organisations need to garner enough profit to be commercially viable (Tomazos and Butler 2012). Lyons et al. (2012) suggest that it is too early to say whether volunteer tourism will be fully co-opted by profit interests but that the programmes' emphasis on self-improvement impoverishes notions of 'global citizenship'. Mostafanezhad (2012) notes that while it would be simplistic to construe the motivation to do good as counter-productive, the practices of volunteer tourism have to do better in addressing structural inequalities and focusing on the policies and structures imposed by Western nations. While these critiques outline major inequalities within volunteer tourists' transformations, they are haunted by a narrowly conceived teleology of neoliberal capitalism.

The co-option of good intentions in volunteer tourism has led these critics to express doubt, or assume the worst, of the kinds of futures it projects. However, recognising the play of transpositions in this dynamic industry gives us an insight into the unpredictable becoming of contemporary global transformations. The transpositions of money, data and a mobile imaginary of change do not necessarily challenge dichotomous power structures between volunteer tourists and Third World communities or provide an alternative to commodification, as part of renewed codes of global citizenship. What these transpositions *do* suggest is that both the inequalities of the neoliberal economy and the challenges within it are becoming more diverse. While it may be impossible to verify the good being done in volunteer travel amongst such diversity, returning to the kinds of nostalgia for recognisable change in reference to an identifiable Other, evinced in traditional analyses of travel, may not be the only theoretical road to take. Similarly, the narratives of mutual human change in recent analyses of volunteer travel may be limiting our capacity to make sense of what is becoming our future (Matthews 2008, Spencer 2010). If there is a hope of recognising the potential for good to be done when it makes a transversal transfer into the future, then it must be allowed to be qualitatively different to what is expected, reflecting an ambiguously weighted process of personal and global change. The ongoing transpositions of volunteer travellers, among others, are reasons to remain hopeful because they ensure an imaginative and material vitality. Ask travellers like Jessica where they have been and they will say 'most countries'. It is possible to play a game with them of trying to name places where they have not been, but it proves difficult. Ask them if they have stopped travelling, stopped volunteering, stopped collecting moments of simultaneous self and global transformation in multiple places and they will say that would be impossible. There is a possibility that they are becoming that 'other' future, an alternative to the exclusively destructive teleology imagined for neoliberal capitalism. This 'other' future may just be the only place they have not yet been.

References

Allon, F. 2000. Altitude anxiety: Being-at-home in a globalised world. Unpublished PhD thesis. University of Technology, Sydney.

Allon, F. 2004. Backpacker heaven: The consumption and construction of tourist spaces and landscapes in Sydney. *Space & Culture*, 7(1), 49–63.

Beck, U., Giddens, A. and Lash, S. 1994. *Reflexive Modernization: Politics, Tradition and Aesthetics in the Modern Social Order*. Stanford: Stanford University Press.

Benson, A.M. 2011. Volunteer tourism: Structuring the research agenda, in *Volunteer Tourism: Theoretical Frameworks and Practical Applications*, edited by Angela M. Benson. London: Routledge, 240–51.

Benson, A.M and Siebert, N. 2009. Volunteer tourism: Motivations of German participants in South Africa. *Annals of Leisure Research*, 12(3–4), 295–314.

Braidotti, R.M. 2006. *Transpositions: On Nomadic Ethics*. London: Polity Press.

Brown, S. 2005. Travelling with a purpose: Understanding the motives and benefits of volunteer vacationers. *Current Issues in Tourism*, 8(6), 479–96.

Coghlan, A. and Fennell, D. 2009. Myth or substance: An examination of altruism as the basis of volunteer tourism. *Annals of Leisure Research*, 12(3–4), 377–402.

Duffy, R. and Moore, L. 2010. Neoliberalising nature? Elephant-back tourism in Thailand and Botswana. *Antipode*, 42(3), 742–66.

Frow, J. 1997. Tourism and the semiotics of nostalgia, in *Time and Commodity Culture: Essays in Cultural Theory and Postmodernity*, edited by J. Frow. Oxford: Oxford University Press, 64–101.

Gray, N.J. and Campbell, L.M. 2007. A decommodified experience? Exploring aesthetic, economic and ethical values for volunteer ecotourism in Costa Rica. *Journal of Sustainable Tourism*, 15(5), 463–82.

Guttentag, D.A. 2009. The possible negative impacts of volunteer tourism. *International Journal of Tourism Research*, 11(6), 537–51.

Haldrup, M. and Larson, J. 2006. Material cultures of tourism. *Leisure Studies*, 25(3), 275–89.

Hardt, M. and Negri, A. 2009. *Commonwealth*. Cambridge, MA: Harvard University Press.

Ingram, J. 2011. Volunteer tourism: How do we know it is 'making a difference'?, in *Volunteer Tourism: Theoretical Frameworks and Practical Applications*, edited by A.M. Benson. London: Routledge, 211–22.

Jokinen, E. and Veijola, S. 2004. The disoriented tourist: The figuration of the tourist in contemporary cultural critique, in *Touring Cultures: Transformations of Travel and Theory*, edited by C. Rojek and J. Urry. London: Routledge, 23–51.

Koleth, M. 2014. Travelling goods: global self-development on sale, in *Managing Ethical Consumption in Tourism*, edited by C. Weedon and K. Boluk. New York and London: Routledge, 122–33.

Lyons, K., Hanley, J., Wearing, S. and Neil, J. 2012. Gap year volunteer tourism: Myths of global citizenship? *Annals of Tourism Research*, 39(1), 361–78.

MacCannell, D. 1999. *The Tourist: A New Theory of the Leisure Class*, 2nd edition. Berkeley: University of California Press.

McGehee, N.G. 2012. Oppression, emancipation and volunteer tourism: Research propositions. *Annals of Tourism Research*, 39(1), 84–107.

McGehee, N. and Santos, C.A. 2005. Social change, discourse and volunteer tourism. *Annals of Tourism Research*, 32(3), 760–79.

Matthews, A. 2008. Negotiated selves: Exploring the impact of local-global interactions on young volunteer travellers, in *Journeys of Discovery in Volunteer Tourism: International Case Study Perspectives*, edited by K.D. Lyons and S. Wearing. Cambridge, MA: CABI, 101–17.

Morris, M. 1988. At Henry Parkes motel. *Cultural Studies*, 2(1), 1–47.

Mostafanezhad, M. 2012. The geography of compassion in volunteer tourism. *Tourism Geographies*, 15(2), 318–37.

Mustonen, P. 2007. Volunteer tourism – altruism or mere tourism. *Anatolia*, 18(1), 97–115.

Palacios, C.M. 2010. Volunteer tourism, development and education in a postcolonial world: Conceiving global connections beyond aid. *Journal of Sustainable Tourism*, 18(7), 861–78.

Pine II, B.J. and Gilmore, J.H. 1999. *The Experience Economy: Work is Theatre and Every Business as Stage*. Boston: Harvard Business School Press.

Pons, P.O. 2003. Being-on-holiday: Tourist dwelling, bodies and place. *Tourist Studies*, 3(1), 47–66.

Ren, C. 2011. Non-human agency, radical ontology and tourism realities. *Annals of Tourism Research*, 38(3), 858–81.

Rodger, K., Moore, S.A. and Newsome, D. 2009. Wildlife tourism, science and actor network theory. *Annals of Tourism Research*, 36(4), 645–66.

Rojek, C. 2010. *The Labour of Leisure: The Culture of Free Time*. London: SAGE.

Scheyvens, R. 2002. *Tourism for Development: Empowering Communities*. Essex: Pearson Education.

Sheller, M. and Urry, J. 2004. Places to play, places in play, in *Tourism Mobilities: Places to Play, Places in Play*, edited by M. Sheller and J. Urry. London: Routledge, 1–10.

Simpson, K. 2005. Dropping out or signing up? The professionalisation of youth travel. *Antipode*, 37(3), 447–69.

Spencer, R. 2010. *Development Tourism: Lessons from Cuba*. Farnham: Ashgate.

Stoddart, H. and Rogerson, C.M. 2004. Volunteer tourism: The case of habitat for humanity South Africa. *GeoJournal*, 60(3), 311–18.

Tomazos, K. and Butler, R. 2012. Volunteer tourists in the field: A question of balance? *Tourism Management*, 33(1), 177–87.

Tomazos, K. and Cooper, W. 2012. Volunteer tourism: At the crossroads of commercialisation and service. *Current Issues in Tourism*, 15(5), 405–23.

Turner, V.W. 1982. Liminal to liminoid in play, flow, ritual: An essay in comparative symbology, in *From Ritual to Theatre: The Human Seriousness of Play*, edited by V.W. Turner. New York: Performing Arts Journal Publications, 20–60.

Turner, V.W. and Turner, E. 1978. *Image and Pilgrimage in Christian Culture*. New York: Columbia University Press.

Van den Abbeele, G. 1980. Sightseers: The tourist as theorist. *Diacritics*, 10(4), 2–14.

Vrasti, W. 2013. *Volunteer Tourism in The Global South: Giving back in Neoliberal Times*. London: Routledge.

Wearing, S. 2001. *Volunteer Tourism: Experiences that Make a Difference*. Wallingford: CABI.

PART II
Transformation, Representation, Story

Chapter 5

Saddos and Saddhus: Transcendence as Breakdown in Geoff Dyer's *Jeff in Venice/Death in Varanasi*

Bianca Leggett

The concept of travel as a spiritual journey in Anglophone literature is one which has its roots in Christian allegorical narratives, that is, texts like John Bunyan's *Pilgrims Progress* (1952 [1678]), in which a naive protagonist chooses to leave the confines of his home in order to expose himself to the harsh lessons and spiritual improvement which comes from a journey through foreign surroundings. Just as it was in Chaucer's time, however, the pilgrim has also historically been a figure of fun, torn between earthly pleasures and the desire for a higher good.

Pilgrimage literature, both reverent and irreverent, continues to exist in a contemporary form. The association between travel and spirituality survives in the largely secular societies of the contemporary age, although travellers are less likely to be seeking a Christian salvation than pursuing the aggregate of spiritual ideals known as New Ageism. The Eastern-inflected ideas of the New Age also found expression in travel to the East, especially in the form of the Hippie Trail, an overland route which typically began in a Western European city and ended in Iran. In his travelogue *The Spiritual Tourist*, Mick Brown defines transcendence as:

> [M]oments of a particular clarity, in which our vision seems to grow larger, and we are no longer looking at the world through the muddy glass of our preconceptions but seeing it as it truly *is*; where we become momentarily aware of some pattern or order greater than ourselves, and of which we are an intrinsic part. (1998: 4)

This enlarging vision is concerned with perception and selfhood, but also with a sense of connection to one's fellow beings. The New Age traveller usually pursues this state through a combination of spiritual instruction and good deeds. It owes something to the Buddhist ideal of Nirvana or Hindu ideal of escaping *samsara*, but mediated and reformulated by their passage into Western popular culture. Geoff Dyer suggests that Eastern spirituality has reached us largely through American writers: 'Thanks to Kerouac, Ginsberg and the Beats, notions of karma and dharma had become common currency' (2009: 196). Travelogues and travel fiction which feature pilgrim-like travellers whose travails lead them to transcendence have proved popular in recent decades. Susan Gilbert's *Eat, Pray, Love* (2007), Gregory David Roberts' *Shantaram* (2005) and Greg Mortensen's *Three Cups of Tea* (2008), all international bestsellers, are examples of the genre.

There exists alongside this strand of literature, however, a counter-narrative of travel writing and fiction which, like Chaucer before them, has a more critical slant on modern-day pilgrims. William Sutcliffe's *Are You Experienced?* (1997) is a light-hearted and satirical story of the gap-year of Dave, an unlikely traveller, whose story records the pretensions of the fellow travellers he meets on his disastrous travels around India. Alex Garland's *The Beach* (1996) was amongst the first to put the figure of the backpacker under the microscope and to suggest a dark side to the utopian ideal behind travelling. Garland's backpackers are motivated more by the desire for thrills and experience than the pursuit of enlightenment or broadened cultural horizons and they are duly punished in the novel's violent conclusion. In the wake of *The Beach* came a string of paperback thrillers and horror films which echoed its parable of the dangers which await naive and hedonistic travellers in foreign lands. The more thoughtful of these novels attempt to confront the historical legacies of colonialism, which continue to shape the encounter between Western travellers and their Eastern destinations, along with the ethical dilemmas which the first-world traveller in the developing world must negotiate.

Geoff Dyer's *Jeff in Venice/Death in Varanasi* (2009) is a highly self-conscious and postmodern text which can be placed in the tradition of pilgrimage literature, but whose comment on the connection between travel and transcendence is highly unconventional. Its diptych structure is an appropriate form for a text which delights in doubleness and playful indeterminacy: its protagonist, like Dyer himself, is an English writer and journalist, whose name, Jeff, a variant spelling of the author's own, indicates the ambiguous position between novel and travel-writing which this text occupies. In this slippery text, which delights in paradox, it becomes difficult to say whether the New Age ideal of transcendence is being ridiculed, or just reformulated. I will be focusing on the *Death in Varanasi* section in which Jeff, who arrives in India on a journalistic assignment, takes up residence in a bohemian hotel on the banks of the Ganges and, under the influence of Varanasi's combination of abject poverty, spiritualism and narcotics, edges ever closer towards breakdown, or just possibly, an ironic form of epiphany. Dyer's traveller is not a typical backpacker: older, more self-aware and somewhat cynical, he is something of an outsider amongst the residents of the Ganges View where he takes up residence and this allows him a more objective position from which to comment on travel culture. Jeff is neither unthinking nor unfeeling about his position as a tourist amongst the abject poverty of Varanasi, yet the deconstructive playfulness of his work does not lend itself to moral certainty. In this chapter, I will both consider Dyer's comment on the possibility of a meaningful experience of transcendence through travel, but also consider the ethical implications of his conclusions.

Travel and living abroad are popular themes in Dyer's work. 'Every day spent in the country you were born is a day wasted', says one of the young characters of *Paris Trance* (1998: 94), the story of a cosmopolitan bunch of young people living in Paris described by reviewer Tim Pears (cited in Bennett 1998) as '*Tender is the Night* for the ecstasy age'. His earlier novel, *Out of Sheer Rage* (1997), records a Dyer-like protagonist moving from one destination to the next, attempting to find inspiration to write about another author with nomadic habits, D.H. Lawrence. Like Lawrence, Dyer's characters are attracted to abroad both from the desire for experience and the rejection of the torpid life which they associate with home. One might argue, however, that torpidity is one of Dyer's themes, a state in which he finds both poetry and profundity. Dyer's first novel, *The Colour of Memory* (1989), the story of bright young drop-outs on the dole in Brixton, begins what Joseph Brooker calls an 'unswerving fascination with vacancy' (Brooker 2004: 148). Dyer's later novels move away from London, but his fascination with stasis proves strangely compatible with the theme of travel. *Out of Sheer Rage* is ultimately a novel about the *failure* to write a book about D.H. Lawrence, a paean to procrastination through the displacement activity of travel. Dyer's collection of short stories about travel is entitled, characteristically, *Yoga for People Who Can't be Bothered To Do It* (2003b).

Travel in Dyer's fiction often becomes a form of dropping out, a creative and countercultural stance. 'The paradox of nomadism', says Sahra, one of the characters of *Paris Trance*, is that once '[y]ou realize you *can* live in other countries you can never quite settle anywhere again. You never feel quite content' (Dyer 1998: 94). Another character returns, however, that contentment is a word which 'should never be spoken, only spat' (Dyer 1998: 94). The rootless nature of travel in *Paris Trance*, like unemployment in *The Colour of Memory*, is a melancholy but enabling state which promotes free thinking and individualism. Like the figure of the tourist as described by Lucy Lippard, Dyer's travellers are 'alienated but seeking fulfilment in his [and her] alienation – nomadic, placeless, a kind of subjectivity without spirit, a "dead subject"' (1999: xvi). The travellers of *Paris Trance* bear a strong resemblance to the modernist conception of the artist-exile as described by Caren Kaplan (Kaplan 1996). As Caren Kaplan argues, '[w]hen detachment is the precondition for creativity, then disaffection or alienation as states of mind becomes a rite of passage for the "serious" modern artist or writer' (Kaplan 1996: 36).

While these ideas of the connection between travel and creativity are pertinent to *Jeff in Venice/Death in Varanasi*, it is a postmodern rather than modernist text, and its central character is not an exile but a tourist. Kaplan distinguishes between the two, saying that '[c]ulturally, exile is implicated in modernist high art formations while tourism signifies the very obverse position as the mark of everything commercial and superficial' (Kaplan 1996: 36). Even so, tourism is often conceived as not an expression of the 'commercial and superficial' nature of contemporary culture, but an escape from it. A somewhat Orientalised notion of Eastern countries which positions them as historic, spiritual and less materialistic than the 'West' perpetuates the notion that travel, that is, tourism, is the pursuit of an alternative to the home culture. Barbara Korte suggests that contemporary appetites for travel writing are fuelled by a feeling that in 'a period of hyper-realities and virtual worlds', travel writing 'offers readers the reassurance that reality exists which can still be authentically experienced' (Korte 2000: 143).

It is often noted, however, that both travel writing and tourism tend to kill the thing they love. While travellers seem to crave danger and unmediated experience, the expansion of the tourist industry has the opposite effect upon the places to which they travel. While backpackers' values recall the anti-materialist ideals and experimentalist appetites of their hippie ancestors, they are essentially consumers, interpellated by the tourist industry whose expansion they perpetuate. Jeff remarks on the hollowness of such an example of 'staged authenticity' when he observes the burning of ghats in Varanasi:

> You didn't have to be a particularly discerning tourist to see that this was an exhausted pageant, drummed up for tourists, a *son et lumière* with a cast of hundreds. Any significance it was supposed to have had been drained, possibly a long time ago or maybe just yesterday, or even now, right before our eyes. The event had bled itself white, but each night it had to bleed afresh, which only made it seem more stale and bloodless. It was like trying to glimpse, in a performance of *The Mousetrap*, the ravaged majesty of *Macbeth*. (Dyer 2009: 173)

The ceremony is a form of simulacrum, indistinguishable from the 'hyper-realities' and 'virtual worlds' from which, according to Barbara Korte, both the reader of travel writing and the traveller wish to escape. The traveller, as such, loses any claim to superiority over those who stayed at home.

Jeff operates, however, at a double-distance, both removed from his home culture but also distinct from other tourists. He is older than his fellow hostel residents and preoccupied with his own ageing, rendered something of an onlooker on the backpacker community of which he is a peripheral member. Like most backpackers, however, he is also, to use the phrase coined by Dean MacCannell (1999), an anti-tourist. 'I don't have camera', Jeff tells someone, 'making it clear that I was not a newcomer, not just off the boat, not Japanese' (Dyer 2011: 170). We might equate Jeff's emphasis on his own individuality and separation from the tourist masses as an attempt to claim the status of the modernist exile-artist, yet there is an element of self-parody here which offsets any serious claim to superiority. His admission of the petty snobbery which underpins the anti-tourist's identity also highlights the fragility of its distinctiveness. As Dean MacCannell (1999: 64) comments:

> The error of the anti-tourists is that they tend to be one-sided and in bad faith. They point out only the tawdry side of tourism and the ways it can spoil the human community, while hiding from themselves the essentially touristic nature of their own cultural expeditions to the 'true' sights.

While Jeff may find himself succumbing to the anti-tourist's vanity from time to time, however, he is less naive in assuming that touristic sights must be either 'tawdry' or 'true'. He acknowledges that his limited understanding of the society around him makes such distinctions impossible. Observing a couple of local men, Jeff wonders, 'Were they imparting wisdom to disciples or just chatting with pals ... about the cricket? Enlightened or completely out of it? Both?' (Dyer 2009: 167).

Jeff is perhaps not so much an anti-tourist as a post-tourist who, 'knows that he or she is a tourist and that tourism is a series of games with multiple texts and no single, authentic tourist experience' (Urry 2011: 91). Varanasi appears to be an apt destination to question the meaning and value of authenticity. The city, he explains, appears ancient but actually,

> [g]ets razed to the ground and rebuilt, razed to the ground and rebuilt. No sooner
> has it been rebuilt than it looks like it's on its last legs. Every atom of the air is
> saturated by history that isn't even history, myth, so a temple built today looks,
> overnight, as if it's been there since the dawn of time. (Dyer 2009: 174–5)

The city is neither antique nor unique, yet it is 'saturated by history that isn't even history' (Dyer 2009: 174–5). Whereas Varanasi might not be described as 'authentic' in conventional terms, then, it seems that Dyer is creating a new understanding of the term which allows for contradiction. The same paradoxical logic is evident when Jeff muses that, 'Even the fake holy men – and I'd been warned, by Jamal, that many of them that were wholly fake – were genuine' (Dyer 2009: 167). As Erik Cohen argues, 'authenticity is frequently a socially constructed concept ... its social (as against philosophical) connotation being not given but negotiable' (Cohen 2004: 104). Jeff's idea of the 'genuine' or 'authentic' is based less in empirical reality than a kind of value judgement expressed in the ludic spirit of Wildean aphorism.

The same confusion between the real and the fake is present in Jeff's interactions with the local people of Varanasi, in which his inability to understand his foreign surroundings tends to mar his judgement. 'And everyone was so friendly', he exclaims, 'I'd only been here a minute and someone was wanting to shake my hand. It was like being a celebrity or a visiting royal. Except he didn't want to shake my hand at all. He wanted to demonstrate the massage he was hustling' (Dyer 2009: 168). Jeff quickly becomes disillusioned with overtures of friendliness in Varanasi since 'one's relations always came down to the bottom line of people wanting your money' (Dyer 2009: 168). As Pico Iyer observes, tourists are wont to feel resentful when submitted to intense commercial pressure by their hosts, particularly when this runs counter to an idealistic view of the host-country as spiritual and unmaterialistic:

> If the First World is not invariably corrupting the Third, we are sometimes apt to
> leap to the opposite conclusion ... we begin to regard ourselves as beleaguered
> innocents and those we meet as shameless predators. To do so, however, is to

ignore the great asymmetry that governs every meeting between tourist and
local: that we are there by choice and largely by circumstance; that we are
travelling in the spirit of pleasure, adventure and romance, while they are mired
in the more urgent business of trying to survive. (Iyer 1998: 26)

Jeff makes a connection between this asymmetry and colonial history, noting that
the abundance of cheap services at the disposal of all tourists means that, '[a]t
some level, the poorest backpacker enjoyed the privileges and perks of the Raj'
(Dyer 2009: 233). The attempt to exercise these privileges responsibly is, however,
a difficult business, as a story in *Yoga For People Who Can't Be Bothered to
Do It* illustrates. Dyer's narrator and his girlfriend are in Cambodia and after
approaching a young girl to buy a can of Coke, they decide instead to favour a
more needy merchant, a young boy with only one leg. The young girl's rage seems
to the narrator to respond not only to the lost sale but to a far greater injustice: 'If
the boy seemed to us the incarnation of Cambodia, to her we were the incarnation
of all the fickle power and wealth of the West' (Dyer 2003b: 41).

It is hard, it seems, to respond responsibly to the neo-Raj of tourism or to
keep one's equanimity amongst the mercantile hustle and bustle of Varanasi.
During his time in India, Jeff's tolerance for the chaos and occasional squalor
of life in Varanasi seems to diminish rather than increase. Infuriated by a queue-
jumper at an ATM machine, Jeff's nationally conditioned responses come to the
fore: 'My own smile had now become a death's head grin, a rictus of suppressed
English rage, the product of years of rainy summers, ruined picnics, cancelled
trains and losing at penalty shoot-outs' (Dyer 2009: 229). In a moment of extreme
disaffection, Jeff urinates in the Ganges, well-aware that this could be perceived
as a blasphemous act. Jeff is frustrated that although 'there must have been a
world of poets, intellectuals and thinkers' in Varanasi (Dyer 2009: 226), he is
doomed to 'the eternal *jugalbandi* of tourist life: "Boat, sir?" "No, thank you"'
(Dyer 2009: 226). In response to his increasing frustration, Jeff begins to shield
himself from his surroundings by listening to his iPod to keep 'the din of India at
bay' (Dyer 2009: 215).

Jeff's response seems to be the very opposite of the ideal of transcendence.
He deliberately dulls his perceptions of his surroundings and shuts himself off
from interaction and the troubling thoughts which it can prompt. In an essay
entitled 'Sex and Hotels', Dyer notes that hotels are liberating because, '[b]y
becoming a temporary resident of this non-place you become a non-person', and
as a result, 'you are granted an ethical equivalent of diplomatic immunity. You
become morally weightless ... You have no history' (Dyer 2011: 298). This might
suggest that travel is not a question of 'finding yourself' but rather of 'losing
yourself', embracing the freedom of becoming an amoral 'non-person'. Rather
than becoming aware that we are part of something 'greater than ourselves', the
hotel-dweller is freed from all context, and therefore any reason to constrain the
pursuit of their individual desires.

Jeff's breakdown is signified not only by his growing detachment from his immediate surroundings, but in the way he becomes increasingly distanced from home. By ignoring incoming assignments, 'the reciprocal momentum of email diminished, faded, petered out completely' (Dyer 2009: 274). Dyer is given a book by a friend staying at the hostel but knows that he will not read it since 'reading was one of the things I no longer did' (Dyer 2009: 276). His estrangement from his two friends, Darrell and Laline, begins when Jeff realises that the two are having an affair, leaving him feeling peripheral to the group. A bad bout of dysentery, which leaves Jeff weakened, seems to alienate him further. The illness is brought on when Jeff is smacked in the mouth by the dung-encrusted tail of a cow, thwarting his attempt to stay at a hygienic remove from the dirt of Varanasi. His increasing disinterest in his own well-being is signified by the relaxation of his anxieties about contagion, culminating finally in his immersion in the River Ganges.

Jeff's illness leaves him looking thinner and more unkempt, more like an 'ageing backpacker' than he did on arrival, a physical change which mirrors a similar shift of mentality (Dyer 2009: 277). Jeff's growing interest in spirituality becomes synonymous with his breakdown, especially as it is dictated by his own idiosyncratic take on Hinduism rather than any scholarly interest. The narrative ends with Jeff in a state of psychosis, wading about the Ganges and attempting to engage tourists in conversation, all the while imagining himself to be in the pouch of a giant kangaroo named 'Ganoona', a god who is his own imaginative creation representing chaos. One of the catalysts of this breakdown is the achievement of one of his chief obsessions: to see the far bank of the Ganges, the place where souls are supposed to rest (Dyer 2009: 269). When he finally achieves his aim, the results are disappointing: the far bank turns out to also be the resting place of 'crushed packets of cigarettes, squelchy plastic bags, the odd animal bone, brown fragments of pottery, an old sandal and a couple of broken, muddy Biros' (Dyer 2009: 246). 'The idea of the afterlife was just what it was revealed here to be', Jeff concludes, 'rubbish' (Dyer 2009: 246). What might be read as an anti-climax, however, might also be understood as a kind of dark epiphany. Jeff's conclusions on the banks of the Ganges recall those of Mrs Moore in the Malabar Caves in E.M. Forster's *A Passage to India* (1979 [1924]). The echo of 'ou-boum' in the cave prompts Mrs Moore's conclusion that 'Pathos, piety, courage – they exist, but are identical, and so is filth. Everything exists, nothing has value' (Forster 1979 [1924]: 132). *Jeff in Venice/Death in Varanasi*, as its punning title would suggest, is a profoundly intertextual work which contains 'unacknowledged quotes in the text', allusions which Dyer insists are either 'too well known' or too submerged to require naming (Dyer 2009: 295). The repetition of the chant '*Aum*' and drum beat 'Boom!' seems to be a submerged allusion to the 'ou boum' noise Mrs. Moore hears in the Malabar Caves (Forster 1979 [1924]: 132). For Jeff, as for Mrs Moore, all divisions seem to have collapsed into a kind of relativism, although his reaction is less despairing, and more manic and gleeful. In this blurred state, it becomes difficult to judge whether Jeff has reached a state of enlightenment or of nervous collapse.

Travel has certainly brought about a kind of transcendence, but not of the kind we would expect. One of the catalysts to Jeff's breakdown is a strong *bhang lassi*, a yoghurt drink laced with liquid cannabis, under whose influence he imagines discussing consciousness with a goat. His friend Darrell comments that he 'won't be doing that again in a hurry', but Jeff suspects that 'part of me was still doing it' (Dyer 2009: 269). Travel and drugs are both strongly associated with the Hippie Trail of which Varanasi is a part, a route which was determined partly by the accessibility of cheap hashish in the destinations along the way. Lindsey Michael Banco (2009) uses the word 'Tripping' to suggest the confluence of travel and drugs, often experienced together, and both of which represent the taking of risks in pursuit of hedonistic highs and deeper self-knowledge. Asked in interview about his travel 'habit', Dyer too makes connections between travelling and taking drugs, also suggesting that the two pursuits are complimentary. Dyer muses:

> I've liked taking drugs for a good long while and it's pretty much always, apart from the few freakouts, been really valuable on the level of this kind of responsiveness to place ... [I]t enables one sometimes to have these really intense responses to a place. There's a long tradition of that. (Dyer, interviewed by Hansen 2003a)

While Dyer seems to accept here that both travel and drugs can produce a kind of insight, he then goes on to note that he is also 'drawn to the confusion that drug use can lead to. That incredible chronic indecision – there's a lot of scope for not just humour. That in itself provides insight into a contemporary malaise' (Dyer, interviewed by Hansen 2003a). Drugs, then, do give the taker a kind of insight, but this insight is neither an uplifting nor a spiritual one, rather it tends to reveal that the true nature of existence is confused and empty.

If it is the revelation of existential emptiness that Jeff finds in India, we are left in no doubt that this rings true with his experience of life at home in London. 'I'd come to Varanasi because there was nothing to keep me in London', he comments, 'and I stayed on for the same reason: because there was nothing to go home for' (Dyer 2009: 241). Jeff watches two musicians absorbed in their work with some envy, wishing that 'there was something in my life like that' (Dyer 2009: 240). He professes to hate writing and lists his only interests as tennis and drug-taking. His satisfaction with life in Varanasi comes, not from its difference to his life in London, but its similarity to his formless, free-wheeling ordinary way of life. The sources of annoyance with life in Varanasi are, likewise, similar. Jeff realises that some of the 'irritation' of life in Varanasi is in fact 'strangely familiar, almost reassuring', as 'it was how I felt all the time in London, the default setting for a life in which a constant drizzle of frustration, annoyance and rush-hour Tube travel was the unremarked-on norm' (Dyer 2009: 230).

In finding these unromantic parallels between London and Varanasi, however, Jeff is not complaining that his touristic experience is too banal to be pleasurable. Instead, he seems to be deliberately working against a domestic/exotic binary to make a, somewhat subversive, connection between Eastern enlightenment and Western disengagement. The playful equation of the spiritual and 'Eastern' practice of meditation with listening to an iPod, an obvious symbol of the materialist West, is an obvious example. During a dangerous rickshaw ride, Jeff muses that the experience could be the basis of a video game entitled 'Varanasi Death Trip' (Dyer 2009: 192). At the close of the narrative, as he gives in to the state of transcendence/psychosis, Jeff muses:

> If it had turned out that I was at home on my sofa watching a documentary about Varanasi or playing a video game called *Varanasi Death Trip*, that would not have altered my assessment of the situation because my situation would not have altered significantly. (Dyer 2009: 290)

These comparisons are deliberately iconoclastic. In comparing the experience of real-life danger to a video game and of meditation to the detachment made possible by a portable media player, Dyer suggests an equivalence between the technology most associated with the debased hyperreality of life in the West to those aspects of New Age travel which are supposed to be their curative, spirituality and an awareness of the fragility of life. Even when Jeff finds an aspect of life in Varanasi to be incomprehensibly alien, its otherness is de-emphasised by comparison to an aspect of Western culture which Jeff finds equally difficult to comprehend. Jeff finds the 'fabulousness of the *Mahabharata*' difficult to accept, but compares it to the world of Marvel comics or magical realism which, likewise, he finds bewildering (Dyer 2009: 196). He compares the amassing of religious imagery in Varanasi and the purpose of prayer to 'its secular equivalent, the worship of celebrity. The more celebrities were photographed, the stronger their aura of celebrity became' (Dyer 2009: 196).

Dyer's play on the similarity between the words 'saddo', a socially inept person, and a 'saddhu', collapses the division between the person who Jeff was in London, a middle-aged man with few attachments, achievements or passions, and the person he becomes, someone resembling a 'saddhu', an ascetic who has extinguished all desire (Dyer 2009: 284). 'I didn't renounce the world', Jeff insists, 'I just gradually took less interest in it' (Dyer 2009: 279). One might ask whether Dyer is reducing the spiritual realm to the level of the prosaic and mundane, or whether conversely, he is venerating the mundane to the level of the poetic and profound? The answer seems to be that in the paradoxical logic of Dyer's work, both intentions are simultaneously possible. Dyer's intention is less to satirise the possibility of transcendence than to deconstruct it through unlikely comparisons. There is, of course, an element of mischief in this deconstructive exercise. Jeff insists that '[i]t's possible to be a hundred per cent sincere and a hundred per cent ironic at the same time' (Dyer 2009: 207). To attempt to classify Dyer's commentary as either wholly a joke or wholly serious is to wilfully misunderstand the text's equivocality.

The collapse of the division between London and Varanasi, between home and abroad, echoes a broader anxiety in travel writing and travel fiction that the homogenising effect of the globalised economy and global mobility, of which tourism is an expression, has flattened the difference between cultures. The response to this fear is often to travel to increasingly remote or dangerous locations in order to escape the bland and commercialised experience of 'backpacker land', as Alex Garland calls it (Garland 1996: 7). Jeff, however, seems to be commenting less that Varanasi is too much like home, than that the experience of Varanasi makes him realise that home is not enough like home, that he feels alienated everywhere. Caren Kaplan suggests that in the contemporary world, '[f]or many of us there is no possibility of staying at home in the conventional sense – that is, the world has changed to the point that those domestic, national, or marked spaces no longer exist' (Kaplan 1996: 7).

We might understand *Death in Varanasi* to be an example of what John Zilcosky terms 'an uncanny travelogue' (2004: 232). Zilcosky, in his essay 'The writer as nomad', considers 'the art of getting lost' in travel writing, that is, the part which the trope of 'lostness' plays in establishing the writer's sense of self (Zilcosky 2004: 232). Zilcosky suggests that nineteenth-century European travel writing 'involved the traveller's attempt to find or "take hold" of himself and, in the end, "return" to a fantasy of a temporally regressed *Ur*-home' (Zilcosky 2004: 232). While the trope of getting lost may seem to suggest a destabilising of the writer or protagonist's subjectivity, an openness to new perspectives or transformation, a narrative arc which Zilcosky dubs the 'romantic recuperation' plot actually tends to return the lost character home with a reinforced sense of the superior values of home (Zilcosky 2004: 239). 'Lostness', Zilcosky says, 'presupposes its own recuperation' (Zilcosky 2004: 239). This plot arc requires, however, a distinct sense of the differences between home and abroad. Zilcosky then proposes a postmodern variation on the familiar lost-and-found narrative arc typified by Roland Barthes' *Empire of Signs* (1982), which he terms an 'uncanny travelogue' (Zilcosky 2004: 239). Zilcosky argues that '[t]he uncanny travelogue asserts that one can never lose one's way' (Zilcosky 2004: 239). The postmodern traveller, he continues, is 'someone who wants to get lost but cannot, because he keeps inadvertently travelling the same paths' (Zilcosky 2004: 239). This, in a sense, is Jeff's dilemma, in which Varanasi becomes an uncanny double of London in which the problems of home are not so much solved as amplified. By ending the narrative, not with Jeff's return, but in a continuing state of 'lostness', Dyer might be said to have broken with a neo-colonial plot arc which repeatedly shows its protagonists mastering their surroundings and profiting by their experiences. For Stephen M. Levin, the search for 'self' is a modernist mission: 'narratives of the self's discovery reflect the structure of modernism much more than postmodernism, while narratives of the self's negation highlight the failure of the postmodern to underwrite any sustainable form of subjectivity' (Levin 2008: 102). Jeff's story, not of 'finding himself' but of losing himself makes a comment on a lack in his English-self more than his India surroundings.

Zilcosky (2004) goes on to argue, however, that the uncanny travelogue is not such a radical break from the romantic recuperation plot after all. The experience of lostness, Zilcosky argues, is really a means of finding a 'situation of writing', that is that in a 'neo-Romantic twist, the writer gets lost in order successfully to find himself as an authorial nomad' (Zilcosky 2004: 239). While *Death in Varanasi* represents Jeff's negation, it could be argued that the text itself represents a part of how Geoff Dyer establishes himself as a cultural authority of the modernist exile-artist type. Jeff is a frustrated and unproductive writer, but Geoff is a thriving one, and the book itself is testament to this. The logic by which Zilcosky undermines the writer of the uncanny travelogue and suggests that his or her practice is linked to a colonial mentality is, however, a somewhat self-defeating one. If we accept that the travel writer, simply by virtue of writing about the places they visit, makes claims to understanding which are arrogant and bolsters their identity as a writer in a way which is self-serving, it seems that travel writing ought to be abandoned completely. If the aim of postcolonial theory is to not only to challenge representation when it perpetuates a colonial ideology, but also to promote cross-cultural understanding, then this seems damaging. Robert Spencer (2011: 164) complains that 'once arguments about the unfeasibility of representation have been deemed credible then we are left with a sort of separatist ideology'.

Dyer's novel is perhaps less guilty of Zilcosky's charge, that postmodern travel writing is founded on colonial ideas of the author-subject, than Spencer's, that postcolonial writing undermines the worthiness of attempting to communicate outside of one's own culture. Dyer deliberately undermines his narrator's claims to authority and understanding by leaving open the possibility that Jeff's 'lostness' teaches him only about himself and his own culture. This is well demonstrated in an incident in which Jeff attempts to talk with a 'friendly-looking holy man' but, on discovering the man speaks no English, is content to pay him simply in order to look into his eyes.

> I'm not sure what I was looking for, what I expected to see – that's why I was looking, to find out what I was looking for. What I didn't see was any affinity between us. He was in his world and I was in mine … If I looked closely, I could see my own face reflected in the dilated pupils of his eyes. It was as if I was there, a little homunculus. (Dyer 2009: 248)

Jeff's breakdown may be a kind of epiphany to him, but like his attempt to look into the holy man's eyes without knowing what it is he is looking for, the only insight he can get is into himself. He may appear to have merged with the chaos of Varanasi, but he remains on the outside of the experience of Indian people and culture with seemingly no means of accessing a better understanding.

I am reminded of a complaint of Chinua Achebe (1993): 'A Conrad student told me in Scotland last year that Africa is merely a setting for the disintegration of the mind of Mr. Kurtz.' Achebe was not comforted by this interpretation of *The Heart of Darkness*. One might comment, similarly, that in Dyer's narrative,

Varanasi is merely a setting for the disintegration of the mind of Jeff. Jenny Turner (2009: 23) comments that, 'Dyer writes with such poise – self-conscious but not self-serious, brainy but not opaque, aware but not self-flagellating about the basic indecency of tourism – that he sometimes drains a situation of its spontaneity and danger'. Dyer's laconic style is not suited to moralising, which often makes his voice an entertaining and unpredictable one, but it limits the depth with which he can depict his subject matter. The detached flippancy of Jeff's tone risks trivialising the spectacle of suffering and poverty in Varanasi which it sometimes depicts. The detached tone which is sometimes troubling in *Death in Varanasi* is not so much a flaw of the writing, however, but a manifestation of Dyer's central theme. What we see through Jeff's eyes is not a view of India but a tiny reflection of Jeff, or maybe even Geoff, himself.

References

Achebe, C. 1993. An image of Africa. *The Massachusetts Review*, 18(4), 782–94.

Banco, L.M. 2009. *Travel and Drugs in Twentieth Century Literature*. London: Routledge.

Barthes, R. 1982. *Empire of Signs*. New York: Hill and Wang.

Bennett, O. 1998. Let's get cerebral, *The Independent*, 11 January. [Online]. Available at: http://www.independent.co.uk/life-style/lets-get-cerebral-1137944.html [accessed: 12 June 2012].

Brooker, J. 2004. Shades of the eighties: *The Colour of Memory*, in *The Swarming Streets: Twentieth-Century Literary Representations of London*, edited by L. Phillips. Amsterdam: Rodopi, 139–52.

Brown, M. 1998. *The Spiritual Tourist: A Personal Odyssey Through the Outer Reaches of Belief*. London: Bloomsbury.

Bunyan, J. 1952 [1678]. *The Pilgrim's Progress*. London: Oxford University Press.

Cohen, E. 2004. *Contemporary Tourism: Diversity and Change*. Oxford: Elsevier.

Dyer, G. 1989. *The Colour of Memory*. London: Abacus.

Dyer, G. 1997. *Out of Sheer Rage: In the Shadow of D.H. Lawrence*. London: Little Brown.

Dyer, G. 1998. *Paris Trance*. London: Abacus.

Dyer, G. 2003a. Interviewed by S. Hansen. A drug user's guide to not writing, [online] 24 February. Available at: http://www.salon.com/2003/02/24/dyer/ [accessed: 14 April 2010].

Dyer, G. 2003b. *Yoga for People Who Can't Be Bothered to Do It*. London: Time Warner.

Dyer, G. 2009. *Jeff in Venice/Death in Varanasi*. London: Canongate.

Dyer, G. 2011. *Sex and Hotels, Working the Room*. London: Canongate.

Forster, E. 1979 [1924]. *A Passage to India*. Harmondsworth: Penguin.

Garland, A. 1996. *The Beach*. London: Penguin.

Gilbert, S. 2007. *Eat, Pray, Love: One Woman's Search for Everything.* London: Bloomsbury.

Iyer, P. 1998. *Video Nights in Kathmandu.* London: Bloomsbury.

Kaplan, C. 1996. *Questions of Travel: Postmodern Discourses of Displacement.* London: Duke University Press.

Korte, B. 2000. *English Travel Writing From Pilgrimages to Postcolonial Explorations.* Basingstoke: Palgrave.

Levin, S.M. 2008. *The Contemporary Anglophone Travel Novel: The Aesthetics of Self-Fashioning.* New York: Routledge.

Lippard, L.R. 1999. Foreword, in D. MacCannell, *The Tourist: A New Theory of the Leisure Class.* Berkeley: University of California Press, ix–xiv.

MacCannell, D. 1999. *The Tourist: A New Theory of the Leisure Class.* Berkeley: University of California Press.

Mortensen, G. 2008. *Three Cups of Tea.* London: Penguin.

Roberts, G.D. 2005. *Shantaram.* London: Abacus.

Spencer, R. 2011. *Cosmopolitan Criticism and Postcolonial Literature.* London: Palgrave Macmillan.

Sutcliffe, W. 1998. *Are You Experienced?* London: Penguin.

Turner, J. 2009. 'How Dare He?', *London Review of Books* (April), 23–5.

Urry, J. and Larsen, J. 2011. *The Tourist Gaze 3.0.* 3rd edition. London: SAGE.

Zilcosky, J. 2004. The writer as nomad? The art of getting lost. *Interventions*, 26(2), 229–41.

Chapter 6

'Home is Lovelier than the Way Home': Travels and Transformations in Mahmoud Darwish's Poetry

Rehnuma Sazzad

Figure 6.1 Mahmoud Darwish
Source: Don J. Usner 2002.

Mahmoud Darwish, one of the leading figures of World Literature, led the life of a constant wanderer. Edward Said (1994: 112) introduces him as a 'wandering exile', who happened to be a member of pre-Oslo Palestine Liberation

Organisation (PLO),[1] but never an adherent to the group in the strict sense of the term, because 'his mordant wit, fierce political independence, and exceptionally refined cultural sensibility kept him at a distance from the frequent coarseness of Palestinian and Arab politics'. His dissociation from the political 'coarseness' is recognisable from his reputation as one of the greatest contemporary Arab poets, who accomplished a persistent improvement of his poetic sensibility through his humane vision that firmly refused to demonise the 'Other'. Commenting on the 'most public of Palestinians', who filled up football stadiums with his poetry recitations, Sampson (2007) points out that Darwish is not a poet of polemic alone; his profound lyrics transcended rhetorical renderings through 'draw[ing] together the textures of daily life, physical beauty – whether of landscape or of women – longing, myth and history'. I examine the 'longing, myth and history' in his poetry that reflect the universal human condition through the personal and national experiences of occupation and exile. I elaborate how his long and varied trajectory contributed not only to the ever-increased sophistication of his poetry but also to the transformation of his perception of belonging. Ultimately, we realise that the 'fierce political independence' he represents originates from his ability to transform himself through the constant travels that refine his poetic sensibility towards reaching a transcendent realm, which he envisages as home.

Darwish was born in a now-erased Palestinian village called Al-Birwa. Having entered the changed (home)land after the catastrophe of 1948 called the Nakba, the six-year-old discovered that he had become an 'illegal infiltrator' there. His primary school teachers had to hide him during the Israeli officers' visits, since he had been classified as a 'present-absent alien'. During the school's celebration of the second anniversary of Israel's establishment, he recited a poem of his own lamenting the reality that disallowed an Arab and a Jewish boy to play together. An instant wrath of the state apparatus was incurred with him being castigated, his father's job at the quarry threatened (they had lost their agricultural land due to the Nakba), and his language belittled (see Akash 2000: 12). The wrath lasted until 1970 in the form of long periods of house-arrests and repeated imprisonments, when he left for Moscow for higher studies. The Russian city became a launching pad for his extended and varied travels around the globe spanning almost three decades. What made him determined about embracing this vast exile, despite causing criticism among his community, was that his life in the usurped land was proving to be too constricting. The 'present-absentee' became fully existent for the authorities, whenever they needed to put him in prison for his poetry and ostensibly for travelling inside the state without a permit. Besides, he was required to report at a police station in Haifa at every sundown.

---

1 On 13 September 1993, Israeli Prime Minister Yitzhak Rabin and PLO Chairman Yasser Arafat signed the Oslo Accords in the White House lawn. Darwish gave up his membership in the organisation soon afterwards, since the 'peace' treaty had betrayed almost all crucial Palestinian claims including the refugees' rights to return.

Interestingly, though, the daily travels to the police station paved the way for his transformation of the caged situation into an occasion of revolt. In his 1980s memoir, Darwish (1995: 174) reminisces about the time of the travail by referring to his poem 'Identity Card' written in the 1960s:

> 'Put this in your record: I'm Arab!' I said that to a government employee ... in Hebrew to provoke him. But when I put it in a poem, the Arab public in Nazareth was electrified by a secret current that released the genie from the bottle.

Evidently, his interchanging of the languages of two politically opposed peoples transformed his humiliating experience of attending the police station everyday into a source of resistance. Darwish's Hebraic assertion of his Arab identity to the Jewish officer was a poignant reminder to him that his culture is a sign of his humanity. This was to provoke him, though, because Darwish was turning the ground of his annihilation into a basis of his strength. Having been translated back into Arabic, the declaration naturally gathered its full force in the midst of the vilified people and 'the genie' of the spurned spirit of the Nazarethians appeared as an electrifying power; they realised that being Arab could not be a justification for being denigrated by the state authority. Thus, Darwish's declaration transported Arabness into the arena of a rich history that enkindled hope in the people.

Said (1980: 155) calls 'Identity Card' 'a national poem', due to its successful reversal of Palestinians' loss of dignity into an empowering proclamation:

> The curious power of this little poem is that at the time it appeared in the late sixties, it did not *represent* as much as *embody* the Palestinian, whose political identity in the world had been pretty much reduced to a name on an identity card. (Emphasis in original)

To me, however, the declaration is not simply an embodiment of a thwarted identity but also a reinvigoration of the truth that humans are irrevocably the same, despite their cultural differences. Needless to reiterate, Darwish's intra-cultural travels made this transforming assertion possible. This explains his vehement refusal to recite the poem when he travelled outside Israel, especially around the Arab world. He was discerning enough to know that this would undo the transformative power the declaration contains and reduce it to a sheer slogan of stultifying sameness.

Indeed, Darwish's politics changed soon, as he first stepped into the Arab world through his move from Moscow to Cairo. The city not only initiated his long wandering in the Arab world but also inaugurated a new era in his writing by transforming the poet from a resistance writer of the Occupied Territories to a steadfast Arab voice of deep lyricism. In the documentary made on his life entitled, *As the Land is the Language*, Darwish describes that Cairo was pleasantly surprising for him, where he first discovered an all-Arabic-speaking world. This new experience of being in the all-Arab environment surely honed the poetic sensibility of this Hebrew-speaking Arabic writer.

   This will be evident from two prominent Darwish poems from this period, both
of which commemorate two travelling figures, one a major Palestinian poet and
the other a classical Arab poet. Clearly, Cairo began to shape Darwish's national
consciousness more assuredly in the light of his linguistic heritage. In any case,
the first poem remembers Rashid Hussein, who was not only a poet of resistance
but a pioneer of Israeli–Palestinian literary exchanges through his translations.
However, he met a tragic death in exile when his New York apartment caught fire
on a lonely winter night. Darwish (1986: 35) pays this moving lyrical tribute to the
great Palestinian littérateur and orator:

>   He came to us a blade of wine
>   And left, a prayer's end.
>   He flung out poems
>   At Christo's Restaurant
>   And all of Acre would rise from sleep
>   To walk upon the sea.

Darwish remembers Hussein's charisma and the Palestinians' loss at his sudden
disappearance that defied their prayers, for he could invigorate the occupied Acre
through the magic of his poetry. Therefore, our poet remembers the son '[f]rom
a limb of Palestine' in his own exile in an Arab city to celebrate his compatriot's
'prose of meadows' and 'poetry of wheat' (Darwish 1986: 36) so that the feeling
of exilic disorientation and directionlessness do not swallow him. He remembers
seeing Hussein, the distraught traveller in Cairo, whose wanderings had made him
feel that he would be free even in the prison, if he were in Nazareth. Unlike him,
Darwish wanted to overcome the dejectedness to protect him from the desire to
vanish at sunset 'Over the deep Nile' (Darwish 1986: 38).
   Cairo reaffirmed that his poetry could save him, since he could look for the
essence of his existence in his language. This resolve remains the first decisive
influence of his long-drawn travels on him, despite the fact that his 'initial
enthusiasm for Cairo, as the first Arab city he lived in, changed over the course of
time due to Egypt's position regarding the PLO and the signing of the Camp David
agreement in 1978' (Nassar 2008: 198). The influence is evident, as he turns to
Al-Mutannabi, one of the most renowned Arab poets, who also had a troublesome
relationship with Egypt. Al-Mutannabi was a literary icon who became ambitious
for political power in Arab countries, the persistent failure of which took him
from one city to another. Darwish writes about the legend's visit to Egypt, where
he won a dubious patronage. The tenth-century poet, then, is an apt parallel to
his twentieth-century counterpart in the same country. However, Darwish neither
coveted political power nor idealised Al-Mutannabi for his misplaced ambition.
Instead, he utilised the poet's travels from Aleppo to Cairo in order to project his
disillusionment with Egypt, his unending voyages, and his resolve to rise above
'the royal ladder' and 'swords' (Darwish 1986: 14–15) through his ideas and lyrics.
In other words, Al-Mutannabi becomes a mouthpiece for the Palestinian poet,

whose resolve to cling to his language becomes stronger in his homelessness. The transformation that Cairo's exciting and frustrating experiences brought to Darwish (1986: 15) is captured in the following verse, where Al-Mutannabi declares:

> Egypt's silence breaks me
> Here is her slave prince
> Here are her hungry.
> I sell the palace a song
> I break the palace with a song
> I lean against the wind and wound
> And am not sold.

Egypt faces socio-cultural difficulties of its own, which probably leads the country to exercise its 'silence' towards the Palestinians through Camp David and its unfriendliness to the PLO. Unlike Al-Mutannabi, Darwish was no friend of 'the palace'. But like him, the Palestinian poet realised in Egypt: 'My country is my latest poem' (Darwish 1986: 11).

We can already see that Darwish's poetry was getting enmeshed with the politics of liberation. This took a new turn when he moved from Cairo to what was then the political heartland of the PLO, Beirut. The city united him with the hotbed of liberation struggle and rendered his verses overtly political, which he later resented. However, the mixture of politics and aesthetics that Beirut matured was the hallmark of his writing in the period, which Paris later refined. Hence, the travel to Beirut creates the watershed moment when Darwish's politics enters into the seething cauldron of revolution through poems like 'In Praise of the High Shadow.' This was 'written on the deck of one of the ships carrying Darwish, along with thousands of Palestinian fighters, from Beirut to Tunisia after Israel's barbaric destruction of Lebanon in 1982' (Ammous 2008). Since the poem is an immediate response to the Israeli aggression that took the shape of bombing Beirut with a fury, murdering the Palestinian refugees of the Sabra and Shatila camps, killing the civilians indiscriminately, and banishing the PLO from its exilic shelter, Darwish describes the dreadful predicament as the moment of eclipse for his people. The symbolism of the shadow is significant here. Since a shadow implies a lack of light, its rise suggests a dark, bleak and doomed prospect for the individuals and the collective of people concerned. Obviously, then, Darwish's ironic praise for the highly risen shadow is meant to be a sarcastic slash at the dark side of human civilisation that pushes an already stateless people into such a dreary state.

As almost all hopes for the Palestinians had evaporated, the poet experienced the feeling of nothingness on the deck of the ship. He felt as if he was en route to Golgotha, the site of Jesus' crucifixion; because he was journeying towards a totally unknown future. Hence, the comparison is a fitting corollary to his people's existential crisis anew in Beirut. Darwish blasts out:

It is for you to be, or not to be,
It is for you to create, or not to create.
All existential questions, behind your shadow, are a farce,
And the universe is your small notebook, and you are its creator.
So write in it the paradise of genesis,
Or do not write it,
You, you are the question.
(See Ammous 2008)

The nada the Palestinians face makes a farce of all other existential questions. Since their shadow rises higher and higher, they are left with absolutely nothing but their willpower to subsist.

Because of the dramatisation of the nihilistic time, Darwish later disapproved of the anthologisation of the poem. However, it is evident that the verses are no mere outcries. The aesthetic is still ingrained in the refusal to surrender, especially as words are employed to buoy up the spirit of survival:

So leave,
For the place is not yours, nor are the garbage thrones.
You are the freedom of creation,
You are the creator of the roads,
And you are the anti-thesis of this era.
And leave,
Poor, like a prayer,
Barefoot, like a river in the path of rocks,
And delayed, like a clove.
(See Ammous 2008)

The precision of the repetitive single words creates a poignant picture of the total loss the Palestinians came to experience after Beirut. Besides, Darwish addresses them as 'you' to differentiate between their usual image in the world and their hidden strong self that can still be rescued from the heavy strikes. Especially, they are compared with cloves, the buds of which ripen through a gradual process of transformation from a pale colour to green, which then develops into bright red. Thus, the poet seeds hope even in the most desperate situation through the nature imagery that bears the indelible proof of his agrarian Palestinian identity. Perceivably, his words are not just politically effective in bearing witness to the aggression but also aesthetically sharp in keeping alive the hope that their thwarted freedom will materialise one day, despite the delay caused by the dispossession and the incessant Israeli attacks. The mingling of politics and aesthetics 'becomes the Palestinian artist's tool of *resistance against the assassination of liberation*' (Hamdi 2011: 24; emphasis in original).

Beirut thus transforms Darwish into a revolutionary voice that is uncompromising in demanding the rights of freedom and dignity for the wretched of the earth. In any case, as the PLO is uprooted from the city, Darwish hits the road again. Tunis becomes his next destination, which is soon changed for Paris. The hub of aesthetics brought a complete overhaul of his rhetorical outburst in the 'High Shadow' declaring, 'Let every barricade be a homeland' (see *As the Land is the Language*). Paris transformed the poet in two fundamentally significant ways. First, it changed his eloquence into a mode of reflection. His verses became more evocative, suggestive, and enriched with imagination. Secondly, the home of art gave birth to the 'cosmopolitan modernist' (Deane 2008) that Darwish became so remarkably known as. The distance from homeland happenings, the paradoxical freedom of unfamiliarity, the company of other exiled poets, and the creative inspiration the city provided all contributed to the enhanced refinement of his verses. Hence, the poet affirms that '[h]ere, I wrote my best works: *It Is a Song, It Is a Song, Fewer Roses, I See What I Want, Eleven Stars*. The last work I wrote here was *Why Have you left The Horse Alone?*' (see *As the Land is the Language*).

The last book mentioned above is an autobiography written in verses, which does not include details associated with the varied events of Darwish's life. Rather, he paints the pictures of the significant phases of his life through 'cultural, historical, and literary allusions' that offer the microcosm of his life as a macrocosm of 'the tragedy of modern Palestinians' (Boullata 2007: 70). I will emphasise the beauty underlying the arrangement of the collection to highlight the Paris influence on the poet. Apart from the introductory poem that contains the essence of the tragedy, the rest of the book is organised in sections the lyrical titles of which evoke the different stages of the poet's life by conjuring up a composite picture of his loss of homeland and identity.

The first section, entitled 'Icons of the Place's Crystal', weaves the representative patterns of his free childhood, the village he knew and 'The Owl's Night' of the Nakba. As the opening lines of the 'The Eternity of the Cactus' capture the Nakba-generated directionlessness, we realise the power of the cactus, which is a sign of resilience working behind the succinctness of Darwish's utterance:

> – Where are you taking me, father?
> – Where the wind takes us, my son ...
> (Darwish 2006: 28; ellipsis in original)

The poignant pain in the couplet needs no explanation, just as young Darwish's concern about the fate of his favourite companion is inescapable:

> – Why did you leave the horse alone?
> – To keep the house company, my son
> – Houses die when their inhabitants are gone ...
> (Darwish 2006: 30; ellipsis in original)

The pathos generated by the lines find an echo in every human heart. We can see that the lines have begun to be as bright as lapis lazuli, Darwish's favourite

gemstone and his allusion to ancient Babylonian and Egyptian cultures, where it
was highly valued. The gemstone that featured prominently in their hymns makes
an appearance in a later Darwish poem:

> I was a robbed man looking at his coffers and asking himself:
> Was that field, that treasure, mine?
> Was this lapis lazuli, wet with humidity and night dew, mine?
> Was I, one day, the butterfly's student in fragility and boldness at times?
> and her colleague in metaphor at others?
> Was I, once, mine? Does memory fall sick with me and have a fever?
> (Darwish 2008: 10)

Lapis lazuli not only contains the wondrous beauty of the dark blue sky but also
symbolises harmony, the lack of which reigns in the Israeli-Palestinian territory.
Since Darwish can claim nothing but the memory of his homeland, he takes lesson
in 'fragility and boldness' from the butterfly, which also becomes his metaphoric
companion in maintaining a dual existence as a 'present-absentee'.

From this perspective, 'Abel's Space', the title of the next phase of the
poetic autobiography under discussion, is noteworthy. Darwish's identification
of himself with Abel represents his victimisation by his own brother, Cain. The
suggested kinship with the Jews is apparent here, which he also developed as a
predominant trope through other Biblical stories. Through his allusions to one
of them, this section relates the episode of Darwish's youth at the newly formed
state. The aptly named first poem, 'Ismael's *'Oud'*, recreates the music of the
instrument to delineate the poet's longing for the lost harmony. Obviously, he
refers to the Old Testament story of Ishmael, who was Abraham's firstborn with
his wife Sarah's handmaiden, Hagar. However, due to the custom of the day, he
came to be identified as one belonging to Sarah, rather than to his own mother.
For this reason, Darwish draws himself as a new Ishmael by depicting the Biblical
precedence of his disinheritance of the motherland.

Evidently, Paris transformed Darwish into a poet who aimed at the depth of
his depictions, instead of their thunderousness. This is not to say that politics
disappeared from sight at this stage. On the contrary, politics became part of
his aesthetics that made the profound sense of his loss more powerful owing to
the sophistication of his thought. This is comprehensible from the tightly knit
structure of the book. Every time he tells his story here, it gets intertwined with the
counter-claim by his 'others', who have now 'saddled the horses at the end of the
night' (Darwish 2006: 12) of their own endless travels. However, Darwish's effort
throughout the collection is to remind them of his ghostly presence that rises from
'the cracks of the place ...' (Darwish 2006: 14; ellipsis in original) Through all his
memories, thus, the poet proclaims the presence of his ghost in the landscape of
his lost homeland only whose resuscitation will rectify the wounds of the Nakba.
Thus, the poet advances his unflinching demands for justice with no involvement
of the bombast he abjures.

Alessandrini (2009) reminds us of the effectiveness of the employment of the ghost-figure in the post-Oslo period, especially as the treaty denied the internationally recognised rights of the exiled Palestinians to return to the homeland. As Darwish's apparition hovers over the historic land, Alessandrini (2009) asserts that it becomes:

> a figure that also brings together past, present, and future. The ghost comes from a past that has been buried, forgotten, or actively obscured; he returns to haunt the present precisely as a reminder of this forgotten past and as a vision of a just future that might redress the crimes of the past.

The 'revenant', as Alessandrani calls it, powerfully opposes the destruction of Palestine and the obliteration of its people's history. But I add that the apparition is a subtle means through which Darwish shows a more aesthetic command in advancing his inalienable right to exist as a living being. Evidently, Paris changed the tones, modes and expressions of Darwish's poetry; but not his humanist politics. Rather, the politics was enhanced by the honing of his aesthetics.

The improvement is seen in the next section of the autobiography as well. 'Chaos at Resurrection's Gate' records Darwish's memory of the revival of the nationalist spirit. However, the style could not have been further removed from that of the writings in the Occupied Territories or in Cairo, in the sense that the cosmopolitan poet now defends his fundamental rights through connecting his indigenous world with the varied cultural spheres of humanity. When he reminisces about the dried up and abandoned well in front of his erased home at Al-Birwa, he connects it with the Sumerian myth of Gilgamesh. Having been thrown out of the well's vicinity, he imagines that the area is surrounded by the footsteps of his ghost. In order to restore it to life, he awaits the return of the king of the Sumerian city of Uruk, from which Iraq derives its name. Thus, Gilgamesh represents the poet's hope of being rescued from the nameless existence and the dream of beginning a national epic, which is more open to the world. Consequently, the key French influence of cosmopolitanism becomes foregrounded in his poetry.

The openness to the multiplicity of belonging continues in the fourth section as well. 'A Room to Talk to Oneself' presents his pluralistic worldview through the memory of his first experiences of exile. He remembers that he was searching for a self-definition in his lonely life and discovered that it is impossible to be pinned down to one particular culture, due to Palestine's being a historic crossroads of influential civilizations, colonial powers, and major religions. Hence, the tension that currently sways the land is not entirely unforeseen. Darwish (2006: 130) pithily states:

> ... I was born of my language
> on the route of India tucked between two small tribes. Above them was
> the ancient religions' moon and the impossible peace
> They had to grasp the astrology of their neighbour Persia

and the great anxiety of the Romans so that the burdened time
would release itself over the Arab tent.

The two conflicting peoples are clearly acknowledged as the equal claimants on
the land. However, they have to comprehend the place's sophisticated and multi-
faceted heritage as well as the pressures of empires it withstood since the Roman
time. With the understanding of 'the burdened time' that hit the 'Arab tent', they
have to work towards an 'impossible peace'. In other words, an expansive and
integrative vision is required from them to rise above the conflict.

    With this aim, the fifth section of the autobiography, 'Rain On the Church
Tower', works towards the reconstruction of harmony between him and his
Israeli beloved, despite their unfulfilled longing symbolised by the rain. The
cosmopolite beseeches his beloved to write 'a song of songs' for him that will
inscribe his name on 'the trunk of a pomegranate tree in the gardens of Babylon'
(Darwish 2006: 148). As she fails to do so, he takes recourse to ancient cultures to
keep alive his search for:

    Jasmine
    on a
    July
    night ...
    (Darwish 2006: 150; ellipsis in original)

Thus, he is 'in pursuit of "opening a space" for not just any flower, but jasmine,
at once the most ordinary and yet the sweetest-scented of free-growing vines'
(Omer 2005: 72). What needs to be emphasised here is that Jasmine works as a
complex symbol of the poet's effort at bringing grace and elegance in his poetry,
his attachment to his beloved, and their sensuality. Since the poet keeps singing the
songs of Jasmine despite their failed relationship, the flower also becomes a sign
of his resolute hope for peace in the land. He further asserts in the last section of
the autobiography, aptly entitled 'The Curtain Fell', that the ordinary is sufficient
inspiration for him to look beyond his sordid reality. Even though we see in this
section that his imaginary attempt at communicating with the Jewish settler in his
village meets an unsuccessful end, he keeps creating his 'Sequences for Another
Time'. Surely, the transcendent and multifarious vision is another significant result
of his transformation in Paris as a cosmopolite.

    The relentlessly evolving poetic psyche had to go through a final transformation
in 1996, when the poet was allowed to return to the Occupied Territories after 26
years of wandering, whereupon he divided his time between Ramallah and Amman.
He preferred to withdraw to solitude in Amman whenever the events at West
Bank proved to be too tumultuous for him. In any case, his return did not fulfil
his longing for his lost homeland, since he could not go back to the completely
destroyed village of his childhood, Al-Birwa. The profound sense of loss and the
perpetual search that we have encountered in Darwish so far originate from his

being uprooted from the village's iconic 'open spaces, fields and watermelons, olive and almond trees' (see Cook 2008: 18). The clarity with which he remembers the contours of the village reveals his intrinsic connection to it:

> I remember the horse that was tied to the mulberry tree in the yard and how I climbed on to it and was thrown off and got a beating from my mother ... I remember the butterflies and the clear feeling that everything was open. The village stood on a hill and everything was spread out below. (See Cook 2008: 18)

Like the memory, his writings preserved these features during his far-flung travels in a way of being rooted to the environment. We have seen earlier that the reassertion of his denied identity is with which his poetic mission started in 1960s Palestine. His late phase verses re-embodied the spirit as if by completing the cycle of transformation his poetic sensibility went through. However, his later poetry proclaimed the land in the light of the sea changes the 'wandering exile' experienced during his long period of absence from the homeland.

The point is that Darwish's travels not only created specific influences in his writing but also rendered the constant traveller incapable of calling a particular place home. I think his realisation of this fact became more potent after his ambiguous return to Ramallah. His very last poem, 'The Dice Player', which he recited there just six days before his final departure, records this ambiguity through depicting human connections (and lack there of) to particular places as chance-governed:

> I'm the way the dice fall
> sometimes winning sometimes losing
> I'm like you
> or maybe slightly less ...
> (Darwish 2009c: 55; ellipsis in original)

His being a Palestinian from Al-Birwa is a chance occurrence, just like the Israelites' being a people with a mythical claim. This does not undermine his historical ties with the land, nor does it overweigh his deep-rooted devotion to it, despite the fact that his standing in the world is less powerful than his opponent's:

> O land I love you green
> Green
> an apple dancing in water and light
> Green
> your night green, our dawn green
> so plant me with the tenderness of a mother's hand
> in a handful of air
> I am one of your seeds
> Green ...
> (Darwish 2009c: 67; ellipsis in original)

This is no exclusive assertion of belonging to the land, despite the express spontaneity and depth of the tender feelings. Hence, immediately after this desire to be planted in the soil of the motherland, he casts doubts on his honest utterance through reinserting the refrain about the power of chance over our identity and belonging:

> I might not have been a swallow
> if the wind had wanted it that way
> the wind is the luck of the traveller
> I went north, east and west
> but the south was far and impenetrable to me
> because the south is my home
> So I became a metaphor of a swallow soaring above debris.
> (Darwish 2009c: 59)

The lines emphasise his lucklessness with his southern home, which paradoxically brought the wind of the three other hemispheres to his favour. As the poet sees Ramallah through the prism of his previous wanderings, the city makes him assert that our sense of belonging could be rooted to a place not of our own choosing; but our identity is always a construct, open to influences, and hence, reconstructions. For this reason, he never stops reformulating his lines. This transforms him into a metaphor of 'soaring above debris' of dispossession and exile.

Therefore, I agree with Alshaer (2011: 99) who believes that the poem accentuates the fact that our 'identity has more elements than politics or even history could suggest, and the consequence is the way humanity and identity is asserted in relation to the human essence that binds all people'. But I also think that this highlights the poet's uncertainty about his identity. Darwish (2009c: 67) continues:

> Who am I to say to you
> what I'm saying?
> It would have been possible not to be who I am
> It would have been possible not to be here ...
> (Ellipsis in original)

As these questions are thrown into the void, a perennially unsettled poetic soul emerges. The loss of Al-Birwa and the greater Palestine, the long-lasting travels around the globe, and the constant transformations due to the phenomena left him face to face with ontological questions about belonging. In *As the Land is the Language*, Darwish stands near one of the very many checkpoints of the Palestinian enclave to explain why he feels like an exile inside the territory. Just as the checkpoints curb his freedom, his existence as a citizen of an 'absent' country renders him a stranger even to himself. As this painful truth makes him choke for a moment, he pinpoints the effect of non-freedom: 'I feel that I am like a tourist but without the rights of a tourist. This feeling of being a visitor is devastating' (see *As the Land is the Language*).

However, being an optimist through and through, he transforms this devastating feeling of perpetual 'out of placeness' into an imaginative travel to historical times in order to find a sustainable place of belonging. The poet who was in search of Al-Birwa's 'open spaces, fields and watermelons' thus saw in his poetic vision the 'butterflies' of the village flying in the multi-ethnic landscape of Andalusia, the Arab-governed part of Spain that reached the apex of its glory between the ninth and twelfth centuries, when the three monotheistic religions formed a relatively coherent whole. Writing five centuries after the fall of Granada that marked the end of the 700 years of Muslim rule in Spain, Darwish (2009b: 61) dreams of the Andalusian model of coexistence:

> Five hundred years have come and gone, and the rift between us
> isn't complete, right here, the letters between us haven't ceased, and the wars
> haven't changed my Granada gardens.

The 'out of time' place he always travelled to in his mind's eye transforms his definition of home. Home now becomes synonymous with a journey towards a non-existent but a humanistic model like Andalusia, the details of which, including its marvellous gardens, his poetry relentlessly sketches.

Therefore, in his posthumously published journal, he imaginatively travels to Cordoba, which was first the eighth-century city of the Damascus Caliphate and then the capital of all Andalusia. Thereupon, he resides in the atmosphere of one of the most advanced cities of the time:

> Cordoba's wooden doors do not invite me in to give a greeting from Damascus
> to a fountain and a jasmine bush. I walk in the narrow alleys on a gentle, sunny
> spring day. I tread lightly as if I am a guest of myself and my memories, not an
> archaeological fragment passed around by tourists. I do not tap on the shoulder
> of my past with melancholy joy, as expected of me by a poem I've postponed
> writing. (Darwish 2009a: 113)

He feels happy, as he is not typically expected to be 'an archaeological fragment' of Palestine. Instead, he is basking in the company of other exilic poets, who are discussing poetry's future, until Derek Walcott brings back his contested past, his 'melancholy joy' (Darwish 2009a), by asking whether Jerusalem belongs to him or his 'Other'.

Clearly, even in his imagination, he cannot gain restfulness. This represents his historico-political reality of remaining unhoused even in his poetry. This is why the relationship between his travels and his art is always nuanced, as his poems create a continuous picture of his journey towards an imaginary but more humane abode on earth. Instead of the finality of arriving at the destination, though, carrying on with the journey becomes his poetic mission. In other words, home is such a beautiful dream that being on the road to it becomes increasingly more significant for him. His conversation with Al-Jarrah (1997) confirms this, as a result of which she concludes that home is lovelier 'than the way home' for the poet. Al-Jarrah (1997) recognises that Darwish affirms his Arab and Palestinian identities in order to deepen them *'with a human existence that is receptive to the soil and air of the whole world'* (emphasis in original). Given the patterns of his travel-inspired transformations discussed above, I could not agree more.

References

Akash, M. 2000. Chronology, awards and publications, in *Mahmoud Darwish: The Adam of Two Edens*, edited by M. Akash and D. Moore. Syracuse: Jusoor and Syracuse University Press, 11–15.

Alessandrini, A.C. 2009. *Darwish's Revenants* [Online]. Available at: http://reconstruction.eserver.org/093/Alessandrini.shtml [accessed: 15 March 2010].

Al-Jarrah, N. 1997. *Mahmoud Darwish: Home is More Lovely Than the Way Home* [Online]. Available at: http://www.aljadid.com/interviews/0319aljarrah.html [accessed: 30 March 2010].

Alshaer, A. 2011. Identity in Mahmoud Darwish's poem 'The dice player'. *Middle East Journal of Culture and Communication*, 4(1), 90–110.

Ammous, S. 2008. *Mahmoud Darwish: Palestine's Prophet of Humanism* [Online]. Available at: http://electronicintifada.net/v2/article9758.shtml [accessed: 6 April 2010].

Boullata, I.J. 2007. Review of *Why Have You Left the Horse Alone? World Literature in Review*, 81 (July), 70–72.

Cook, J. 2008. Mahmoud Darwish: A poet for the people. *New Statesman*, 25 August, 18.

Darwish, M. 1986. *Sand: And Other Poems*, translated by R. Kabbani. London: KPI Limited.

Darwish, M. 1995. *Memory for Forgetfulness*, translated by I. Muhawi. Berkeley: University of California Press.

Darwish, M. 2006. *Why Did you Leave The Horse Alone?*, translated by J. Sacks. New York: Archipelago Books.

Darwish, M. 2008. At the station of a train which fell off the map, translated by S. Antoon. *Banipal*, 33 (Autumn/Winter), 6–15.

Darwish, M. 2009a. *A River Dies of Thirst: Diaries*, translated by C. Cobham. London: Saqi Books.

Darwish, M. 2009b. *If I Were Another*, translated by F. Joudah. New York: Farrar, Straus and Giroux.

Darwish, M. 2009c. *Mural*, translated by R. Hammami and J. Berger. London: Verso.

Deane, R. 2008. *A Guest of Eternity: Mahmoud Darwish in Memoriam* [Online]. Available at: http://electronicintifada.net/v2/article9761.shtml [accessed: 10 April 2010].

Hamdi, T. 2011. Bearing witness in Palestinian resistance literature. *Race & Class*, 52(3), 21–42.

Nassar, H.K. 2008. Exile and the city: The Arab city in the writing of Mahmoud Darwish, in *Mahmoud Darwish: Exile's Poet*, edited by H. K. Nassar and N. Rahman. Massachusetts: Olive Branch Press, 191–214.

Omer, M. 2005. Opening a space for Jasmine: Mahmoud Darwish, poet of Palestine – and the world. *Washington Report on Middle East Affairs*, 27 July, 72–3.

Said, E. 1980. *The Question of Palestine*. London: Routledge & Kegan Paul PLC.

Said, E. 1994. On Mahmoud Darwish. *Grand Street*, 12(4), 112–15.

Sampson, F. 2007. *In the Serene Land* [Online]. Available at: http://www.guardian.co.uk/books/2007/dec/08/featuresreviews.guardianreview1 [accessed: 3 August 2012].

Documentary References

As the Land is the Language (dir. Simone Bitton, 1997).

Chapter 7

The Nomad, the Refugee, the Developer and the Migrant: Four Stories of Inner-City Travellers in Johannesburg, South Africa

Shannon Walsh

Introduction

When we think of travel, we don't often think of the urban migrant, the nomad, the vagabond, and the many people who eke out a living on the excesses of capitalism. But these figures are also part of the shifting geography that produces and reproduces the contemporary city. As Zygmunt Bauman (2000: 23) wrote, 'the vagabond is the alter ego of the tourist'. Urban spaces around the world teem with tourists, migrants, refugees and nomads of a plethora of dispositions. How do these disparate identities both intersect and construct one another? Are nomads, refugees and migrants the cyphers creating possibility for the tourist to exist, and vice versa?

In Johannesburg, South Africa, enactments of power are continually created through the movement of bodies through space. From slums to skyscrapers, elite gated communities to hijacked tenements; Johannesburg is ripe with human and spatial contradictions. Migrants, refugees, tourists and nomads continually journey from suburb to inner-city, disrupting smooth understandings of an urban whole. Yet it is through their movement in and between spaces that both the visible and invisible worlds of the city are revealed. In each crossing we catch glimpses of capitalism in its continual transformation and adaptation. Even the minute urban territory of the neighbourhood captures these contradictions, intersections and slippages.

This chapter emerges from research developed as part of a documentary film, *Jeppe on a Friday*, created with a group of South African filmmakers in 2012. It tells the stories of four diverse people who travel through the neighbourhood of Jeppe, each in radically different ways. Over the course of eight months Arya Lalloo and I, along with various other filmmakers, explored the neighbourhood, doing interviews, ethnographic study, wandering the streets, taking photos and video: spending time learning the beats and rhythms of Jeppe. The final documentary, *Jeppe on a Friday*, was filmed over the course of one day in March 2012. The stories here contain traces and remnants that were filmed and included in the documentary, as well as additional video interviews, in-person interviews and ethnographic observations that were not part of the documentary.

Figure 7.1 Jeppestown from above
Source: © Parabola Films.

Critically, for the South African context, apartheid tore apart and ghettoised whole communities based on crude definitions of racial difference and identity. While 1994 marked the end of political apartheid, its history still scars the city, as new practices of economic separation superimpose themselves on the landscape. In the last two decades there has been an explosion of gated communities and other practices that attempt to retain a sense of 'comfort', safety and separation for the wealthy as violent crime escalated. Johannesburg has become a city of walls, gates, grills and divisions. At the same time, since the racist divisions of space legislated under apartheid have been lifted, thousands flock to the city, and migrants from across the continent make the journey towards more prosperity in one of Africa's richest economies. Mobility has come to mark multiple experiences of urban life, as divergent 'worlds' co-exist in opaque and visible modes and juxtapositions, often in direct conflict with one another. Globally, this continual mobility marks the experience and existence for many in and of the city, though on radically different terms:

> While tourists and vagabonds are separated by their dissimilar experiences of
> travel, their movements within the global economy are structured and shaped
> by overlapping and intersecting forces that allow a privileged few to enjoy
> the freedom of movement and at the same time deny these options to others.
> (Murray 2010: 14)

The four stories I tell here reframe the meaning of travel and mobility in one neighbourhood in Johannesburg, revealing how the city continues to function as a human ecosystem of scales, each element interlinking to the larger whole. Vusi, a garbage reclaimer, moves 26 kilometres with his trolley from the rich white suburbs into the inner-city every day and reinterprets the language of travel in his own project of transforming waste, wealth and social space. Arouna is a migrant entrepreneur from Benin who survived 10 days blockaded with his family in his apartment while xenophobic violence raged in the streets below, only to establish a West African restaurant catering to migrants from across the continent. Nathi, who along with a few hundred other blind people, fled to Johannesburg from Zimbabwe, and now occupies an inner-city building on the edge of the soon to be gentrified neighbourhood. Finally, JJ, a young white venture capitalist who returned to South Africa from Europe hoping to develop what he believes might be the next New York-style urban environment in the inner-city up against building hijackers and slum lords. Each travels through the city, transformed by their journeys in very different ways, while still sharing close physical proximity to one another. Their movements throw into question relationships to territory, and 'freedom' of movement in a time of vast economic disparity, economic migration, class and racial conflict. At the heart of their journeys the question remains: who is allowed to move and why do they move? Bauman argues that:

> [T]ourists move because they find the world within their reach irresistibly *attractive*. The vagabonds move because they find the world within their reach unbearably inhospitable ... The vagabonds are, one may say, involuntary tourists, but the notion of 'involuntary tourist' is a contradiction in terms. (Bauman 2000: 23)

'Involuntary tourist' may sugarcoat displacement and forced economic migration, but it also indicates ways in which mobility is prized in a globalised world. There is a danger of romanticising the nomad, as increasingly the tourist (and for my purposes here, the urban developer or venture capitalist) sees himself in just such an idealistic light. Kirstner (2004) challenges a romantic idea of the nomad, or 'lifestyle nomads' as she calls them; self-styled wanderers who appear to be held together by 'nomad capitalism', subverting boundaries and creating new kinds of affinities:

> Post-industrial millennial culture has discovered its affinity with nomads – in their mobility and subversion of boundaries. This self-stylization obliterates any distinction between the dislocation that has become the condition of movements of people across the globe driven by war, civil strife, poverty and starvation, ecological disasters, and political exigencies and those who are on the move either by virtue of 'lifestyle' or profession or as a matter of commuting between various sites across which they have pitched their everyday lives. (Kirstner 2004: 243)

Whether self-stylised, or forced by the conditions of everyday life, movement comes to mark and shape our lives within 'nomad capitalism'. Is there meaning in the intersections weaving together the nomad, the refugee, the developer and the migrant? How do these divergent ways of moving through the city tell us something about the larger processes and scales of urban life, and capitalism, more globally? While I can't hope to elucidate all these questions here, I turn to the stories of people in movement as a way to begin through looking at the traces of everyday life.

Four Stories

The Nomad

Figure 7.2 Vusi in Jeppestown
Source: © Parabola Films. Photo by Blake Woodhams.

Vusi moves swiftly through the city. At only 27 years old, Vusi has lived on the streets for most of his life, and has been a waste-picker since he was a boy. He is a nomad, moving 'from point to point':

> The nomad has a territory; he follows customary paths; he goes from one point
> to another; he is not ignorant of points (water points, dwelling points, assembly
> points, etc.). But the question is what in nomad life is a principle and what is only
> a consequence … the nomad goes from point to point only as a consequence and

as a factual necessity; in principle, points for him are relays along a trajectory. (Deleuze and Guattari 1988: 380)

The city is built of different zones that Vusi is able to translate and navigate as a way of survival. For Vusi the city is not opaque. It is intercut with the lines he weaves with his trolley. It is visible, even behind its walls. While in some ways he is blocked from entry by the walls, gates and barriers that mark the suburbs along his journey into the inner-city, he also has an intimate knowledge of the lives and 'being-in-the-world' behind those walls, as he roots through the suburban trash.

Because the garbage bins of the rich are much more lucrative than those in poorer areas, Vusi walks over 26 kilometres a day, starting before dawn, and making his way into the inner-city recycling facility in Jeppestown that is his home base. His journey traces the deep scars of apartheid, and the ongoing separation that exists in Johannesburg. 'People are cutting up money like dust', he says as he pulls out a piece of a 20-rand note from one bin. From another he finds a working pen and a binder, both of which he knows he will be able to sell on the streets of the city. He tells the story of a foetus he finds wrapped in paper in a garbage bin, never to be found, that sits like a scar in his memory. He also talks, with knowing confidence, of the ideals of cleanliness and order that dominate the suburbs. Things he is all too happy to oblige. To keep the bins clean and tidy is part of the job he has created for himself: 'these people, they don't like mess', he insists.

During the violent clashes between Inkatha and the African National Congress (ANC) in the 1990s, Vusi lost both of his parents and wound up as a migrant to Johannesburg from KwaZulu-Natal province when he was just a boy. He soon entered the world of informal work. Growing up on the streets of Johannesburg with other kids, washing cars and making a living hustling in any way he could was hardly easy. At that time, he worked in a team of nine boys, collecting recyclables together and sharing what they earned. He talks about those times wistfully: 'they are all gone now. A few of them died or went to jail. Others I lost touch with. Now I like to work alone, it's better that way.' He explains:

> I need to try and get what God gave me and express that to people. So I tried to make [it with] this trolley. Okay, but that is not the only thing I'm good at. I do a lot of other things in life you know. I just could not get the things in my life to be good. I'm short with money. The reason I am hustling is so that I can get the tools I need [to be a gardener]. I see, my brother, I cannot survive without this job. I must survive with this, this is the better way, and I like this. I'm proud my brother.

Waste-pickers work in dirty and dangerous conditions, mostly for little return. Scattered throughout Johannesburg's city streets, they are some of the most vulnerable workers in the informal economy. Police often confiscate their goods and arrest them for pushing their trollies on the streets. 'I've never worked at anything else, but this is real work', he laughs. From the quiet streets of the suburb Vusi admits:

> I have dreams. Serious dreams too, like any human being. I am a gardener. I can change the lawns, I can change anything – flowers, trees, roses. You name it. I can change it … I like to decorate. That is the thing I like to do.

The nomad is a traveller of another kind altogether. One gets the feeling that Vusi will disappear whenever he decides too. He is not attached to this space, but he knows its usage. He goes *through* the landscape, and is transformed by it. He rides the surface of the territory, alone and bound to no one but himself. The injustice and exclusion of the city, something that apartheid planning made manifest in very distinct ways, operates in the present, punctured with holes and fissures in which people can move through. Yet the city itself is hardly transformed, even with the possibility to *move*. It is still not possible to *inhabit* the city freely. As such, Johannesburg is a place in which at one point or another, almost everyone feels like a tourist, or rather, a stranger.

Figure 7.3 Vusi digs in the suburban trash
Source: © Parabola Films.

Marie-Hélène Gutberlet (2012) talks about the contradictions of the bourgeois concept of 'freedom of movement' which evolved from the French Revolution and only includes the movement of citizens, not subjects. Translating that onto the streets of Johannesburg, she finds that here in fact her freedom was dominated by the proscriptions of where she should not walk, not go, apart from those 'safe' white spaces and places in the city.

> With whom can I come together, apart from those it has been decided I should meet? Is it possible for me to move between different segregated and racialised territories without being identified with them? Can one walk through a territory without being occupied by it? (Gutberlet 2012: 17)

Gutberlet speaks as a white traveller/tourist, but we might wonder how the space occupies Vusi as he makes his way through such contradictory territories. Moving through the city also means being transformed by interactions within it. Catherine is the floor manager and administrator at the recycling facility where Vusi brings what he has collected to sell. A petite young white girl, she loves the place. 'Everyone is equal here. There is no pretence. I never thought as a white person I'd be working in the inner-city, but tell you the truth, I really love it here.' The recycling plant is a central stabilising space in Vusi's life. It is here where he is known. He is relaxed in this warehouse crowded with recycling, and perhaps somewhat understood. Vusi and Catherine are both strangers in the city, voyagers into the small off-limits confines of South African segregation. They have built an easy but strong friendship amidst the trash. Both are 'occupied by the territory', as their social relationships become informed and transformed by the spaces in which they are able to exist. Their relationship is a testament to the possibilities still present within division through *movement*.

The Migrant

> The nomad is not at all the same as the migrant; for the migrant goes principally from one point to another, even if the second point is uncertain, unforeseen, or not well localized. (Deleuze and Guattari 1988: 380)

When you walk into the 'Odumaya Republic & African Restaurant' the first thing you notice is the smell. Fragrant and tantalising, smells of West Africa permeate the space. The décor is simple. Zeinab stands behind a metal grill, serving up to the continuous stream of people coming through her doors. A television mounted high on the yellow wall blares Al Jazeera. Zeinab's West African specialties tantalise their patrons, often recalling the tastes of home. A smattering of languages and laughter fill the space. Most of the clients are men, working in the area, but West Africans from as far as 80 kilometres away will drive here to get a taste of this home-cooked, familiar food. Only a few years ago Zeinab was selling her dishes out of a small blue cooler, walking through the streets of the city trying to entice passers-by. Now they have opened a stable restaurant in the heart of Jeppestown.

Zeinab is from Mali, and her husband Arouna is from Benin. They met in a building housing foreigners in Johannesburg and have been living in Jeppestown for the last eight years. They are like many other Africans who find their way across the continent under harsh conditions and attempt to make a decent living. As Murray (2010: 15–16) points out, '[p]ulled by the illusive dream of steady income or pushed by despair and hopelessness, tens of thousands of recent arrivals have come to the greater Johannesburg metropolitan region in search of a better life'. Arouna says that Jeppestown is the only place he has lived since coming to South Africa: 'I had never been anywhere before …' he says. Asked why he chose to migrate to Jeppestown, he replies:

> It is just God. From home [in Benin] they give me a number of a guy who I have to meet here. Because I know no one here before I came. So the guy lived in Jeppestown. So when I came, he come and get me [from the airport], and take me to Jeppestown, that's why I'm staying in Jeppestown.

Figure 7.4 Arouna at home
Source: © Parabola Films.

Arouna overflows with enthusiasm and tells his complex story of migration with an easy manner, smiling all the while. It was a difficult journey to get to South Africa, and not where he originally wanted to go. He had his sights on the United States, and had gone a long way towards securing some contacts to get there. But he was unable to obtain a visa to get on a flight, and so he decided to come to South Africa. At the time, he saw this as an interim measure, still hoping to get to the United States. That idea is long gone. He has settled happily in Jeppestown now with a wife and two young children. He laughs when he remembers his first impressions: 'When I came here I couldn't believe South Africa was beautiful like this! I thought they had made a mistake of the flight and brought me somewhere in Europe. But no, I realized, this is South Africa.'

In Benin, Arouna was an electrician, mainly making his living as a television repairman. But his profession led to dead-ends when he came to South Africa. He explains:

I start to ask people about this job here in South Africa, I want to do it. They say 'No, here they don't repair a TV. When it's broken you don't fix it. You throw it away and buy another one'. I said, 'What am I going to do now?' I've got no papers, no [work] permit, except my passport for living in South Africa.

With no papers or permit in South Africa, Arouna tried to get asylum status. After two weeks of going everyday and being turned away, he discovered that people sleep outside the Home Affairs office in a queue in order to get in. Arouna did the same and was lucky enough to be one of the first five in the door in the morning, receiving his asylum papers, starting him on the road towards his own business.

After many ups and downs it was a fateful day when a wall tumbled down beside his parked car, smashing it beyond repair. It was the last straw. Piece jobs had been allowing him and his wife to survive, and he was using the car to make money as a taxi driver. When the car was smashed it seemed like the last thing that could provide an income was gone too. For Arouna, a devout Muslim, he felt this turning point must be fated. His wife was not so sure. In the depths of despair and increasing poverty, she convinced him that she should start cooking and sell the food she made. Armed with a small blue cooler, she hit the streets selling her cooking to pedestrians and workers. Within only a few weeks she began making money.

In the meantime, Arouna asked his landlord and neighbour, Abdullah, for a loan. Abdullah was one of the last remaining Indian businessmen in the area. Jeppestown was once the site of over 42 tailors, the majority of which were Indian shops. This population has slowly died off, and the younger generation does not seem interested in following in the family footsteps. Abdullah, though, still had a few shops in the neighbourhood and he had taken a shine to Arouna. An unlikely alliance cemented when Abdullah lent Arouna both the money and the space to try his hand at opening a small restaurant. There is a beautiful irony in this interaction, since Abdullah was part of an earlier wave of migrants who came from India, and did exactly what Arouna was trying to do now: open small businesses and create a life and family in Jeppestown. Even though they were from very different backgrounds, there was a common idea of what it takes to come from very far and attempt to establish a life as an entrepreneur. Ironically, almost all of the former Indian shopkeepers have abandoned Jeppe as businesses closed in the inner-city and it became increasingly unsafe. It is once again a wave of migrants, this time from West Africa, that keep the neighbourhood alive. Yet many do not see it that way.

While business was booming, the country was racked with a wave of xenophobic violence, and Jeppestown became a site of terror. Arouna recalls how they spent 10 days barricaded in their flat above the restaurant, waiting for the violence to subside. They hid a family of six from Mali who had been chased out of a building next door by hauling them over the vicious razor wire, one person at a time. He is not bitter about the experience though: '[t]here is a saying in my country. If you are scared that something is going to eat you, you will never have something to eat. So I'll go like that.'

Figure 7.5 Arouna at the mosque in Jeppestown
Source: © Parabola Films.

While Arouna is proud of his business and seems settled in Johannesburg, he hopes one day to return to Benin. He wants to return to his homeland, because there he is free. 'I'm not free here', he emphasises. Being a foreigner, he explains, means he is never really free. He is continually harassed at every turn: 'Not all of them, but many South Africans don't like foreigners.'

For Arouna, travel has meant possibility, but return is inevitable. 'We had the heart to leave our country, after that you can never be scared, you just put scared to one side and try to do something.' Coming to Johannesburg has transformed Arouna's life entirely, as it does for millions of migrants around the world, yet Johannesburg is for taking what you can, producing what you can, and returning to a place where you can *live*.

Arouna moves 'principally from one point to another, even if the second point is uncertain, unforeseen' (Deleuze and Guattari 1988: 380). Arouna is part of the continual flow of bodies back and forth across the continent, who move because of necessity, who carve out points between places that become worn, like footpaths through a forest, collecting many of the others who feel displaced, far from home, and without stability. Unlike Vusi, Arouna knows where he comes from and where he will return. He travels with a faith that allows this movement to gain meaning, but it is not Jeppe where he imagines his journey ends, even if his presence in the neighbourhood is doing a great deal to keep it alive.

The Refugee

There are many ways migrancy happens, some creating much more severe forms of displacement than afforded to Arouna. In Johannesburg, the practice of occupying, or hijacking, abandoned buildings in the inner-city has been a widespread phenomenon since the end of apartheid. The conditions in these buildings are terrible and threats come in multiple, mind-boggling ways.

In 2008, after the outbreaks of xenophobic violence that affected Arouna and his family, a group of blind Zimbabwean refugees occupied an abandoned building on the perimeter of Jeppestown. Many of the blind beggars support the children and families they have left behind as economic hardships worsened in Zimbabwe. On a monthly basis they scrape together their meagre earnings to send back to Zimbabwe: bags of groceries are sent on buses and bits of money are wired home. A few times a year many of the blind beggars, along with thousands of other Zimbabwean refugees, attempt to make the treacherous journey across the border in order to be with their families.

There are hundreds of blind Zimbabweans living in South Africa, and thousands of refugees that make the very difficult journey back and forth to Zimbabwe. Their stories remain largely unknown, but these kinds of migrations are happening all over the world. It is estimated that close to 600 blind Zimbabweans live in Johannesburg, a majority of them earning a living by begging. Throughout the city you find blind beggars with their sighted companion standing at the traffic lights, hoping to catch a few coins from passing motorists.

More and more of these blind beggars started migrating across the border into South Africa about six years ago, as political and economic turmoil in Zimbabwe escalated. Many of the blind refugees are illegal migrants who have come across the border without identity documents or passports. The trip to the border can take as little as 48 hours, but it is an extremely dangerous journey. Often touts prey on the Zimbabweans, stealing money and possessions.

On the edge of Jeppestown just over 350 people have occupied an abandoned building, over 100 of whom are blind Zimbabweans living under threat of deportation, eviction, disease and violence. The conditions are deplorable, with limited electricity, no running water and few toilets. Police have started raiding the building frequently, looking for bribes or arresting people to be deported. There are constant worries that there will be a mass raid, followed by evictions and deportations. The South African government has recently overturned its amnesty for Zimbabweans, and migrants fear what this will mean for the thousands who live in the country.

Many of the blind people in Jeppe lost their sight in early childhood due to measles and found their way across the border after learning from blind friends that there were opportunities for begging in South Africa. One group of friends we followed met each other at the School for the Blind in Zimbabwe and slowly helped each other cross the border into South Africa. The meagre assistance they had been receiving in Zimbabwe from the state had dried up, and begging in Zimbabwe did not provide enough money to survive. Forced economic migrants, they made their way to where some money could be made.

Figure 7.6 Living in occupied spaces in Johannesburg
Source: © and photo by Mujahid Safodien.

Given these conditions it is amazing that Nathi is always smiling. He has a sharp intellect and inquiring mind. He talks about how much he wishes people understood that blind people have many things they are able to contribute to society. He dreams of having a grinder so he could make peanut butter to sell, or maize that he could distribute to the many hungry people in Zim. Nathi has three children he supports back home. On average he is able to make around 50 rand (US$8) a day if he is lucky. From that money he must pay and feed his sighted assistant, and pay transportation to and from their work location. In the end, he is left with only a few dollars. He saves bits of this money so he can buy groceries to send back to his children by bus, and slowly tries to save enough that he can get back himself. Each night after work begging he comes to Elisabeth's small room where the five or six blind people prepare, eat dinner and pray together. There seems to be some light in their support and friendship with each other, always tempered, though, by the terrible conditions that surround them. As one article reports of the situation in these buildings:

> there is no electricity – the darkness inside the hijacked building leaves anybody blind. Water is stolen from fire extinguishers. Some walls are daubed with human faeces and the stench of urine permeates. The warehouse-like building has been almost entirely plundered of any metal that can be sold off and the elevator shaft is now completely exposed. In the pitch-blackness of the building it is a danger to both the blind and the sighted. The labyrinthine of floors have been individually partitioned, using cardboard, bits of wood and election posters, into small rectangular homes. (Tolsi 2011: n.p.)

The hollowed-out building has what appears to be a shack settlement built inside its walls. The perils of the situation are numerous. When xenophobic violence broke out across South Africa in 2008 foreigners were targeted, some were beaten and even killed. While Arouna was hiding out with his family a few blocks away, many other foreigners in the inner-city were forced out of their homes and had to seek refuge in local police stations and a Methodist church. Shelter in the church did not last for long, and many of the blind people moved to occupy derelict buildings in the city centre. This is how the building in Jeppestown came to be occupied. This is the starkest separation of the difference between travel, tourism and involuntary *movement*. This is movement in which each displacement further deepens human crisis and hardship.

In 2010, those occupying the building came under threat of eviction, but the Methodist priest who had housed many of the blind during the xenophobic attacks helped launch a stay of eviction which is still in court. The threat of eviction looms every day. Harassment comes from many directions. Occasionally blind beggars are arrested, jailed and fined by police, and city social workers have been known to harass and even abuse them (IRIN 2011: n.p.).

Never before have there been as many people crossing borders both as either refugees or tourists (Russell 2003). In our times, it is the economic refugee that is the real counter-point to the tourist as the stories of these migrants make plain. Theirs is an invisible journey. Forced into darkness, they cross the border through cover of night and through clandestine and dangerous practices, and find ways to live in the cracks and crevasses of the city which remain invisible to scrutiny. Their displacement is total. Can Nathi ever cease to travel, to move from streetlight to streetlight, from building to building, from country to country?

The Developer

Nathi's invisibility is the flip side of JJ's visibility. JJ's movement affords opportunity, privilege, risk and reward. In the last decade a new breed of urban developer has been transforming Johannesburg. While Vusi, Arouna and Nathi carve lives in the cracks and spaces of invisibility that allow for innovative life-sustaining practices to exist, JJ uses those same fissures in an entirely different way. JJ epitomises the new breed of developers who are transforming Johannesburg from top to bottom. Young and idealistic, he is dreaming big, thinking not only of the buildings he is transforming, but radically rethinking the entire social space, from parks to sidewalks to arts spaces.

After working in Europe, he found his way back home to South Africa to a decaying Johannesburg open to risk-taking young entrepreneurs willing to try their luck in restructuring the city. Riddled with high levels of crime, many affluent whites living in the northern suburbs can still not even imagine making the trip into the inner-city, still considered dangerous ever since people flooded the spaces that had been illegal for non-whites under apartheid. Here again you see the stark racial and class divisions built into post-apartheid Johannesburg, where for some coming 'into town' takes on a dangerous yet titillating appeal for those making the trip, while for others of the upper and middle classes, the inner-city continues to remain a no-go zone.

Figure 7.7 JJ – property developer
Source: © Parabola Films, photo by Manielle Brits.

Yet new developments are transforming the urban centre into arty New York style lofts for the up-and-coming jet set, hipsters, students and the aspirational middle classes. These new developments sit uncomfortably beside workers' hostels, rundown buildings occupied or hijacked by migrants from across the continent, and locals trying to eke out a living in the city. The juxtaposition of these contradictory worlds reinforces the invisible walls of a new segregation.

The term enclave describes those territories occupied and guarded in various ways, and inaccessible to those beyond its walls (Harvey 2006). But an enclave can also describe the spaces that are outside these opaque zones: where citizenship has little meaning, where 'illegality' is the norm, where people live in sprawling shack settlements or occupy abandoned buildings, where people are on the move, displaced by economic and environmental crisis. Behind walls, in free trade zones, behind fences and borders – sometimes along state lines, sometimes not – we can see spaces in which the power is consolidated, but more importantly than power, territory. Between and among these new geographic separations contestations are continually taking place.

JJ is of the new generation that sees their role as taking over from government, doing it better where the state fails and rebuilding an urban metropolis in the image of New York or London. It is about money, for sure, but JJ insists it is about more than that too. Young venture capitalists like JJ see themselves at the centre of the rejuvenation of Johannesburg. And they are putting their money where their mouths are. He explains his approach and his philosophy:

> We are in an age of abundance. All of the technologies are there. I don't believe we're in the same phase of scarcity that other generations were in. The money is there. There's lots of money, it's retro-designing it. Not asking people what they want, but going back to the basic questions of what are their principle needs.

JJ is another young upstart like developer Jonathan Lieberman who is behind the Maboneng Precinct, a new artsy development that has transformed the area beside Jeppestown with urban lofts and penthouses, retail outlets and hip restaurants. As Lieberman says of his multi-use development, 'I'm trying to bring back and encourage knowledge of the history of Johannesburg, and so develop a sense of pride in the city'. Unlike the other developers in the city, JJ still has a long way to go to start making his dream a reality. He calls his approach 'human-centric', focusing on what it would take to construct an ideal community. These are new fiefdoms to be sure, with developers buying up whole neighbourhoods, using private funds injected with public monies, renaming and reshaping them. It is hard to see where Vusi and Nathi would fit into such a planned, smooth space the developers envision, yet it is most certain they will not vacate this area easily. Sinking further, perhaps, away from the visible, yet still an inherent aspect of the city as such.

In the meantime, the movement from inside and outside the city, across and through its spaces, is transforming it. Private security companies take over from police, private developers take over road maintenance and other services from the state, and public space is transformed into controlled, private and inaccessible property. Much like the Enclosures movement in the sixteenth century,[1] the use of public space is once again transformed. Racial segregation has transmuted into class division, as Johannesburg becomes marked once again with new kinds of geographic separation. In tracing the 'evolution of white strategies to find comfort zones', Richard Ballard suggests that 'assimilation, emigration, semigration, and integration have come to dominate the repertoire since the demise of formal segregation ... Spatial practices such as gated communities and enclosed neighbourhoods are examples of this' (Ballard 2004: 51). In the inner-city, the new developments have invisible walls in the form of 24-hour street security,

---

1   The process of land enclosure, from the sixteenth through to the nineteenth century in England, saw land formerly held in commons deeded into private property. This ended a system of traditional farming and grazing rights for peasants and farmers. Enclosure was often a violent process and created a landless working class.

fingerprint-controlled entry, and homogeneity of the visitors and residents that would make a worker or beggar a certain stranger.

On the rooftops of one of the new developments at the edge of Jeppestown, ironically named Revolution House, were spray-painted the words: 'We won't move'. The reference directly recalls the same slogan painted on walls during the forced evictions that happened not far from here in the racially mixed area of Sofiatown by the apartheid government. The slogan asks for many readings. One might think residents being displaced by the swanky new lofts and penthouses had painted it there. But a more likely reading is that it was the developers and city hipsters themselves who had painted it, in an even more ironic twist: that the once displaced (white) wealth that used to inhabit the city is now coming to claim it back.[2] This is a strange twist to the idea of 'the right to the city'. It is a right claimed by those who can afford to be citizens, and are politically able to mobilise such a claim.

Passages and Movements

The movements of the migrant, refugee and nomad are inseparable from the tourist and the affluent urban developer. As territory that once allowed communities to exist is accumulated, people are displaced, looking constantly for cracks in which they can create new possibilities for life. Migrants like Arouna create value in spaces abandoned by traditional capital by opening businesses and building families and communities. At an even more invisible scale, Vusi creates informal work and contributes to the possibilities and flows of capital accumulation through his cheap human labour, collecting and recycling the excesses of production. Through the small change of the rich driving through the city, Nathi is able to maintain his family back home, tracing and retracing a path between borders. In it all, JJ moves through the space watching for possibilities to accumulate wealth, to see rewards in the remainders and the discarded or disused built environment. Through all their stories, an entrepreneurial energy drives their everyday lives, as they create possibility in absence.

These passages and movements between the cracks in advanced capitalism, what David Harvey (2006) has called combined and uneven development, might also be seen as a continuation of the processes of capital accumulation since its origin. The effects of the original land privatisation and Enclosures phenomenon from the sixteenth through nineteenth century meant a breakdown of social cohesion as families disintegrated, young people left home in search of work and vagabonds and itinerant workers increased (Federici 2004), much as today's so-called precariat like Vusi or Nathi. Displacement and movement are a fundamental aspect of the destructive, and disruptive, forces of capitalism. Displacement of some in order for others to invent anew sites of accumulation, is a continual

---

2   Thanks to Arya Lalloo for this insight.

process, and tracing bodies in movement shows us how and where (Glick Schiller and Caglar 2011, Harvey 2006). Yet movement and displacement also create new realities that in turn influence and change the city. As Glick Schiller and Caglar (2011: 12) insist, migrants in the city are *scale-makers* who have a transformative power 'as part of the labor force upon which cities build their competitiveness; as historical agents; [and] as agents of neoliberal restructuring who contribute to or contest the changing status and positioning of neighborhoods and cities'. Much like Ruba Salih and Bruno Riccio (2011) found in their study of small towns in Italy, migrants like Arouna have invested time, money, energy and human capital in Jeppestown, a neighbourhood that had undergone massive deindustrialisation and depopulation in the preceding decade. This investment from migrants allowed Jeppe to remain economically vital and competitive, even if decaying, part of what now makes venture capitalists gravitate towards the area.

Figure 7.8 Jeppe train station
Source: © Parabola Films.

Acknowledgements

The South African Research Chair in Social Change supported this research. The Chair is funded by the Department of Science and Technology, administered by the National Research Foundation and hosted by the Faculty of Humanities at the University of Johannesburg. The Social Sciences and Humanities Research Council of Canada also supported this research. Thanks to Thulani Sundu for translations from isiZulu. I also wish to acknowledge the contribution of Eugene Arries, Lucilla Blankenburg, Ryley Grunenwald, Kitso Lelliott and Mujahid Safodien who conducted some of the above interviews as part of the documentary film project *Jeppe on a Friday*, and, finally, I am indebted to Arya Lalloo for the overall intellectual and creative partnership throughout this project.

References

Ballard, R. 2004. Assimilation, emigration, semigration, and integration: "White" peoples' strategies for finding a comfort zone in post-apartheid South Africa, in *Under Construction: 'Race' and Identity in South Africa Today*, edited by N. Distiller and M. Steyn. Johannesburg: Heinemann, 51–66.

Bauman, Z. 2000. Tourists and vagabonds: Or, living in post-modern times, in *Identity and Social Change*, edited by J.E. Davis. New Brunswick: Transaction Publishers, 13–26.

Brenner, N., Marcuse, P. and Mayer, M. (eds) 2011. *Cities for People, Not for Profit: Critical Urban Theory and the Right to the City*. Oxon and New York: Routledge.

Deleuze, G. and Guattari, F. 1988. *Thousand Plateaus: Capitalism and Schizophrenia*. London: Athlone Press.

Federici, S. 2004. *Caliban and the Witch: Women, the Body and Primitive Accumulation*. New York: Autonomedia.

Glick Schiller, N. and Caglar A. (eds) 2011. *Locating Migration: Rescaling Cities and Migrants*. Ithaca, NY: Cornell University Press.

Graburn, N.H.H. and Barthel-Bouchier, D. 2001. Relocating the tourist. *International Sociology*, 16(2), 147–58.

Gutberlet, M.H. 2012. On walking, in *Shoe Shop*, edited by M.H. Gutberlet and C. Snyman. Johannesburg: Jacana Media, 13–23.

Harvey, D. 2006. *Spaces of Global Capitalism: Towards a Theory of Uneven Geographical Development*. London: Verso.

IRIN. 2011. South Africa: Blind beggars go south. *IRIN: Humanitarian News and Analysis*. [Online June 2011]. Available at: http://www.irinnews.org/Report/92969/ SOUTH-AFRICA-Blind-beggars-go-south [accessed: 28 August 2012].

Kirstner, U. 2004. Raison d'état. *Interventions*, 6(2), 242–51.

Murray, M.J. 2010. *City of Extremes: The Spatial Politics of Johannesburg*. Durham, NC: Duke University Press.

Russell, R.V. 2003. Tourists and refugees: Coinciding sociocultural impacts. *Annals of Tourism Research*, 30(4), 833–46.

Salih, R. and Riccio, B. 2011. Transnational migration and rescaling processes: The incorporation of migrant labor, in *Locating Migration: Rescaling Cities and Migrants*, edited by N. Glick Schiller and A. Caglar. Ithaca, NY: Cornell University Press, 123–42.

Tolsi, N. 2011. Blind beggars search for a better life in Jo'burg's darkest corners. *Mail & Guardian*. [Online September 2011]. Available at: http://mg.co.za/article/2011–09–30-blind-beggars-search-for-a-better-life-in-joburgs-darkest-corners/ [accessed: 28 August 2012].

PART III
Transformation in Motion

Chapter 8

Temporality, Technologies and Techniques of the Self: Long-Distance Walking as Secular Pilgrimage

Leila Dawney

Introduction

The South West Coast Path is one of the 15 'national trails' in the United Kingdom that pass through 'some of the most stunning and diverse landscapes in Britain' (www.nationaltrail.co.uk). It runs for 630 miles around the coastline of Somerset, Devon, Cornwall and Dorset, and as such affords the possibility for a continuous waymarked trek, as well as shorter walks and strolls.

In recent years the path has been a space of geographical experimentation and the focus of debates in human geography regarding landscape and subjectivity (see also Sidaway 2009, Wylie 2005).[1] This chapter revisits the path to further explore the role of body practices such as walking in the production of subjectivities, paying attention in particular to the role of cultural tropes of self-transformation, and to the practice of walking as a 'technique of the self' (Foucault 1988). The empirical material in this chapter derives from a 'loose ethnography' of the South West Coast Path, which involved a combination of research methods including walking interviews, group walks and autoethnographic research, as well as archival research on the many diaries and journals kept at the headquarters of the South West Coast Path Association (SWCPA). These modes of enquiry were used to investigate how the space of the path is both performed and practised, and how these performances and practices contribute to the production of subjectivities, imaginaries and forms of life. Attention was paid particularly to the role of materials and practices in the production of subjectivities. In this chapter, empirical examples are used to discuss the material production of the self in transformation, referring to specific ways through which participants use walking, photography and diaries in order to 'work on themselves'.

---

1   This research was commissioned as a collaborative doctoral award from the Arts and Humanities Research Council, with Professor John Wylie and the South West Coast Path team as partners.

Pilgrimage: Walking as Transformation

Many of the walkers encountered during fieldwork, both in interviews and through their diaries, articulated and narrated their endeavours with reference to ideas of challenge, self-transformation, or marking a particular milestone in the life course. The focus on walking as a technique through which work on the self was performed and enabled emerged from these subjective framings of the long-distance walk. This practice can be described as a 'secular pilgrimage', a term that refers to a particular mode of being and attention that was identified in walkers, a mode that encouraged reflection and self-transformation. Whether or not the goal of self-transformation is a primary reason for undertaking long-distance walking, the trope of the transformative journey is almost ubiquitous in the ways in which these walks are narrated and described by participants in diaries, interviews and during walks. This trope is further augmented through the appeals to history and to the tradition of walking seen in guidebooks and promotional material about the path, particularly through reference to histories of ancient trackways, migratory and pilgrimage routes, which further associate the long-distance walk with the idea of pilgrimage.

The accounts of journeys along the South West Coast Path in this chapter are 'secular pilgrimages', firstly because most rely to some extent on the trope of the transformational journey for their social legitimation and, secondly, because through their performance *as* pilgrimage, they contribute to a genealogically related set of ideas, concepts, technologies and practices of the body that feed into the cultural trope of the transformational journey or challenge (Adler 1989, Reader and Walter 1993, Slavin 2003, Solnit 2002, Turner 1974, Turner and Turner 1978). Many discussions of pilgrimage, and also many common-sense understandings of the concept, draw on Durkheim's idea of the sacred as that which is removed from the everyday (Durkheim 1964). The concept of the secular pilgrimage has been used to describe journeys to sites of remembrance, identity construction and religious or quasi-religious experience, such as journeys to Glastonbury, to war graves in northern France, to Graceland, Memphis, or to Anfield, Liverpool (Reader and Walter 1993). Here, it refers to the practice of journeying undertaken, in part, as a process of self-transformation, as a labour through which the self is worked on through bodily practices and adopting a particular relation to the self, thus moving the focus from destination to practice. The state of the body when on pilgrimage is often self-reflexive and in transformation (Adler 1989, Desforges 2000, Slavin 2003, Solnit 2002). Rebecca Solnit (2002: 46) discusses pilgrimage as labour or work, in a 'spiritual economy in which effort and privation are rewarded', arguing that pilgrimage is almost universally embedded in human cultures as a spiritual journey, where asceticism and physical exertion are means of spiritual development. One of the problems with some of the literature on pilgrimage is that much is made of an attempt to define the essence of 'pilgrimage' and the extent to which these practices can be seen to correspond to that essence (Turner 1974, Turner and Turner 1978).

Rather than relying on an *a priori* definition of pilgrimage or transformation, this chapter focuses on the way in which ideas of transformation are mobilised and enacted in practice. Hence this discussion of walking as secular pilgrimage is concerned with the techniques, practices and processes through which these ideas are enacted; how walkers make their journeys transformational and what materials, practices, ideas and imaginaries contribute to the practice of walking such that it becomes a 'secular pilgrimage' rather than an afternoon stroll. The discussions outlined in this chapter focus specifically on the 'transformational' aspects of research participants' accounts. Central to this is an investigation into the way that the self in transformation is imagined by those participating in these endeavours. Elsewhere, I have discussed how the imagination, as a material, embodied capacity, enables particular subjectivities and the production of certain historically situated modes of experience (Dawney 2011, 2013a, 2013b). In the course of this chapter, I draw on a theoretical framework informed by Foucault's later work on the self, supplemented with a concern with the role of *time* in the subjective processes through which the self comes to be thought of, or imagined, as in a process of transformation.

In the first section, Foucault's writings on technologies of the self are drawn upon in order to understand how participants enacted change through adopting a specific ethical relationship to themselves during the course of their journeying. Many of the participants in the research articulated their choice to walk and also their experience of walking in terms of giving themselves time to think, in terms of their bodily and mental health, or of connecting with a past or with some idea of nature or the divine. The practice of undertaking such an endeavour is then figured as a way of working on the self – a technique of the self. The accounts of walkers (and runners) in the SWCPA's archive, where narratives of self-transformation are drawn on, point to their practices being undertaken as what I refer to as an *extraordinary technique of the self*: a practice that is extraordinary because it happens over an extended period that marks a spatial and temporal removal from the ordinary.

In the second section, the discussion turns to how this attention to the self is supplemented through technologies of recording. Archival research at the South West Coast Path Association, as well as ethnographic conversations with walkers, led to a recognition of the importance and prevalence of documentation of long-distance walks through technologies of recording (blogs, cameras, diaries, notebooks), technologies that are later referred to in recalling past experiences. In this section I argue that these technologies of recording and documentation assist the presencing of memories and future possibilities into the here and now, and through attempts to 'hold onto' experience for future memory. The archive of diaries and photo-diaries produced by coast path walkers is drawn upon to discuss how technologies and bodies are co-constitutive of this project of the self, and serve to augment the transformative power of long-distance walking. This draws on Foucault's discussion of the *hypomnemata*, an ancient Greek notebook that was used for practices of reflection, for working on and thinking about the self

(Foucault 1997). Here we can consider these diaries, blogs and photograph albums as contemporary *hypomnemata*: they serve as active participants in the practices and technologies of reflection, imagination and transformation of the self.

Through this theoretical framing, the concept of time is introduced as a means of considering how imagined temporalities are central to the ways in which subjects imagine and understand their practice in terms of self-transformation. This chapter argues that imagining the self in transformation involves an invocation of previous and future selves, and this is apparent in the ways through which narratives of transformation are discussed by walkers. It concludes with a discussion of how these theoretical approaches enable a closer analysis of the material and subjective processes through which a walk becomes a practice of the self, and in doing so, provides a means of analysing those technologies, practices, imaginaries and cultural tropes through which walking as secular pilgrimage is enacted and through which walking becomes transformational.

Techniques of the Self

In his later work, Michel Foucault became interested in the idea of the self, and the processes through which subjects take control of their own governance through working on their selves. This form of governmentality, or self-policing, was shown to be a feature of the dispersal of power in modernity and, alongside biopower, formed one means through which governance takes place as sovereign power declines in significance. In particular, the second and third volumes of *The History of Sexuality* (Foucault 1988, 1992), and accompanying lectures at the Collège de France and the University of California, Berkeley (Foucault 1982, 1983, 1987, 2005, 2008), discussed the relation of the self to the self in terms of techniques and technologies through which that relation is produced. Here, the idea of the self as stable and persisting through time is called into question, and instead is understood as the effect of particular practices and techniques of the body. For example, in Nikolas Rose's (1996) work a specific idea of the self is shown to have emerged through the techniques and practices associated with psychiatry and psychology. As such, the self is performative: it emerges through its ongoing practice and performance (Butler 2006).

The self, then, is seen as a product of its immanent production through regimes of power and relation, meaning that different understandings of the self, and different relations to the self, emerge during different historical formations. For example, Foucault makes the distinction between 'care of the self' (the *epimeleia heautou*) – a particular relation of oneself to oneself found in ancient Greece – and 'knowing the self' considered as the product of modern regimes of psychiatry and self-help. Care of the self involved an ethic of taking care of the body, soul and others through a concern with, and vigilance of, the self, which was made manifest through particular practices such as the adoption of regimens. An analysis of various texts of the first centuries revealed an:

insistence on the attention that should be brought to bear on oneself; it is the modality, scope, constancy, and exactitude of the required vigilance; it is the anxiety concerning all of the disturbances of the body and the mind, which must be prevented by means of an austere regimen. (Foucault 1988: 41)

Ancient practices of cultivation of the self also involved a medicalisation or somaticisation of the relation to the self through particular attention to the body, which was seen to threaten the soul with its weaknesses. This ethics of care of the self in relation to the body discouraged excess while favouring particular measured activities such as 'regimens, physical exercises without overexertion, the carefully measured satisfaction of needs' (Foucault 1988: 51). The body was controlled through regimen as a structure of conduct, seen as both voluntary and rational, involving a concern with regulation and avoidance of excess, and also of passivity, seen as morally inferior to activity, in the sexual role and in other areas of life. Practices, spaces and relations thereby all became valorised in terms of their healthy or unhealthy properties.

Foucault shows that the idea of the self, and the relationship that we have with ourselves, is the product of sets of discursive formations and practices through which we establish this relationship. To consider the self as a surface effect of particular practices enables a materialist and non-foundational reading of subjectivity, allowing us to investigate the subject through the processes through which it comes into formation. In the research discussed here, cultural tropes such as that of the pilgrimage, the quest, the challenge and the idea of self-discovery, have all been significant in participants' accounts of their walking practices, both during and after their walks. Walking was referred to as a way to 'test oneself', to 'go beyond where I'd usually stop and head to the nearest café' (interviewee near Lynmouth, Devon). Others discussed walking as a way of taking time to think about their lives, to reflect on family and friends, or to work out solutions to personal dilemmas. In this way, they used the embodied practice of walking as a meditative technique, the rhythmic movement of the body enabling a particular mode of reflective engagement, as discussed by Solnit in her social history of walking: 'the rhythm of walking enables a rhythm of thinking, and ... creates an odd consonance between internal and external passage, one that suggests that the mind is also a landscape of some sorts' (Solnit 2002: 5–6). Cultural associations of walking with thinking, of the idea of pilgrimage as a time of reflection, as well as the material forces of rhythm, exertion and the sheer amount of time spent away from other distractions, then, provide the conditions of possibility for the walk to be performed as a reflection and meditation – as a pilgrimage.

Central to many of these narrations of the self in transformation is the *temporalisation* of the self through imagining 'before and after' versions. This imagining takes place through the practice of walking through a calling into presence of past and future selves in order to position the temporal self in transition. Future selves may materialise in the activation, for example, of deferral – a deferred feeling of achievement: 'You need to have pain in order to feel pleasure' (walker near Newquay, Cornwall). The future self may emerge as improved; different: 'I'm going to be a stone lighter by the end of this' (coast path walker, Lands End, Cornwall). The present of bodily fatigue becomes displaced through summoning to presence an imagined future self as 'having done that', as having achieved, as this ethnographic extract illustrates:

> It is pouring with rain and very windy. I have fallen over many many times. My feet are killing me in these walking boots, so every step is agony. I can't even see anything because of the misty rain! All I can do is think about getting to Perranporth, and sitting down in a warm pub, taking off my boots, and thinking – I made it! I didn't give up. (Field notes, near Newquay, Cornwall)

The phrase 'I want to have done it', echoed in many diaries, interviews and conversations, defers the pleasure, and also the recognition of transformation, until afterwards – in the pub, at home, in comfort. Bodily discomfort was seen to enable the deferred pleasure of comfort which, in its doubling over into the experience of discomfort, enabled a positive reading of discomfort in terms of its 'improving' impact on the self. Once again, the effort and privation associated with pilgrimage is drawn upon in order to 'read' feelings of exertion and discomfort positively, in terms of transformation and work on the self. Equally, ideas of physical health and fitness involve a focus on bodily discomfort in the present moment being displaced through the future fitter self. Narrating transformation through body techniques may also involve the invoking of past and future selves. The following field note extract demonstrates how these selves emerge:

> I met a man today who had just been made redundant, and was walking along the coastal path from start to finish, carrying camping equipment. He had an enormous green rucksack which looked incredibly heavy. He was in his early forties, and slightly dishevelled. He smiled and we started chatting. He had been walking for 7 weeks, and was nearly at the end of the path. He was in no rush to finish, however – time was not a constraint for him. He told me that he saw walking as a new way in which he defined himself, and a practice that enabled his reinvention of himself as someone who views time differently.
>
> This man discussed how, after a few weeks he started to not worry about getting to the next place, and to relax into the idea that there was no hurry, no time limit, and that the next place would not offer up anything more than what he was experiencing at that moment. This was described as a revelatory moment of relaxing into the new temporalities afforded by a long walk. (Field notes, June 2009, Hartland, Devon)

In this extract, walking, as an extended body practice and technique of the self, enabled this man to reconsider his past as remembered in terms of someone who worked too hard, who did not spend enough time in his own company and who neglected his physical and mental health. It then helped to actively produce a different self in contrast to this recalled and reconsidered past self, which was assisted through the production of a different, more indeterminate, but more contented, future self.

Through this example we can consider how temporally aligned imaginaries of the self are invoked, in order to colour experience and enact walking as transformative. The embodied practice of walking also involves an imagining of past and future selves, figures that are invoked in the process of making the self otherwise. They fed back and fed forward through his embodied perception of the world and shaped the way in which he understood and narrated his self. The experience of the material present (a lowering of levels of stress hormones, the sensation of fresh air in the lungs, exercise-induced endorphins, pleasing landscapes and open views) enabled a rethinking of the future self as someone content, calm and in control. The remembered past folded into the present as an undesirable future state, giving his walking a symbolic value as a boundary marker between the rejection of one imagined self and the beginning of another.

Hypomnemata

In 'Self-writing', Foucault discusses various practices of the 'aesthetics of existence' and the governing of the self through writing. The ancient Greek *hypomnemata* notebook is seen as both constraint on the self and central to 'self-work' – for example practices where the written artefact is reflected over and meditated on (Foucault 1997). The contents of the notebook were seen to actually form part of the self – 'the soul must make them not merely its own but itself ... into tissue and blood' (Foucault 1997: 2–5) meaning that self-writing performed an infolding of the texts of others such that they appear as internal to the self of the reader. The *hypomnemata* can thus be considered as part of the substance of the self, and it is for this reason that I consider certain technologies that are involved in the production of the self as 'prostheses'. In a similar way, Lury discusses the concept of the prosthesis in terms of how the photographic image is involved in 'novel configurations of personhood, self, knowledge and truth' and how this technical reconfiguration can call into question bounded notions of bodies and embodiment towards a more topological understanding of bodies as collections of capacities and technologies (Lury 1998: 2). In the *hypomnemata*, and in subsequent practices of correspondence and diary writing, there is an awareness of recording for future review, or for assessment by others. The present of writing contains within it the imagination of future selves, and also the possibility for future memory to be augmented through the act of reading and re-reading.

The archive of the South West Coast Path Association contains diaries, poems, photograph albums and notebooks sent in by those who have walked along the path and documented it in some way. Interviews undertaken after walking the path often focused on photograph albums or diaries. Recording experience through photography, blogs or diaries, for many of the participants I worked with, provided a record of a self in transformation, a focusing of attention onto the self and the production of future memory as a way of working on the self – the bringing into presence the possibility for the event of that memory, either individual or collective; the concretisation of the significance of the practice through an attempt to materialise experience in the text. We can consider the production of documentation of experience a type of *hypomnemata* for the present – a process of writing and recording that encourages a particular type of self-reflection participates materially in the process of self-transformation.

Technologies of memory such as photographs and diaries can be considered as prosthetic devices for recording and storing experience for the production of future memory, or to 'hold on' to a particular moment as practised by walkers.[2] One research participant, who kept a wildflower notebook while walking, suggested that it was 'like having a journal without having to write one'. Every day she noted down the flowers she saw along the way, sometimes sketching them, including the date and place where the flowers were spotted. She had done this for the 15 years she had walked along the coastal path.

> Sometimes, we go back to the same place, and I look at what I saw before and compare it to now. It depends on the time of year, of course, but it's lovely to see what is the same and what is different. It's also nice to see my drawing has improved. (Interview near Valley of Rocks, North Somerset)

For this participant, the flowers spotted on the walk offered a route to memory, a means of ensuring continuity between past, present and future selves. The notebook accompanying her on the walks provided a means of accessing memories of past walks and past selves. By contributing to the ongoing documentation of her walks, she created a constant; something to refer back and forward to, to place her walks in terms of season and geographical space. The attentiveness towards the flowers she spotted along the way brought about a particular mode of attunement, a way of focusing the mind and body and producing a more contemplative subjectivity. The writing of the wildflower notebook was a technology of memory and allowed those memories, and the selves that become tied to those memories, to take specific forms. Over time, this process of attending to, documenting and reflecting on the flowers in her walks assisted her recollection of past events and the production of a specific relation to herself that contributed to her ongoing subjectivity and identity formation.

Walking and photography were often tied together as practices which foreground the temporalising of the self through the material production of future

---

2   For further discussion on the use of technologies of memory such as photography in tourism literature, and on the practice of photography in shaping tourist subjectivities see for example: Bærenholdt et al. (2004), Haldrup and Larsen (2003), Robinson and Picard (2009), Scarles (2012), Urry (1995), Urry and Larsen (2011).

memories. The production of images that archive and order experience serve to situate the walk and the self in time, providing a way of thinking about the self in transformation. The practice of photography, when used to document a particular practice of the self, enables the camera to testify to one's presence and to produce a catalyst for the recalling of a future memory, which may be static and visual or may summon the senses into a displacement of bodily sensation into new times and spaces. As such, the photographer both performs the self and contributes to the ongoing production and becoming-other of the self through producing technologies of future memory. The writing of a journal, or the taking of photographs, can be considered in terms of the construction of a testimony, a present or perfect tense account. We testify to ourselves and to others: *I was here*. It may be revisited in times of self-doubt, at times of sorrow, as melancholy reflection or to remember good times.

Pip is a young photographer with whom I spent five days walking and camping. In the following, she describes how and why she takes photographs whilst walking. For Pip, walking involved a combination of physical challenge and the practice of paying attention to the world. As such, the self as photographer and nature lover was practised through specific embodied ways of focusing attention to light, weather, mood, and the technical practice of photography as a means and outcome of this attention: 'I want to practise how to act quickly – how to know your tools, even when it might be horrendous weather' (walking interview, North Cornwall).

Those who combined walking and photography referred often to post-production practices – the editing and construction of an archive after the moment which would testify to presence at the site of capture. As Pip goes on to reveal, photography involves an attempt to:

> recreate the feeling as if you were here ... I think on it and act on it and edit them after – I try and create an essence of the trip or wherever you are, where half of you is engaged and half is keeping a foot on dry land. (Walking interview, North Cornwall)

The self as photographer, as future editor of photos, as an individual who pays attention to the sensory aspects of landscape were being performed as conscious ways of working on the self, of improving skill levels and becoming a better photographer. 'I find it more involving when you're walking and doing something as well – there's no pressure and you can go with it more, but it's keeping in practice as well, like training – you have to keep doing it' (Pip, walking interview, North Cornwall). The photographic practice involved a doubling of the present and future self through an attempt to absorb the moment – the feel of a place, the sense of being there, while also projecting a future of review, edit, print and display. Photography, in this example, was about both paying attention to the moment and the production of future memory: 'it engages you in where you are at the time ... it's instantaneous – you react to how you're feeling at that moment even through that might change when you're looking back on it afterwards' (Pip, walking interview, North Cornwall).

Through practices such as photography, the production of future memory occurs. A consideration of the way in which future memories are involved in experiencing the present can demonstrate how imagined futures contribute to the ongoing production of the self. The future recalling of memory through the material artefact of the photograph summons memory into the moment of engagement with the image. The camera here is co-constitutive of both an attunement to a field of experience (landscape, walking) and to the production of the self. It cannot be separated from the ongoing process of performativity through which bodies come to be known as subjects (Lury 1998). Photography, and other techniques of recording, demands attentiveness. Taking photographs in particular marks a moment when a reflexive sensibility occurs – the act of photography as part of the archiving of an extended practice of the self, a reflecting on the here and now in order to attune thought to the production of a self that takes place in the present, but also in the future in the storing up of experience. The camera, the diary and the flower notebook can be considered as prosthetic devices in the production and recording of experience, and in the production of time, through their mobilisation in techniques of the self: they store future memories outside of the body. The camera participates in this production through its role as a technology of memory – its producing of future memories which allows the production of experiential forms that resonate through memory and through their participation in imaginaries based on ideas of nature, pilgrimage and the transformation of the self.

Conclusion: Selves in Transformation

In the above discussions of the practices of walking as transformation and the technologies used to store memory and capture experience, the reflexive playing out of life and of biography involves rewind and fast forward: a comparison of past and future selves. To situate the self in time is to position life as a linear trajectory, and those technologies that break up that trajectory through allowing other times to ingress onto the present actually reinforce that sense. The imagination positions past and future selves together in order to produce the experience of the self in time. I now consider the role of time and the imagination in this process of self-production, and suggest that my concept of the 'embodied imagination' is central to the understanding of self-production in terms of how the self is imagined or dreamed during techniques of the self (Dawney 2011a, 2011b, 2013b).

We might think of the self as a product of the foldings in of these other selves, an incorporating of imagined selves into the way in which the self is practised and performed in the present. This 'folding in' provides a way of thinking through the relationship between temporality and techniques of the self, where transformation of the self takes place through various practices, often in conjunction with technologies such as cameras or diaries. These practices fold inwards, creating the idea of the self. Time, and in particular the concept of the self in time, is central to this production of the self: futures and memories gain ingress into the experience of the present as part of this self-production. Imagined futures and pasts are folded into present, 'lived' experiences such that they are productive of contingent temporalities and subjectivities, and contribute to the structuring of experience.

Techniques of the self, then, may involve the imagination of the self as a subject of a biography – a process which occurs through narrativisation, temporalisation and the employment of particular vocabularies and techniques in order to stabilise the self as that which is concrete and continuous. The process of subjectivation takes the form of particular patterned practices of narrative, performance and reflection.

The capacity of the subject to think, to imagine and to dream otherwise is a central part of the way in which the self is produced as an effect of techniques of subjectivation. The capacity to imagine the self otherwise, and to enfold doubled past and future selves into the experience of the moment as a temporalisation of the narrative of the self is what enables the self to exist as a continuing idea. Memory is a necessary part of the experience of the self, as is the projection of possible future selves and the production of future memory.

The accounts of walkers (and runners) in the SWCPA's archive illustrate my discussion of long-distance walking as an *extraordinary practice of the self*: extraordinary because their practice takes place over an extended period that marks a spatial and temporal remove from the ordinary. While some participants engaged in specific thought techniques in order to bring about changes in the self, or in their relation to the world, others experienced transformation of the self as a by-product. Indeed the body is by its very existence involved in ongoing transformation and modification, and this necessarily reflects on the self as the surface effect of the body's actions.

This chapter has focused on some of Foucault's writings on technologies of the self in order to think about transformative practices such as 'secular pilgrimages'. Central to this analysis has been, firstly, the role played by the imagination – how bodies imagine themselves as being-in-transformation and, secondly, the role of temporality in the imaginative production of the self. Certain techniques and technologies (walking, photography, diaries) assist in this temporalising of the self, where the self is narrated and so produced as an effect of that narration in terms of a singular and continuous presence through linear time. Past and future selves are imagined and folded into the experience of particular practices, allowing them to be experienced as transformative or part of a narrative of progression enacted through techniques of the self.

In discussing how participants enact transformation in their walking, , this chapter has thought through the material conditions of possibility for that transformation of the self and of the subject. In doing so, I have drawn attention to the specific material practices that give rise to the experience of the self in transformation, arguing that the subjective experience of transformation emerges through a conscious practice of working on the self, accompanied by temporal imaginings of the self in transition. This provides a means of considering the processes whereby walking is made into secular pilgrimage, where the self is worked on and performed through the collaborative work of particular modes of attention, landscapes, imaginaries, aching, weary limbs, cameras, memories and texts. Through a consideration of the significance of temporality, and a mobilisation and interrogation of the practices and technologies through which the experience of transformation is enacted, we can consider how bodies make the self in transformation, negotiating with past and future selves in the active pursuit of becoming-other as becoming-self. In doing so, the notion of linear time is destabilised through its own infolding in the spacing and temporalisation of the world, where pasts and futures collide in the ongoing production of present experience.

References

Adler, J. 1989. Travel as performed art. *The American Journal of Sociology*, 94(6), 1366–91.

Bærenholdt, J., Haldrup, M. and Larsen, J. 2004. *Performing Tourist Places*. Aldershot: Ashgate.

Butler, J. 2006. *Gender Trouble*. New York: Routledge.

Dawney, L. 2011a. Social imaginaries and therapeutic self-work: The ethics of the embodied imagination. *The Sociological Review*, 59(3), 535–52.

Dawney, L. 2011b. The motor of being: a response to Steve Pile's 'Emotions and affect in recent human geography'. *Transactions of the Institute of British Geographers*, 36(4), 599–602.

Dawney, L. 2013a. The interruption: investigating subjectivation and affect. *Environment and Planning D: Society and Space* 2013, 31, 628–44.

Dawney, L. 2013b. "Feeling connected": practising nature, nation and class through coastal walking in *Coastal Cultures: Revisiting Liminality and Leisure*, edited by P. Gilchrist, T. Carter and D. Burdsey. Eastbourne: LSA, 87–101.

Desforges, L. 2000. Traveling the world: Identity and travel biography. *Annals of Tourism Research*, 27(4), 926–45.

Durkheim, E. 1964. *The Elementary Forms of the Religious Life*. London: Allen & Unwin.

Foucault, M. 1982. The subject and power. *Critical Inquiry*, 8(4), 777–89.

Foucault, M. 1983. *The Culture of the Self* [Online]. Available at http://dpg.lib.berkeley.edu/webdb/mrc/search_vod.pl?avr=1 [accessed: 24 January 2011].

Foucault, M. 1987. The ethic of care for the self as a practice of freedom, in *The Final Foucault*, edited by J. Bernauer and D. Rasmussen. Cambridge, MA: MIT Press, 1–20.

Foucault, M. 1988. *The History of Sexuality. Vol.3, The Care of the Self*. Harmondsworth: Penguin.

Foucault, M. 1992. *The History of Sexuality. Vol.2, The Use of Pleasure*. London: Penguin.

Foucault, M. 1997. Self writing, in *Ethics, Subjectivity and Truth (Essential Works of Foucault, 1954–1984, Vol. 1)*, edited by P. Rabinow. New York: The New Press, 207–22.

Foucault, M. 2005. *The Hermeneutics of the Subject: Lectures at the Collège de France, 1981–82*. New York: Picador.

Foucault, M. 2008. *Le Gouvernement de Soi et des Autres – Cours au Collège de France 1982–1983*. Paris: Seuil, Paris Gallimard.

Haldrup, M. and Larsen, J. 2003. The family gaze. *Tourist Studies*, 3(1), 23–46.

Lury, C. 1998. *Prosthetic Culture: Photography, Memory and Identity*. London: Routledge.

Reader, I. and Walter, T. 1993. *Pilgrimage in Popular Culture*. Basingstoke: Macmillan Press.

Robinson, M. and Picard, D. (eds) 2009. *The Framed World: Tourism, Tourists and Photography*. Aldershot: Ashgate.

Rose, N. 1996. *Inventing Our Selves: Psychology, Power, and Personhood*. Cambridge: Cambridge University Press.

Scarles, C. 2012. The photographed other: Interplays of agency in tourist photography in Cusco, Peru. *Annals of Tourism Research*, 39(2), 928–50.

Sidaway, J. 2009. Shadows on the path: Negotiating geopolitics on an urban section of Britain's south west coast path. *Environment and Planning D: Society and Space*, 27(6), 1091–116.

Slavin, S. 2003. Walking as spiritual practice: The pilgrimage to Santiago de Compostela. *Body and Society*, 9(1), 1–18.

Solnit, R. 2002. *Wanderlust: A History of Walking*. London: Verso.

Turner, V. 1974. *Dramas, Fields and Metaphors*. Ithaca, NY: Cornell University Press.

Turner, V. and Turner, E. 1978. *Image and Pilgrimage in Christian Culture*. Oxford: Blackwell.

Urry, J. 1995. *Consuming Places*. London: Routledge.

Urry, J. and Larsen, J. 2011. *The Tourist Gaze 3.0*. 3rd edn. London: SAGE.

Wylie, J. 2005. A single day's walking: Narrating self and landscape on the south west coast path. *Transactions of the Institute of British Geographers*, 30(2), 234–47.

Chapter 9

Memories of Forced Transformation through Travel in 1948

Lynda Mannik

The concept of 'liminality' was developed in the mid-twentieth century, following the Second World War, through ideas about 'strangers' in an attempt to understand the in-between social status of travellers who were attempting to enter a group, culture or territory. Alfred Schultz (1944: 499), philosopher and sociologist, defined a stranger as 'an adult individual ... who tries to be permanently accepted or at least tolerated by the group which he approaches'. Schultz claims that the most outstanding social example is the immigrant or the refugee. Movement is expressed in his idea of the 'approach', which also allows for a permanent space between the inside of a culture and the outside of a culture. The stranger's approach creates an innate form of cultural liminality because 'strangers' do not have the ability to truly comprehend the cultural patterns of a new society, and therefore, will never feel safe or loyal and will always be seen as ungrateful (Schultz 1944: 507). Georg Simmel (1950: 402) conceptualised the stranger as the common denominator between movement and place,[1] entities that facilitated 'the unity of nearness and remoteness'. Although cast as an outsider, Simmel's stranger is a critical component of any society. Imagined as the essence of objectivity and freedom, the stranger is relegated to the position of the ultimate other, yet also elevated as a component of society that neutralises the innate subjectivity and closed-mindedness central to the nepotism associated with locality (Simmel 1950: 404–5). However, it is Arnold Van Gennep's (1960) work concerning 'rites of passage', which was elaborated on and made popular by Victor Turner in the 1970s,[2] that has inspired contemporary anthropologists and other scholars to theorise about a state of 'refugeeness', a state that is ambiguous and unstable; a negative, soulless void, where suffering reigns, and conversely, an empty space where new cultural identities can emerge.[3] In anthropological literature, refugee camps have been the spaces most commonly examined. In this chapter I will situate refugee travel by boat as a similar space

---

1   Simmel (1950: 404) specifically explains that 'the mobile person' comes in contact with society, but is not organically connected through established ties to locality and kinship.

2   Victor Turner (1969) is most famous for the development of this theory in *The Ritual Process: Structure and Anti-structure*.

3   Scholars who have discussed these aspects include: Mallki (1992), Robertson (2002), Bhabha (1990) and Kumsa (2006).

or liminal experience and discuss aspects of transformation for those seeking refuge in this manner. In particular, the passengers aboard the *Walnut* and how their memories of this type of voyage reflect determination, creative thought and action, and shifts in identity.

In 1948, 347 passengers, who were primarily Estonian refugees, undertook a dangerous and illegal journey from Sweden to Canada on the HMS *Walnut*, a decrepit, British minesweeper. All had initially fled to Sweden in 1944, in small fishing vessels, to escape Soviet occupation; however, fears that the Swedish government was weakening under constant pressure from Russia to repatriate all Baltic citizens caused them to flee again. Between 2006 and 2009 I had the opportunity to interview over 30 of the *Walnut*'s surviving passengers about their memories of life in Sweden as refugees, this voyage, and their first impressions of Canada. Many referred to their experience as 'a trip of a lifetime' and all described it as an experience that had permanently marked their identity and transformed the way they looked at life in general. They endured 32 days with little food or water, only two toilet facilities for 347 people, five severe winter storms, and numerous mechanical problems before landing at Pier 21 in Halifax's harbour.

According to Michel Foucault (1986: 27), in symbolic terms, travel by boat is representative of the perfect heterotopia – a space reserved for infinite imaginations that move nowhere and somewhere at the same time; 'a floating piece of space, a place without a place, that exists by itself, that is closed in on itself and at the same time is given over to the infinity of the sea'. In this context, the *Walnut* was not only moving people and cultural capital between places, but also fuelling cultural fantasies, dreams of adventure, hope and fears of demise. This voyage represents a liminal period in all of the passengers' lives when they were 'betwixt and between' (Turner 1969) social status and state protection. It also represents a time of ambiguous memories about travel, transformation and being a refugee, which are illustrated in comments made by Elmar Peremees (interview 2006), one of the passengers. When asked to describe his experiences as a refugee he said:

> I don't really consider myself to ever have been a refugee. I consider myself just
> to be another person who went from one place to another place. I don't think of
> myself as a refugee ... more like a traveller or a tourist.

This chapter will examine discrepancies between self-representation and collective representation conveyed through memories about this voyage, and the various ways the *Walnut*'s passengers talked about their experiences in this liminal period of their lives when they were searching for safety, refuge and renewed political status. It will argue that this type of transformation through travel, which inherently shifts cultural boundaries and identities, does not fit the traditional, anthropological model of a 'rite of passage', but similarly is remembered as both dramatic and empowering. The outcome of being uprooted twice, experiencing near-death during ocean travel twice, and ascribed refugee status for four years is remarkably remembered 60 years later in a positive light.

Choice and Agency: Choosing to Leave

Every interview and, therefore I would argue, many memories about the *Walnut*'s voyage were bracketed by the experiences undergone during the Second World War, and this group's first migration by boat from Estonia. In 1940 the Soviet army occupied Estonia. By June of 1941 over 12,000 Estonians were sent to concentration camps in Siberia. In July 1941, Estonia was overtaken by German occupation and there was a new wave of persecution. As well, all Jewish people and Estonian gypsies were annihilated. In 1944 the Soviets occupied Estonia once more. All of the *Walnut*'s passengers were part of a mass exodus that took place at this time when over 70,000 Estonians attempted to cross the Baltic Sea in small fishing boats, often under fire from Soviet planes. It is estimated that during this period Estonia lost over one-third of its original population (approximately one million Estonian citizens) and over 1,000 died while making this crossing.[4]

This first episode of a double migration was vividly remembered as being terrifying and, for some, much worse than their experiences aboard the *Walnut*. Several spoke candidly about intense physical and psychological trauma experienced while crossing the Baltic Sea in 1944:

> We came with a very, very small boat. It only had five young people on it and the oldest one was the owner of the boat. We had a lot of trouble ... and the storm took everything. We didn't have anything. We just lied on the bottom of the boat and when the storm was over somebody saw a big ship or something and took some white linen and put them up so they could see us. They noticed us and came very close to us and we thought it was the Germany army or something like that, or the Russians, we didn't know where we were. (Lige interview 2007)

> Like I said, I was sick and I was on the bottom of the boat and we were like, if you have read those stories about when they brought the slaves over from Africa to America, it was something like that. We were stuck on the bottom. I really don't know who was upstairs. (Kuusk interview 2007)

> My uncle Walter was late. He arrives on the beach and the Russians were already there and they just shot him. This is not an uncommon story. (Laumets interview 2007)

There were no nostalgic comments or reminiscences suggesting that this travel experience by boat was even slightly touristic in nature. Leaving was not a choice, but a necessity.

Sweden was supposed to be a temporary stopping-off point. However, throughout the mid-to-late 1940s, the state refused to protect Estonian refugees

---

4   For statistics and details about the impact the Second World War had on Estonia see Kangilaski et al. (2005).

from attempts by Soviet officials to repatriate them andin 1945, 167 Baltic citizens were returned. Several tried to commit suicide while being escorted onto Soviet ships. By 1948 the threat of repatriation by the Soviet government was still looming and was the motivation for a second migration, as reiterated throughout the *Walnut*'s passengers' narratives, who emphasised a dire need to get as far away from Russia as possible. The 'push factors', a term coined by Fethi Mansouri and Michael Leach (2004), for those fleeing illegally by boat are generally severe because of the understood risks inherent in this type of passage. In this case, 'push factors' were primarily based on fears of Soviet repatriation. When asked why they chose to leave the majority said that leaving Sweden was a necessity, not a choice. Liisa Ester (interview 2007) explained: 'When you are young and you are scared of the Russians, you have to go because they might put you in jail any way. We were honest people. This was a very scary time.'

Nonetheless, some of the *Walnut*'s passengers did talk about choices they made within the parameters of this fear. A general feeling that was implicit in many comments was that 'it was a hard choice'. They were comfortable in Sweden except for the lingering tensions concerning the proximity of Russia and recurring Soviet threats. Some claimed to have just followed the crowd; their friends or acquaintances were going and so they decided to go. Aleksander Seero (interview 2006) made a spontaneous decision to go to Canada in two days because his brother and uncles were leaving. Others spent months deciding. Some had no choice due to their age. Adele Nyman (interview 2006) was only 16 at the time. She said that if she had been older she would have stayed in Sweden because she loved her life there. Comments about choices emerged in reminiscences to challenge the notion of a fixed type of refugee; nevertheless they were couched under a dominant narrative of fear.

Most often there are limited choices for refugees in terms of entering a territory or finding a new homeland. In this case over 50 voyages were organised by Estonian refugees between 1945 and 1951. Sailing vessels of various sizes carried them to a variety of locations. Between 1947 and 1950, approximately 50 ships, nicknamed the 'Viking boats', left Sweden. These vessels, which ranged in size from small, 30-foot sailing sloops to 164-foot trawlers, were mostly filled with Estonians. According to Karl Aun (1985: 25), 17 ships went to the United States; 10 to Canada; six to South Africa; five to Argentina; three to England; one to Brazil; two sunk and two were deemed to have disappeared. Eleven landed in Canada, the largest of these was the *Walnut*. Depending on who you knew, you may have had a choice about your final destination.

Interestingly, most of the *Walnut*'s passengers said they knew very little about Canada prior to leaving. Canada as a specific destination was definitely secondary to leaving Sweden, and most said they virtually knew nothing about the country, or so little that it did not matter. Some said they knew that it was a big country and northern, so similar in climate to Estonia. The most common secondary response was that they knew Canada was close to the United States, therefore possibly a gateway into the 'promise land'. Canada was easier to get into, but the United States was the desired destination. The 'American Dream' was a well-known concept and it was also assumed that someone could live the American Dream of democracy, freedom and prosperity while living in Canada. A less common, but still popular, response revolved around cowboys and Indian stereotypes gleaned from films and literature, including a Blackfoot comic book series, as described by Leho Jogeva (interview 2007). Canada was understood to be a wild place, primitive, but exciting; a place where you still might see Indians roaming around. In an unconscious reference to the Pocahontas myth, Aleksander Seero (interview 2006), who was 19 at the time, said, 'I always thought, worst case scenario, maybe an Indian woman would take me in and take care of me'. Obviously, adventurers and explorers have far more agency than refugees. Nevertheless,to fantasise or imagine oneself as a stranger entering a new land with advantages creates positive motivation and a vision of hope that can possibly assist in imagining a new identity.

Figure 9.1 Boarding the *Walnut* in Sweden, November 1948
Source: Photographer: Manivald Sein. Courtesy of Manivald Sein, private collection.

Choice and agency are conjoined and complicated terms when allocated to refugee experiences. Agency is rarely discussed because international legal definitions emphasise 'well-founded' fears as a core requirement for protection. If an individual does not express a 'well-founded' fear, which propels them into homelessness and helplessness, they cannot expect to acquire protection. This would suggest that any form of agency on their part could be viewed as detrimental to the attainment of refugee status. However, in reality, fear and agency are most often conjoined in the refugee experience. Individuals would not risk 'their lives in unseaworthy boats [if] they [we]re not in danger' (Mansouri and Leach 2004: 121). In the media, so-called 'boat people' are described as particularly threatening because it is imagined that their agency is increased through movement in uncontrolled waters. Words such as *engulfed, swamped, flooded, washed away* and *inundated* are used to describe the effect they have on the national spaces they arrive in (Pugh 2004: 54–5, also in Mansouri and Leach 2004). Realistically, individuals do not risk their lives, and in many cases their family's lives, in unseaworthy boats if they do not feel that they are in extreme danger. Remembering choices, even if they fall under the umbrella of forced migration, has empowering implications that negate one-sided stereotypical narratives of victimhood most often relegated to refugees and their imagined liminal, or void-like, state.

Memories of the Voyage

Most commonly, refugees' migrating by boat experience humiliating and debilitating conditions onboard and the *Walnut*'s voyage was no different. The risks associated with travelling across the Atlantic on this ship were not necessarily apparent when they bought their tickets. The primitive accommodations and size of the ship did not become an issue for most of the passengers until they boarded. Two days into the voyage they were hit by a massive winter storm in the North Sea and, from all reports, this is when it became obvious that they were in for a rough passage. Unfortunately, most had sold what little belongings they had acquired in Sweden in order to buy their ticket(s) and were left with very limited funds,[5] so there was no turning back. Contrary to the severe conditions onboard mentioned earlier, memories about this voyage range from horrifying to fun. They add an extra dimension to literature that focuses solely on the struggles and trauma associated with refugee experience, while complementing the literature that positions liminality as a creative space.

During our interviews, the *Walnut*'s passengers spoke candidly, many for the first time in a semi-public atmosphere, about what it was like to experience migration by boat as a refugee. For many, the only memories they had of the actual voyage revolved around seasickness and lying in a cramped bunk unable to move. Others distinctly remember violent storms, very cramped quarters, freezing temperatures, rotting food, dangerous toilet facilities and generally feeling panicked throughout this experience.

> I don't want to think about it anymore, how it was. We were sleeping head to feet. That is just the way we were on the boat. There were sick children, bringing up. They were seasick, so seasick. No food! Ohhhh! It was murder staying on a boat like that for one month. I was lucky though. I was healthy, I wasn't sick.

---

5   One passenger recalled how he only had about five dollars in his pocket when he arrived in Canada (Seero interview 2006).

I only brought up once, but then I was ok all the rest of the way. (Martsen interview 2007)

Figure 9.2 A family in their bunk, November 1948
Source: Photographer: Manivald Sein. Courtesy of Manivald Sein, private collection.

Memories associated with several storms that occurred throughout the voyage were also common and prominent. One story told by Aleksander Seero (interview 2006) explains the ferocity of the winter weather at sea:

146   *Travel and Transformation*

> There was one bad storm, one night where I heard those two girls Unita, what's the other girl's name, Mina or Nina. They had been going to one end of the boat to the food area in the middle of the boat and a big wave came over board and threw them down and luckily they were stopped by the railing that was outside the boat, because if they had gone overboard they would have been goners. Apparently it was a really big wave that came right across the top of the boat.

The crowded conditions aboard, little food and lack of fresh water and toilet facilities left all of the passengers in discomfort and stress. These conditions also added to the constant worry that the *Walnut* would not survive the Atlantic. Several passengers spoke of seeing others suffer deep emotional and psychological distress throughout the voyage. Anna Himmist (interview 2007) remembers a stranger in her cabin:

> I may be completely wrong but my impression was ... there were some people, there was a man in my cabin that was almost out of his mind with worry and thinking when he heard the water moving from side to side, he kept thinking that the boat was going to sink. He kept thinking that there was a hole in the boat somewhere and we were going down with the boat.

These memories are invaluable in understanding the experience of refugees travelling by boat. They give a voice to individuals who migrate in this way and are similar in some ways to comments made by Iraqi and Afghan refugees travelling to Australia, which have been documented in *Lives in Limbo* (2004). Mansouri and Leach (2004: 10) argue that '[m]uch of the frustration experienced by refugees and asylum seekers is the feeling that their stories and experiences are misrepresented, distorted, or, perhaps most distressingly, completely ignored'. I was told that memories of the *Walnut*'s voyage are rarely brought up in conversation with outsiders because disbelief is the usual response. Over the years they have retreated in silence or struggled to find ways to tell stories so that others will believe them. When asked if they would ever take a trip like that again, there was a resounding 'No, no, never'! Some said that although it was quite an adventure, they would never go on a voyage like that again (Arens interview 2007) and a few claimed to have remained afraid of water and therefore unable to travel by boat ever again, particularly ocean travel (Adosaar interview 2007, Muursepp interview 2007, Nyman interview 2006).

Nevertheless, refugees' narratives do not just portray melancholy. Under an umbrella of fear, loss and trauma many survivors recalled positive memories of everyday life while aboard the ship. These types of memories were more common for male passengers and individuals who had been children at this time. Positive, happy memories were often associated with socialising while in transit, playing cards, listening to music and feeding seagulls. This memory was spontaneously incited by a photograph of the deck of the *Walnut* while it was crossing the Atlantic:

Yes, well I spent a lot of time right here (pointing to the crowded deck), all of the young people, we stayed in between the boats here because it was warm and there was a smoke stack up there. We put our back against the smoke stack to keep warm. All the children you know, our age 11–15, were here coming across the Atlantic. On a nice day we could all sit up there. (Muursepp interview 2007)

There was little space for moving around the boat and few places to sit or stand, yet several passengers fondly remember playing cards in their bunks to pass the time:

Yes, some people played cards, but I can't remember if I played cards. Oh yes, some people were playing 21, Black Jack, for cigarettes. We had lots of duty free cigarettes on the boat and so they were playing for cigarettes. They were mostly Camels and the cost, one dollar a carton. (Alle interview 2006)

Leho Jogeva (interview 2007) described his daily routine on the Atlantic. He was 15 years old at the time:

LM: Where were you on the ship?

LJ: We were in the stern and that is the worst place to be. Up and down, up and down, I couldn't take it. Early in the morning we would head up and sit by the chimney back there, we would be sitting back there by the chimney. We had no problem there what-so-ever. We opened up cases of apples and ate oranges and that is the most stable part of the ship. We would come down a ladder if you want to call it that. The mess hall, if you want to call it a mess hall was on this side of the ship here. I think there was a small kitchen. Nobody like the food but any ways, my job was to take a bowl of soup to my parents.

The word *adventure* was used on several occasions to describe the voyage, particularly by passengers who had been children or young adolescents at this time. These reminiscences provide examples:

No we just thought it was supposed to be safe, when really it wasn't, but we didn't know that. In those days I don't think we worried, at that age, being a young lad, everything was fun. It was just an adventure really. I thought it was lots of fun. Some people didn't think so, they were very sick. (Melts interview 2006)

But it is funny, I don't ever remember ever really being scared. I don't know … it was just quite an adventure. In the evening we used to gather on the top of the ship and this guy, Heinsaar, he used to be a sailor and he used to tell us all kinds of stories and when we were at the camps we had a lot of fun really. (Arens interview 2007)

Figure 9.3 Socialising onboard, November 1948
Source: Photographer: Manivald Sein. Courtesy of Manivald Sein, private collection.

The range of memories about this experience suggests that there were a wide range of emotions felt during this strenuous voyage. As well, I believe that talking positively during our interviews aided in normalising oral narratives about this voyage. Becker et al. (2000) also noted in their conversations with Cambodian refugees that extremely emotional memories are often couched in everyday topics in order to make them more believable in contemporary renditions. Documenting this range of emotions reminds us that those who are labelled 'refugees' also converse, tell stories, play games, socialise, have fun and help each other; again, shifting conversations away from a stereotypical focus on victimhood. Added to that, there is a certain amount of nostalgia incorporated into all remembering, and in the case of traumatic or distressing memories, nostalgia can serve an important psychological function. Nostalgia has been described as a positive emotional 'reservoir that people delve into to deal with existential threats' (Sedikides et al. 2004: 206). It is a coping mechanism that serves to protect and affirm identity. In this way it can also serve as a type of forgetting, a creative way to alter past traumatic experience (Mannik 2011: 87).[6] Diverse memories and perspectives

---

6 In *Remembering, Forgetting and Feeling* (Mannik 2011) I provide a detailed account of the types of memories that were recalled about this voyage while looking at photographs of this voyage approximately 60 years later. Here, I would simply like to provide an overview of the range of memories and emotions, from traumatic to enjoyable, that were expressed.

brought forward by the *Walnut*'s passengers support the notion that this experience allows for continual exploration of identity.

'Trip of a Lifetime'

Piotr Sztompka says, '[t]rauma occurs when there is a break, displacement, or disorganization in the orderly, taken-for-granted universe' (2000: 457). Individuals who have escaped totalitarian regimes and survived two dangerous migrations have experienced disruption on several levels. The trauma of forced migration 'touches the core of collective order – the domain of main values, constitute rules, [and] central expectations' (Sztompka 2000: 457), therefore it is deeply felt. When these experiences are given a voice through narratives it is often with the intention of making sense of painful memories and losses so that they can be integrated into present time. The relation between trauma and memory is complex. For example, symptoms of post-traumatic stress dissipate over time, yet acute memories and extreme emotions can lay dormant for a lifetime. Memories and stories told about this group's first migration were thick with emotion, no uplifting memories were recalled. Their narratives were powerful and it was obvious that well-told stories masked highly charged personal feelings. However, memories about experiences onboard the *Walnut* were somewhat different – grounded in dignity. When asked to reflect 60 years later on the question, 'What does this trip mean to you now?' most often positive, upbeat responses based on being adventurous, making the right choice, and having gained strength of character through adversity were offered.

The tension that exists between memory, traumatic experience, nostalgia and everyday activities was made clear. 'Strength through adversity' was one of the prevailing themes within a complex web of ideas concerning being a refugee that surfaced. This is not an uncommon theme for those who have experienced forced migration (Holt 1997: 251). It was explained to me on several occasions that there was a 'certain type of strength' gained from having been a refugee that very few people can understand unless they experience it themselves. Some felt they were better people for having gone through it. A few made the same joke, 'what doesn't kill you, makes you stronger'![7] Valter Pass (interview 2006) stated, 'I firmly believe it made me a better person. I appreciate life more ... learning it the hard way ... experiencing something like that definitively does something to you'. Even though the meaning of 'strength' was often obscure, this sentiment was clearly stated by most of the passengers interviewed.

There was also a sense of pride in being determined enough to get to Canada illegally, being hard workers, and in being strong enough to start over again

---

7   This phrase was coined by his mother and then made famous by Friedrich Nietzsche. The original phrase, written by Nietzsche in 1888, was in *Out of Life's School of War: What Does Not Destroy Me, Makes Me Stronger* (see Nietzsche (1977: 463–4) 'Twilight of the Idols').

Figure 9.4 Departing from stopover in Ireland, November 1948
Source: Photographer: Manivald Sein. Courtesy of Manivald Sein, private collection.

after losing everything. This pride was linked to being Estonian and to having been a refugee. One interviewee stated, 'When I used to be called a DP, I used to think, "They are Canadian by birth; I am Canadian by choice"' (Laumets interview 2007). 'DP' was a popular acronym in the 1940s and the 1950s in Canada and the United States that meant 'displaced person'. It was commonly used to refer to individuals who had been displaced due to the events of the Second World War and it was commonly used for self-identification by many of the *Walnut*'s passengers. As well, many of the passengers' feelings of pride superseded any negative connotations about being labelled a 'refugee' or a 'boat person'. They considered their experiences to be a unique and valuable factor in the formation of their identity that superseded what others might think. Rudolph Laumets (interview 2007) was brought to tears when asked what this trip meant to him now and responded: 'I am very proud of having done that. To know that my parents, my ancestors, and that community have that strength of will and determination and courage to do that.' For others looking back made them feel like an explorer of sorts, which transcended all negative connotations. For Aet Lige (interview 2007), for example, the different way they came, not standard air travel, made her life interesting: it 'made it like an adventure'. And again, it could be argued that this discourse of strength serves to normalise past struggles, and even more so, add value.

The theme, 'strength through adversity', can be conjoined with retrospective comments made about choice, some of which were discussed previously in terms of choosing to board the *Walnut*. The majority of the passengers did not feel that they had a choice concerning whether to stay in Sweden or leave due to the fear of Soviet reprisal, nevertheless, their choice to come to Canada was highlighted as 'the right choice'. August Maaniit (interview 2007) stated, 'It was a good move. It was the right move at the time and still is today' and Anna Himmist (interview 2007) said, 'I am happy I am here. It was a good country to come to and we have been happy from the beginning'. Some were a bit more reticent due to age and loneliness:

> I have a satisfying life and I do not have any complaints about that, except that I am not getting back home. In your old age you like to have a relative that is either living with you or caring for you. (Berendson interview 2007)

Regardless of their current circumstances, passage on the *Walnut* offered an opportunity for a new life. Decisions were frequently made based on fear, but in the hopes of a better future. As August Maaniit (interview 2007) put it, 'it takes a vision or a feeling or a drive' to follow through on this type of life choice or perhaps it takes a combination of all three.

In general we compose memories and retell memories that help us feel at ease with our lives, our pasts and our identities; memories aid in the creation of appropriate contemporary meanings. The past is not filed away waiting to be resurrected, but 'reconstructed on the basis of the present' (Halbwachs 1992: 40). However, traumatic experiences are so powerful and unusual that meaning cannot always be allotted to them because there is no appropriate context. Theorists have suggested that trauma can only be experienced in a belated form, 'when it returns in the form of dreams or flashbacks' (Edkins 2003: 40). Talking positively about past traumatic experience can aid in creating a buffer between contemporary identities and distressing memories; again, normalising narratives of past refugees' experience. Gaining some sort of strength from traumatic experience is one way of transcending and transforming negative and numbing emotions. Ideas about strength contradict and challenge socially imposed ideas about 'liminality'.

Conclusion

Tensions are inherent in the process of constructing self-identities. Reflections on the past experiences of the *Walnut*'s passengers revealed that forced migration has a profound impact on individual identities, which is multi-faceted in nature. In reference to Palestinian refugees, Laleh Khalili (2007) explains that through mnemonic narratives, it is possible to see how political performances concerning identity shift over time from an emphasis on heroic nationalism to tragic victimisation. Each serves a different political motive and each is also part of a continuous dialogical interaction with various audiences and institutions. According to Kumsa (2006: 230), 'belonging is both fixed and constantly shifting', even for individuals who experienced forced migration many years ago. Sharing personal memories allows for the restructuring and rejuvenation of present identities that often incorporate and recycle past identities. The sense of self of those who have experienced disempowerment through forced relocation can become more easily fragmented and composed of 'intense personal and emotional upheavals regarding place, location, identity and desire' (Shalhoub-Kevorkiam, cited in Holt 1997: 248). No one is born a refugee, and no one wants to become a refugee. The difficulties in making sense of these life-altering experiences are dealt with in a subjective fashion, which rely on a wide variety of determining factors.

Having said that, Liisa Malkki (1997), Prem Kumar Rajaram (2002) and others[8] have argued that victimisation, as a generalised form of representation, is detrimental to understanding the individuality and personal agency of refugees; yet it is perhaps the type of representation that individuals who have undergone forced migration are most comfortable with. Using the language of collective victimisation is protective. It allows for an anonymous space with which to enter the political arena without being viewed as defiant. During my conversations with the *Walnut*'s passengers they talked about both trauma and agency, including experiences on board that mimicked tourist activities as well as subtle moments of happiness, joy and fun. When asked about the ultimate meaning of this trip they unanimously focused on the courage and determination needed to survive such an ordeal, as well as the strength gained through adversity as a central life lesson that builds character. Traumatic experience, in the end, did not have a crippling effect.

I would argue that there are a variety of reasons for an emphasis on this sentiment. Firstly, people do not always see themselves as fitting into stereotypes; however, they do internalise these ideas, and therefore, their self-representation is melded with collective representation, yet remains ambiguous. Secondly, the act of consciously deciding to undertake a voyage (as was the case in leaving Sweden) was different than their first migration from Estonia when they were being forced to leave at a moment's notice and travel under more severe and desperate circumstances. Therefore by comparison, their experience onboard the *Walnut* seemed better or easier. As well, the *Walnut*'s voyage had been organised by Estonians over a fairly lengthy period of time and seemed planned and, therefore, safer. Thirdly, movement on water represents a type of freedom of sorts, a place or space where your imagination can run wild, as opposed to confinement on land in a refugee camp for example, where there are clearer physical boundaries, borders and fences. And finally, time and age. Most of the individuals I spoke with were between 16 and 23 at the time and 60 years had passed since this experience. A retrospective view is often more nostalgic. The majority remembered the trauma experienced at sea, but many preferred to also think and talk about more mundane or pleasant moments that normalised contemporary narratives. For a

---

8   For example, Peter Gale (2004) focuses on representations of victimisation in the media. On another level, Barbara Harrell-Bond (2002) discusses the role victimisation plays in representation of refugees by the UNHRC.

few, memories of constant seasickness predominated, could not be forgotten, and were often accompanied by physical reflexive feelings. Conversely, for others all suffering aboard the *Walnut* was erased in favour of memories about adventure and fun.

Unanimously, this group's collective memory of transformation through this type of travel was not solely focused on the legalities that concern either refugee status or the attainment of citizenship status. When they looked back 60 years later, and when asked to think about what this trip meant to them now, two themes prevailed: one was centred on pride and the strength gained through adversity; the other was centred on making the right choice – living without regrets. This voyage, which radically challenged their identity on many levels, was remembered as changing their lives in primarily positive ways, but not with a sole focus on legal, economic or state-centred ramifications. Scholars suggest that language often falls short of enabling a memory of a traumatic experience due to severe confusion over the actual events, which cannot be understood in a logically way, and therefore, emotions take over. Ernest Van Alphen (1999: 32) uses the metaphor of 'killing the self' to emphasise the dynamic way that trauma can kill memory and meaning. For this group, the adversities they suffered during their liminal experiences as refugees travelling by boat created a new more empowered sense of self, a sense of belonging and contributing that outshone the loss and trauma of relocation.

Acknowledgement

The research for this article has been supported by the Social Sciences and Humanities Research Council of Canada through the Joseph-Armand Bombardier Canada Graduate Scholarships (CGS) Program.

List of Personal Interviews

(The following is a list of interviews that were conducted with surviving *Walnut* passengers. Pseudonyms have been used.)

Name, Place of Communication, Date

Adosaar, Rein. Ancaster, Ontario, March 2007.
Alle, Peter. Don Mills, Ontario, November 2006.
Arens, Lia. Toronto, Ontario, January 2007.
Berendson, Lydia. North York, Ontario, February 2007.
Ester, Liisa. North York, Ontario, 6 March 2007.
Himmist, Anna. North York, Ontario, February 2007.
Jogeva, Leho. Toronto, Ontario, April 2007.
Kuusk, Melanie. Toronto, Ontario, April 2007.

Laumets, Rudolph. North York, Ontario, June 2007.
Lige, Aet. Toronto, Ontario, January 2007.
Maaniit, August. North York, Ontario, February 2007.
Martsen, Eve. Toronto, Ontario, March 2007.
Melts, Oskar. Etobicoke, Ontario, November 2006.
Muursepp, Vulfi. Toronto, Ontario, January 2007.
Nyman, Adele. Toronto, Ontario, November 2006.
Pass, Valter. Richmond Hill, Ontario, November 2006
Peremees, Elmar. Etobicoke, Ontario, September 2006.
Seero, Aleksander. Peterborough, Ontario, October 2006.

References

Aun, K. 1985. *The Political Refugees: A History of Estonians in Canada*. Toronto: McClelland and Stewart Ltd.
Becker, G., Yewoubdar, B. and Pauline, K. 2000. Memory, trauma and embodied distress: The management of disruption in the stories of Cambodians in exile. *Ethos*, 28(3), 320–45.
Bhabha, H. 1990. The third space, in *Identity, Community, Culture, Difference*, edited by J. Rutherford. London: Lawrence and Wishart, 207–21.
Edkins, J. 2003. *Trauma and the Memory of Politics*. Cambridge: Cambridge University Press.
Foucault, M. 1986. Text/context of other space. *Diacritics*, 16(1), 22–7.
Gale, P. 2004. The refugee crisis and fear. *Journal of Sociology*, 40(4), 321–40.
Halbwachs, M. 1992. *On Collective Memory*, translated by L.A. Cosar. Chicago: The University of Chicago Press.
Harrell-Bond, B. 2002. Can humanitarian work with refugees be humane? *Human Rights Quarterly*, 24(1), 51–85.
Holt, M. 1997. The wives and mothers of heroes: Evolving identities of Palestinian refugee women in Lebanon. *Journal of Development Studies*, 43(2), 245–64.
Kangilaski, J., Kask, V., Kukk, K., Laas, J., Noor, H., Rahi-tamm, A., Ratas, R., Raukas, A., Sarv, E. and Varju, P. 2005. *The White Book: Losses Inflicted on the Estonian Nation by Occupation Regimes, 1940–1991* [Online], edited by V. Salo, Ü. Ennuste, E. Parmastro, E. Tarvel and P. Varju, translated by M. Ets, T. Koitla and M. Vihuri. Estonian Encyclopedia Publishers. Available at: http://www.riigikogu.ee/public/Riigikogu/TheWhiteBook.pdf [accessed: 13 July 2013].
Khalili, L. 2007. Heroic and tragic pasts: Mnemonic narratives in the Palestinian refugee camps. *Critical Sociology*, 33(4), 731–59.
Kumsa, M.K. 2006. 'No! I'm not a refugee!' The poetics of be-longing among young Oromos in Toronto. *Journal of Refugee Studies*, 19(2), 230–55.

Malkki, L.H. 1992. National geographic: The rooting of peoples and the territorialization of national identity among scholars and refugees. *Cultural Anthropology*, 7(1), 24–44.

Malkki, L.H. 1997. Speechless emissaries: Refugees, humanitarianism and dehistoricization, in *Siting Culture: The Shifting Anthropological Object*, edited by K.F. Olwig and K. Hastrup. New York: Routledge, 223–54.

Mannik, L. 2011. Remembering, forgetting and feeling with photographs, in *Image and Memory: Oral History and Photography*, edited by A. Freund and A. Thomson. London: Palgrave Macmillan, 77–96.

Mansouri, F. and Leach M. 2004. *Lives in Limbo: Voices of Refugees under Temporary Protection*. Sydney: University of New South Wales.

Nietzsche, F. 1977. Twilight of the idols, in *The Portable Nietzsche*, translated by W. Kaufmann. New York: Penguin Press, 463–64.

Pugh, M. 2004. Drowning not waving: Boat people and humanitarianism at sea. *Journal of Refugee Studies*, 17(1), 50–69.

Rajaram, P.K. 2002. Humanitarianism and representations of the refugee. *Journal of Refugee Studies*, 15(3), 247–64.

Robertson, S.L. 2002. *Defining Travel: Diverse Visions*. Mississippi: University Press of Mississippi.

Schultz, A. 1944. The stranger: An essay in social psychology. *American Journal of Sociology*, 49(4), 499–508.

Sedikides, C., Wildschut T. and Baden, D. 2004. Nostalgia: Conceptual issues and existential functions, in *Handbook of Experimental Existential Psychology*, edited by J. Greenberg, S.L. Koole and T. Pyszczynski. New York: Guilford Press, 200–13.

Simmel, G. 1950. The stranger, in *The Sociology of G. Simmel*, edited by K.H. Wolf. New York: Free Press, 402–8.

Sztompka, P. 2000. Cultural trauma: The other face of social change. *European Journal of Social Theory*, 3(4), 449–66.

Turner, V.W. 1969. *The Ritual Process: Structure and Anti-structure*. Chicago: Aldine Publishing Co.

Van Alphen, E. 1999. Symptoms of discursivity: Experience, memory, and trauma, in *Acts of Memory: Cultural Recall in the Present*, edited by M. Bal, J. Crewe and L. Spitzer. Hanover: University Press of New England, 24–38.

Van Gennep, A. 1960. *The Rites of Passage*. London: Routledge.

Chapter 10

Young Backpackers and the Rite of Passage of Travel: Examining the Transformative Effects of Liminality

Amie Matthews

I'd say ... [travel is] doing a fine job of helping me find myself again ... I'm not feeling like I've missed the bus of life anymore. (Damien, age 29, email interview)

The changes [that travel has brought to my life] have been so great on so many levels that it is hard to quantify ... All I can say is that experiencing this whole other world out there has kind of allowed me to put my own speck of existence into perspective. (Michelle, age 29, email interview)

Introduction: Travel as Transition and Transformation

The notion that travel can result in change, renewal or greater self-awareness is, as these statements from young backpackers and the theme of this collection suggest, enduring. Travel is considered by many to be a fecund space, a space that is ripe with possibility. Indeed, journeys, touristic and otherwise, are firmly fixed in the cultural consciousness as avenues by which new experience and, by extension, new knowledge can be sought and found. Correspondingly, as a number of scholars have pointed out (see for example, Bauman 1996, Elsrud 2001, MacCannell 1989), pilgrims, pioneers, explorers, sailors, tramps, hikers, exiles, nomads, tourists and wanderers litter our histories, our cultural outputs and our imaginings as symbols of freedom, adventure, progress and discovery. On this basis, many tourist destinations are conceived and constructed by tourism operators, media and tourists, as places where individuals may gain heightened, or at the very least different, perspectives: on themselves, their relationships and on their social and cultural worlds. They are frequently conceived as places and spaces that rupture routine and that provide in the breach that which is unique, extraordinary and Other. With this, tourism is perceived, rightly or wrongly (for more on this debate, see for example Bruner 1991), as providing opportunity for reflection, insight, personal growth and transformation. In short, it is understood as bringing about an experiential and sometimes ontological 'shift' in the lives of individuals; a shift that is aided by exposure to new 'elements that successfully establish the case for an alternative reality' (Lean 2012: 157) or a new way of *doing* life.

Without denying their historical longevity, such expectations for, and images of, travel have seemingly been amplified under late or 'liquid modernity' (Bauman 2000). In the contemporary context, it seems that increased uncertainty and ambivalence has led many tourists to seek experiential knowledge and meaning elsewhere, outside of the known and 'beyond the boundaries of the immediate life-space' (Cohen 1979: 182). As a result, one of the key preoccupations of much contemporary tourism studies literature has been to explain *how exactly* it is that travel comes to play the role of educator, illuminator and transformer, and how such roles can best be conceptualised.

The end results are well-established arguments that tourism involves a search for novelty or difference (Cohen 1972), a search for authenticity (MacCannell 1989, Wang 2000), change (Smith 1992), for sincerity (Taylor 2001) and meaning (Graburn 1989). Tourism is modelled as a space inhabited by the surreal and the carnivalesque (Shields 1991), as a ludic space (Lett 1983, Turner and Turner 1978) and a space ruled by eros (Wang 2000). It is also configured as an arena in which nostalgia and serendipity and the desire for 'self-improvement' and 're-creation' (Graburn 1983: 15) rule paramount. Ultimately, for many it also comes to be conceived as an 'epiphanic' space (Hom Cary 2004: 64), a space where increased self-knowledge is possible and where 'fateful' (Desforges 2000: 935) or crossroads moments are likely encountered. Such moments of discovery are particularly important – or are constructed as being important – to those experiencing transition and transformation through travel (see for example, Desforges 1998, 2000, Maoz 2007, Noy 2004, White and White 2004).

Given how salient the ideas of transition and transformation through travel are, it is not surprising that 'rite of passage' is an oft bandied phrase in traveller and academic discourse. At its simplest, the concept of rite of passage is used with reference to those ritual experiences, behaviours or events that are engaged with as a means of signifying an individual or group's passing from one life stage or fixed socio-cultural state to the next (Turner 1995, van Gennep 1960). Rite of passage is intimately connected then with *both* transition and transformation. Subsequently, those who adopt the model (or at the very least, the language) of rite of passage with reference to tourism recognise that leisure travel performs a symbolic function for many individuals, helping them make or mark significant changes in their lives.

Despite this recognition, or perhaps because of it, the phrase 'rite of passage' is often employed – by tourists, the tourism industry and tourism scholars alike – with limited reflection or criticality. While there are notable exceptions to this (see for example, Cohen 2003, Graburn 1983, 1989, Maoz 2007, Matthews 2008, Noy and Cohen 2005, White and White 2007), there is a need to closely examine the rite of passage heuristic and more fully interrogate its applicability to contemporary tourism practices rather than simply accept it as a given. This, in keeping with the recent recognition that there is a need for tourism scholarship which better reflects the complexity of the travel space as it is experienced (see for example, Franklin and Crang 2001, Robinson and Jamal 2009), is one of the goals of this chapter.

Commencing with an overview of the rite of passage heuristic as it has traditionally been conceptualised, most notably by Victor Turner (1995), the chapter reflects on the ways in which travel as a rite of passage contributes to transformation. It also considers some of the limitations to the rite of passage model that have recently been recognised by tourism studies academics. In order to address some of these limitations, the chapter goes on to examine how the 'liminal' space of travel is actually lived by backpackers. By focusing on backpackers' accounts of what occurs within the travel space, the chapter ultimately strives to provide a more nuanced understanding of the rite of passage model and of the transformation paradigm in which it can be positioned.

Understanding the Rite of Passage Heuristic as a Model for Transformation

As already indicated, the phrase rite of passage is frequently used to refer to a series of practices, events and/or behaviours that demarcate, for the individual and the society that they belong to, one life stage or state from another. These rituals, some secular and others religious, and the meanings they are given, vary according to the socio-cultural context in which they emerge. Typically, though, they are used as a means of assisting individuals (in some cases physically, in others emotionally, psychologically and/or symbolically) as they transition through different life phases and/or social positions (Turner 1995, van Gennep 1960). Thus, rites of passage can be understood as comprising various acts or rituals which enable *and* attest to individual, and in some cases social, change or progression.

On this basis, in one of the earliest works dedicated to the subject (first published in 1908), Arnold van Gennep (1960: 11) contended that rites of passage were not singular rites but rather ritual undertakings which could be 'subdivided into *rites of separation, transition rites,* and *rites of incorporation*' (original emphasis). Each of these types of ritual, he argued, could be mapped onto the preliminal ('separation from a previous world'), liminal (transitional) and postliminal ('incorporation into the new world') phases of a rite of passage (van Gennep 1960: 21). Building on van Gennep's model, Victor Turner (1995) later labelled these three phases or spaces of a rite of passage as 'separation', 'margin' and 'reaggregation'. While it is the marginal or liminal space and its affects that I am particularly interested in here, in order to analyse how this space is experienced during the rite of passage of travel and how it contributes to transformation, it is necessary to understand each of these phases and the interrelationship between them. As such, it is to the key constitutive elements of the rite of passage model that I now turn.

Separation: Moving Away from Fixed Social Spaces and Structures

Separation, as one would assume, refers to the initiate or participant in the rite of passage moving away, or being separated, physically, socially and/or symbolically, from the everyday context and their 'normal' roles, statuses and/or responsibilities. According to Turner (1982: 24), this phase of the rite of passage helps to construct for the 'ritual subject' a 'cultural realm which is defined as "out of time" ... beyond or outside the time which measures secular [what we might conceive of as ordinary or everyday] processes and routines'. Separation, however, is not just temporal but may also be spatial, involving a 'geographical movement from one place to another' (Turner 1982: 25). On this basis, within tourism separation would most markedly be seen as referring to the moment of departure on one's trip or journey. Subsequently, acts such as exiting one's place of residence, knowing that 'home' (however it is conceived) is soon to be left behind; entering an airport, crossing a tarmac and boarding a plane; and traversing state borders or international datelines can be read as tangible and symbolic moments of distanciation and separation. They can, in short, be read, when analysed from the perspective of rite of passage, as 'threshold' moments.

Crossing the Threshold to Enter Liminal or Liminoid Space

These threshold moments are of intrinsic value when it comes to the marginal phase of a rite of passage for it is only by crossing the margin or *limen* – an invisible boundary which separates the known from the unknown – that individuals can enter the middle stage of the rite of passage, where they will be introduced to or 'unite[d] ... with a new world', a world unlike any other (van Gennep 1960: 20). This middle phase was characterised by Turner as being *liminal* or *liminoid*, the latter term used in his later works to refer to those rituals undertaken in 'complex' (non-traditional) societies as a matter of 'optation' rather than 'obligation' (1982: 43).[1]

Irrespective of the terminology used (though for a critical discussion of Turner's distinction between liminal and liminoid see Rowe 2008, St John 2008), these spaces were understood by Turner (1986: 41) as being situated 'betwixt and between the structural past and the structural future'. In such states of indeterminacy or ambiguity, Turner (1995, 1982) argued that it becomes commonplace for norms to be subverted, challenged, played with or inverted

---

1   According to Turner (1982) in these complex, social settings rituals are inclined to be more individualistic than collective in nature, they are likely to be connected to the leisure sphere and in some cases the consumer market, and they are more commonly chosen by, rather than imposed upon, the participant. Despite its increasingly normative nature, I would argue that by this formulation tourism tends to fall into the category of liminoid rather than liminal ritual. However, for present purposes the distinction is not an important one as the effects – namely that the ritual space is transformative – remain the same.

in some way. Indeed, he suggested that a sense of malleability pervaded liminal spaces and that they were occupied with the 'subjunctive mood of culture, the mood of maybe' (Turner 1986: 42). This mood of maybe, which implies that there are no rules, or that the rules that do exist are there to be played with, permeates, as I will demonstrate below, a variety of touristscapes. Most importantly, it is the freedom, licentiousness, creativity, indulgence and experimentation that liminality engenders and the intensified social bonds which may emerge from such experience, which leaves ritual participants changed, renewed or transformed in some way.

Communitas and Transformation

Adding to the transformative impact of liminality is the likelihood of individuals being exposed, while in these 'in-between' spaces/states, to experiences or feelings of *communitas*. Described as an intense 'commonness of feeling' (Turner and Turner 1978: 13) shared by those individuals co-inhabiting or moving through liminal space, communitas creates a strong, albeit fleeting, social bond between those who may not ordinarily see themselves as being similar or united. In particular, it is the shared sense of being outside of 'normal social structural relationships' and instead being immersed in the creative and permissive atmosphere of liminality, which creates a sense of unity between co-liminars (Turner 1982: 46). Subsequently individuals engaged in ritual activity (such as a rite of passage or pilgrimage) may experience a momentary sense of commonality whereby they feel spontaneously 'equal' and as 'one' (Turner 1982: 47). Communitas generates a desire for open, honest exchange and mutual understanding and provides a space in which individuals will feel themselves to be relating to or connecting with others in a direct and unmediated way, becoming as a result 'totally absorbed into a single, synchronized, fluid event' (Turner 1982: 48). In short, communitas enables ritual participants to behave and to connect with others in a way they may not in ordinary, structural space and under ordinary social rules. This, for Turner (1995: 139), is why communitas is 'pleasurable' and 'magical', and why it is deemed to house great 'evolutionary potential' (Turner 1995: 128): it leaves individuals open to new possibilities – individually and socially – and in many cases renders them and/or their relationships, changed in some way.

Returning to Structure

The experience of communitas, as with the experience of liminality more generally, is most likely to occur when individuals are separated from the typical social structures and routines that govern their everyday lives. It is separation from these structures and entry into the marginal phase of rite of passage which enables individuals to encounter, experiment with and reflect upon different ways of being. Such reflection is often amplified after the fact, when individuals return from the marginal, middle phase of the rite of passage to structure and come to recall what was experienced previously and compare or contrast it with their present states.

Transformation requires, then, all three components or phases of the rite of passage model to play out. Certainly greater and lesser emphasis may be placed on each stage depending on the transition being made (see van Gennep 1960). However, all three steps of separation, margin and reaggregation, or what we might conceive of, in the case of travel, as departure, journey and return, are crucial to the rite of passage being lived in its entirety. It is for this reason that the effectiveness of rite of passage as an explanatory framework for tourism has been called into question in recent years. As patterns of mobility become ever more complex, as our lives become increasingly globalised, and as communication and social networks extend, it is harder to see travel as a linear process from home to away, ordinary to extraordinary and back again.

Recognised Limitations to the Rite of Passage Model in Tourism Studies

The rite of passage framework may assist in conceptualising the motivations, experiences and behaviours of those who, through travel, undergo some life transition or transformation. However, it has recently been recognised that changes in tourist practice place traditional conceptualisations of the rite of passage model under some strain. For instance, Sørenson (2003), Cohen (2003) and White and White (2007) have all drawn attention to the fact that shifts in traveller communication – especially increases in contact with 'home' when 'away' and with 'away' when 'home' – affect how the rite of passage of travel, and the stages of separation and reaggregation in particular, are experienced. To this end, Sørenson (2003: 861) observes that traveller use of the Internet has 'reframed the conditions for readjustment, by changing the distinction between home and away'. He argues that increased tourist usage of mobile telephone communication, the Internet, video chat, social networking sites and email (initially to maintain social networks at home and later to communicate with fellow travellers) means that total separation from everyday life or a complete return to it are unlikely (Sørenson 2003). This in turn raises significant questions regarding the nature of the inversion witnessed in the rite of passage of travel (Cohen 2003).

So too does Bell's (2002: 150) observation that as travel becomes increasingly common there arises 'a greater possibility of going to visit' loved ones who are abroad. She argues that this increased mobility, along with growing use of telephone and email communication, results in a situation whereby 'the emotion engendered by the OE [overseas experience] farewell has diminished' (Bell 2002: 150). This diminished emotion is explained by Bell (2002) with reference to an increasingly reduced level of physical and/or social separation in travel, as well as the increasingly routine nature of some international journeys.

Also linked with the routinisation of travel and a growing recognition of some of its more quotidian components, is Lean's (2012: 160) argument that 'reality-maintaining elements' of a personal kind (such as emotional baggage, memory, personal roles and responsibilities, and routine performances) often accompany individuals on their journeys. While Lean (2012) points to the unpredictable nature of transformation, arguing that some experience this because of – not in spite of – these 'reality maintaining elements', it is clear that others inevitably feel that the extraordinariness promised by tourism (and on which transformation is often assumed to hang) is undermined by the haunting spectre of the everyday.

Further complicating this situation is the fact that, thanks to globalisation, many travel destinations are no longer as alternate or remote (physically, socio-culturally and in some cases psychologically or emotionally) as they may once have been. For young travellers, this is particularly so as backpacking becomes increasingly mainstream or institutionalised (see for example, O'Reilly 2006) and as backpacker enclaves, often littered with home luxuries, emerge to cater to the needs and desires of independent travellers (Maoz 2007, Noy and Cohen 2005, Wilson and Richards 2008). Furthermore, for many tourists travel is no longer a 'one-time-only' affair and this again poses a challenge to traditional rite of passage models. Noy and Cohen (2005) note, for instance, growth in 'trampoline' or 'serial' backpackers, and Scott Cohen's (2011) work on lifestyle travellers, those for whom travel is envisioned as a way of life and thus an ongoing rather than transitional state, also brings the idea of reincorporation or reaggregation into question.

These observations point to the need for a fuller examination of how the liminal or liminoid space of travel is experienced, and by extension, how the rite of passage of travel is lived. While there is not scope in this chapter to examine all of the nuances of the liminal lives of those backpacking, the analysis will, from here in, focus on the extent to which the liminoid travel space provides separation from 'everyday' life and, in so doing, attempt to address at least one of these recent critiques. Namely, that communication with home disrupts the rite of passage of travel. More specifically, drawing on extensive ethnographic fieldwork conducted within the backpacking community (in Central and North America, the United Kingdom and Europe, Central and South-East Asia) and in-depth interviews conducted with 35 young Australian backpackers (who at the time of interview were immersed in the travel space), the remaining sections of this chapter will interrogate the freedom and permissiveness of the liminal space of travel. In so doing, the chapter will also examine backpacker communitas, backpacker experiences of time and space and the interconnections between such experiences and feelings of transformation and transition.

Living Liminally: Applying the Rite of Passage Framework to the Backpacker Experience

As I have discussed elsewhere (Matthews 2008, 2009), there is a deep-seated sense of freedom which pervades the extended periods of international travel which young backpackers commonly embark on. Freedom (along with authenticity) is advertised and promoted in tourism marketing materials, actively sought by backpackers, and oftentimes, felt and then recounted in their travel narratives (Matthews 2009). For instance, Jessica, a 22-year-old interview participant that I met in Guatemala, observed that she 'took off overseas' five days after completing her university education and that with her 'studies out of the way' she felt she was '*free* to do whatever' she wanted (emphasis mine). Similarly, Casey, a 26-year-old email interviewee, recalled that she had chosen to go backpacking because she had 'finished university', her 'mate was going' and she wasn't yet ready to 'deal with stuff' in Australia. Travel was positioned by her as a viable alternative to 'starting a career' at home and as a means of being able to 'see the world and explore it', and she noted, herself, '*free* from the pressures' of where she had grown up (emphasis mine).

Such explanations are not unusual. Most of the backpackers that I have encountered during ethnographic fieldwork have framed at least some of their travels in this way, with constant references made to the difference, newness, transience, opportunity or escape that travel provides. In addition, the idea that travel presents a break (or separation) from routine, structure and from the social pressures of being known is a common trope to many backpacker narratives. Mel, a 24-year-old interviewee who I met while she was living, working and travelling in Europe, observed for instance that:

> You can do whatever you want [overseas] because at home everyone knows you and knows what you're meant to be like and so you are always sort of in that mould ... Whereas here you can let loose and you don't care ... You do what you want and you don't think about the consequences ... At home ... you're sort of worrying about what other people are thinking or what your friends are thinking ... here you just lose your inhibitions.

These comments point to the significance that separation from home continues to have for the rite of passage of travel. Despite the fact that the majority of backpackers encountered in this research maintained some connection with friends and family at home (typically via email, mobile communications and/or video chat), and despite the fact that many reported crossing multiple thresholds (arriving in a new place, settling there for some time and then departing once more for another *new* town, city or country), physical, if not social, separation still held for them a symbolic power. Being overseas was frequently seen as the key to being anonymous (if they wanted to be) and to being able to embrace a more opportunistic, open and spontaneous lifestyle. In keeping with this perception, a number of interviewees spoke of the pleasure they took from being able to live a more 'open ended', less structured life while in the travel space and of being able to make spur of the moment decisions. In addition, many spoke of purposively constructing different identities for themselves to those they had at home and shared stories of being more willing to try new things and adopting more adventurous outlooks while abroad.

Overall then, travel was conceived by most of the backpackers in this research as being extraordinary. A few recognised that travelling could occasionally become repetitive or even tiresome and a number of the working holiday makers that I spoke to also reflected on the way in which once extraordinary sights or experiences, or foreign destinations, could become ordinary and familiar with time. These points notwithstanding, for the most part emphasis was placed on the new opportunities, relationships and experiences that presented through travel and the transformative effects these had on conceptualisations of self, home, significant others and, in some cases, even the world. Behavioural inversions that were recounted by interviewees as examples of new and extraordinary experiences they had had while abroad included: eating different foods, learning new languages, engaging in different leisure activities (such as hot air ballooning, hiking, scuba diving and skiing), hitch-hiking and living communally (commonplace in most backpacker hostels). Other research participants spoke of working in new or different jobs, meeting people and forming friendships that they wouldn't ordinarily, increased sexual freedom, consumption of illicit drugs and excessive alcohol consumption. While the latter more hedonistic elements were not reported by all interviewees, the following comments offer insight into how such behaviours were commonly conceived of within the backpacking space – as an intrinsic or normal part of the overseas experience:

> I'd never been pissed [drunk] for so many nights in a row [as I was on my European tour] ... Like, I'm not a hard drinker, in that if it was a celebration, then yes [I'd have a few drinks] ... [but on tour] I did go for twenty days straight drinking. (Claudia, age 19, face-to-face interview)

> A ski resort is not real. I mean it took a few weeks for me to settle in ... because ... at first I was like 'Wow, I have nothing in common with these people!' But after a few weeks I was like 'Wow I'm having so much fun!' ... [Living and working there] I partied like I've never partied in my life ... every night, every second night, just spent y'know drunk to the point where you can't move ... And then you go into work the next morning two hours after you've gone to sleep ... It's just crazy. Like you sleep, you barely sleep, you just party all the time and you work a bit and it's so much fun. (Jessica, age 22, face-to-face interview)

In many of the backpacker narratives that I was privy to there was an acknowledgement that some of what goes on in the liminal space of ski resorts, backpacker hostels, traveller bars and tour buses is in fact *abnormal*, but that it becomes accepted as a way of life when travelling. So much so that some of the ritual inversions common to the travel space – which aren't always inversions per se, but often extensions or amplifications of behaviour that may have been indulged in less frequently at home – seem to help backpackers form strengthened bonds with one another. Thus, though it is easy to see some of these liminal behaviours as trivial, irresponsible, harmful or risky, or simply just as a bit of 'fun' (and backpackers conceive of them oftentimes as all of these things), I would argue that it is important to recognise that they are also behaviours that contrast significantly with home lifestyles and which, when shared, engender a sense of commonality or communitas. Subsequently, many young travellers report such behaviours as being integral to the strengthened bonds they experienced with other backpackers and to a newly developed sense of self or *transformed* identity.

Take, for instance, Jessica's comment above. While she explains that at first she felt that she had nothing in common with the people she lived and worked with in the ski resort, that she was, in a sense, *too* different from them, she notes that after she became more accustomed to the way of life there – that is, after she became accustomed to the liminal behaviours that were 'normal' in that environment – she had a lot of fun and made a lot of friends. Incidentally, she also attested later in the interview to the lasting impact of these and other travel friendships and experiences on her identity and new-found outlook on life. Observing for instance that, travel had changed her 'in every way' and that:

> If I had spent the last seventeen months at home I would be in no way even near who I am right now and I am so grateful for that. It's amazing to me how much I have changed and how much I have grown … [I am] more outgoing, [more willing to] try new things … completely independent of any need of anyone, of anything really … [I am] strong enough to do what I'm doing, like confident enough to go around and make friends wherever I go [and to] … attract people that I want to. Like, [that] I respect, y'know?

In this, Jessica's story is not unique. The following accounts from Mel and Christina also speak to the significance of shared experience (not always hedonistic, but often intensified because of the separation from home) to traveller relationships and, by extension, to the impacts of these relationships and interactions on oneself:

> Because you are away from home and … you're doing the same thing as the people here, like you're all in the same boat … I think … [the connection between people is] just sort of a lot stronger … I mean you've got your friends at home and they'll always be your friends and everything … but I think you make friends a lot more quickly here as well … It's sort of instantaneous. Whereas at home that's not really the case … travel does open up your eyes and it just makes you realize there is so much more out there. Even just hearing [about] other peoples' travel experiences as well, like in hostels [where] people have been to all these weird and wonderful places … that just opens your eyes up. (Mel, age 24, face-to-face interview)

> I think the way you strike up quick and intense friendships with people, I think that's part of travelling … [whereas] the way things are structured say in your

normal working environment [that] isn't necessarily the case. Because when you're travelling on your own you do need people and you're much more receptive to new experiences and new people ... so many of my friends who haven't travelled, even the ones who have, are so alien [removed] from my experiences ... that they don't understand why I've done things ... [So] I don't think it would be hard to go back [to Australia] and make friends. But I think those friends would change compared to the ones I had when I went away ... I've met some absolutely amazing people travelling, who I hope I'll stay in contact with for a really long time and I wouldn't give that experience up for anything. (Christina, age 26, face-to-face interview)

It is clear from these comments that it is the travel environment which is understood as enabling fast or instantaneous bonds to develop between backpackers and that these fast and firm friendships are deemed to be personally significant. Taking this analysis one step further though it is also notable that many research participants spoke throughout their interviews about the difference between relationships at home and relationships overseas and pointed to the fact that while they maintained regular communication with friends and family at home, it was not necessarily the same as the communication they had with their fellow backpackers or co-liminars. Some felt that friends and family at home could not relate to their experience – or did not want to relate to their experience – in the same way as other travellers could. Subsequently, they tended to turn more and more to their fellow travellers for support, guidance and company. Others felt that in the travel space time was compressed in such a way as to strengthen bonds with fellow backpackers whilst distancing them from those friends and family at home, who in many cases were not only living their lives to different rhythms, but were in fact in different time zones. In short, *through* communication with home, some backpackers turned further inward to the liminal space of travel. So rather than communication with home disrupting separation and by extension the promise of liminality, which is what has been pointed to by authors like Cohen (2003), Sørenson (2003) and White and White (2007), communication with home can, for some travellers at least, be understood as *reinforcing* separation and encouraging liminality.

In a sense feedback from friends and family at home can be understood as adding a new dimension to backpackers' understandings of, and appreciation for, the liminal travel moment. Communication with home reaffirmed for some interviewees the strength of the bonds they had with their fellow travellers and, in some cases therefore, increased the sense of socio-cultural separation from home. For others it also served as a reminder, at times when travel was at risk of becoming a little ordinary, of its extraordinariness. The following observation is illustrative of this:

My friends are mostly envious ... when you tell people what you're doing they're like, 'wow, that sounds really amazing!' ... I find it really good to hear [that] because sometimes you just get used to what you're doing and you just become accustomed to it. And then you start telling people about your trip or whatever and they're like 'wow, that's really cool, that's really amazing, you're so lucky!' and you think 'yeah, like I really am, it's really cool!' (Natalie, age 22, face-to-face interview)

So, while contact with home may well prove an interruption to immersion in the liminal space of travel, in other instances it can also enhance one's experiences. As travel becomes mundane or monotonous, as it becomes more everyday than extraordinary, communication with those outside of the liminal space helps highlight the 'Otherness' that backpackers are immersed in. To this end, I would argue that contact with home does not necessitate an end to liminality or necessarily undermine the transformative possibilities of the rite of passage of travel. Rather, for some travellers at least, communication with home may act as a counterpoint to the travel state and can thus trigger a deeper, more reflexive engagement with the liminal space: a reflexive engagement which, given the importance of reflection to transformation (Lean 2012), is likely to increase rather than decrease the likelihood of backpackers experiencing transition, change or growth through travel.

Conclusion

Rites of passage are conceived invariably as 'times out of time' or as social spaces in which things increasingly come to be 'judged by [a] … criteria of the permissible' (Abrahams 1986: 62) and where 'new options for experience and relation that are not possible, or desired, within the constraints of established, conventional order' (Rowe 2008: 130) become more readily available. Rites of passage then – particularly the marginal or liminal phase of rites of passage – are understood as giving rise to 'unique structures of experience' (Turner 1986: 41).

This chapter has considered how permissibility plays out in the travel space, examining the way in which it is encouraged by the traveller's absence from home and the unique behaviours, feelings or experiences that it generates. In short, the chapter has been concerned with examining how the rite of passage of travel – and in particular the middle stage of that rite of passage, liminality – is lived and how living liminally can in turn foster transformation. Though the analysis presented in this chapter is restricted to a specific group of travellers (namely, young backpackers), by seeking to 'flesh-out' how the rite of passage of travel is lived, it responds to recent calls for studies that capture the travel experience in more detail. In addition, it addresses some of the questions that have recently been raised with respect to the applicability of the rite of passage heuristic in tourism studies and sheds light on what Lean (2012: 160) refers to as the 'layers of complexity' that underpin the 'notion of transformation through travel'.

More specifically, taking as my starting point the idea that travel represents a geographic separation from home and is commonly configured as providing a temporal and social shift away from the everyday, I have argued in this chapter that the travel space *is* a liminal space: a space 'betwixt and between'. Configured as providing a break from routine, freedom from the pressures of home, as fostering anonymity, opportunity and as a space governed by different social rules, I have demonstrated, drawing on backpacker narratives, that the travel lifestyle is characterised in terms of sociability, conviviality, enjoyment and pleasure. These characteristics or qualities, while not unique to backpacking, are exaggerated and enabled by the liminal nature of travel and by the fact that the backpacking environment is positioned as being away from home but also as *different* to home (even if home-like qualities may be present). Despite the questionable nature of 'separation' in a global, networked society, the backpacking environment is also conceived as a space beyond the confines of the usual structures that may divide people (such as occupation, class, nationality or ethnicity) at home and as existing without the deadlines, responsibilities and time constraints (like having to go to work or having responsibility at work) of everyday life.

Such factors result in many backpackers feeling as though time and space have been compressed when travelling: as though things (experiences, relationships, unique encounters) happen faster, more intensely and with more serendipity than usual. This feeling, coupled with the excitement of travel and the experiences, indulgences and attitudes that are shared by backpackers, brings them closer together and fosters, as I have argued above, a sense of communitas. This sense of communitas in turn, along with the affective and behavioural possibilities of the liminal travel space, causes many young backpackers to reflect on the contrasts between their lives at home and lives abroad, in turn encouraging transformation.

While some have questioned the extent to which individuals are able to embrace separation and liminality when contact with home is maintained during the rite of passage of travel, I have argued that feelings of liminality and by extension transformation may continue despite – and in some cases because of – such contact. Ultimately it seems that for many young backpackers there is a significant difference between being temporarily united with home through communication technology and being connected socio-culturally, symbolically and/or spatially. While this may only be the case for a particular sub-group of travellers, it does point to the fact that separation and liminality, as two-thirds of the rite of passage (reaggregation being beyond the scope of this study), are more nuanced than has previously been recognised. Further research which examines this nuance and the intersubjective experience of living liminally is therefore warranted, particularly when it seems likely that it is the intricacies of liminal life which contribute, at least when travel is configured as a rite of passage, to the potential for transformation.

References

Abrahams, R.D. 1986. Ordinary and extraordinary experience, in *The Anthropology of Experience*, edited by V.W. Turner and E.M. Bruner. Urbana and Chicago: University of Illinois Press, 45–72.

Bauman, Z. 1996. From pilgrim to tourist – or a short history of identity, in *Questions of Cultural Identity*, edited by S. Hall and P. du Gay. London: SAGE, 18–36.

Bauman, Z. 2000. *Liquid Modernity*. Cambridge: Polity Press.

Bell, C. 2002. The big 'OE': Young New Zealand travellers as secular pilgrims. *Tourist Studies*, 2(2), 143–58.

Bruner, E.M. 1991. Transformation of self in tourism. *Annals of Tourism Research*, 18(2), 238–50.

Cohen, E. 1972. Towards a sociology of international tourism. *Social Research*, 39(1), 164–89.

Cohen, E. 1979. A phenomenology of tourist experiences. *Sociology*, 13(2), 179–201.

Cohen, E. 2003. Backpacking: Diversity and change. *Tourism and Cultural Change*, 1(2), 95–110.

Cohen, S.A. 2011. Lifestyle travellers: Backpacking as a way of life. *Annals of Tourism Research*, 38(4), 1535–55.

Desforges, L. 1998. Checking out the planet: Global representations/local identities and youth travel, in *Cool Places: Geographies of Youth Culture*, edited by T. Skelton and G. Valentine. London: Routledge, 175–92.

Desforges, L. 2000. Traveling the world: Identity and travel biography. *Annals of Tourism Research*, 27(4), 926–45.

Elsrud, T. 2001. Risk creation in traveling: Backpacker adventure narration. *Annals of Tourism Research*, 28(3), 597–617.

Franklin, A. and Crang, M. 2001. The trouble with tourism and travel theory? *Tourist Studies*, 1(1), 5–22.

Graburn, N.H.H. 1983. The anthropology of tourism. *Annals of Tourism Research*, 10(1), 9–33.

Graburn, N.H.H. 1989. Tourism: The sacred journey, in *Hosts and Guests: The Anthropology of Tourism*, edited by V.L. Smith. Philadelphia: University of Pennsylvania Press, 21–36.

Hom Cary, S. 2004. The tourist moment. *Annals of Tourism Research*, 31(1), 61–77.

Lean, G.L. 2012. Transformative travel: A mobilities perspective. *Tourist Studies*, 12(2), 151–72.

Lett, J.W. 1983. Ludic and liminoid aspects of charter yacht tourism in the Carribbean. *Annals of Tourism Research*, 10(1), 35–56.

MacCannell, D. 1989. *The Tourist: A New Theory of the Leisure Class*. New York: Schocken Books.

Maoz, D. 2007. Backpackers' motivations: The role of culture and nationality. *Annals of Tourism Research*, 34(1), 122–40.

Matthews, A. 2008. Backpacking as a contemporary rite of passage: Victor Turner and youth travel practices, in *Victor Turner and Contemporary Cultural Performance*, edited by G. St John. New York: Berghahn Books, 174–89.

Matthews, A. 2009. Living paradoxically: Understanding the discourse of authentic freedom as it emerges in the travel space. *Tourism Analysis*, 14(2), 165–74.

Noy, C. 2004. This trip really changed me: Backpackers' narratives of self-change. *Annals of Tourism Research*, 31(1), 78–102.

Noy, C. and Cohen, E. 2005. Introduction: Backpacking as a rite of passage in Israel, in *Israeli Backpackers: From Tourism to Rite of Passage*, edited by C. Noy and E. Cohen. Albany: State University of New York Press.

O'Reilly, C.C. 2006. From drifter to gap year tourist: Mainstreaming backpacker travel. *Annals of Tourism Research*, 33(4), 998–1017.

Robinson, M. and Jamal, T. 2009. Conclusions: Tourism studies – past omissions, emergent challenges, in *The SAGE Handbook of Tourism Studies*, edited by M. Robinson and T. Jamal. London: SAGE, 693–701.

Rowe, S. 2008. Modern sports: Liminal ritual or liminoid leisure?, in *Victor Turner and Contemporary Cultural Performance*, edited by G. St John. New York: Berghahn Books, 127–48.

Shields, R. 1991. *Places on the Margin: Alternative Geographies of Modernity*. London: Routledge.

Smith, V.L. 1992. Introduction: The quest in guest. *Annals of Tourism Research*, 19(1), 1–17.

Sørenson, A. 2003. Backpacker ethnography. *Annals of Tourism Research*, 30(4), 847–67.

St John, G. 2008. Trance tribes and dance vibes: Victor Turner and electronic dance music culture, in *Victor Turner and Contemporary Cultural Performance*, edited by G. St John. New York: Berghahn Books, 149–73.

Taylor, J. 2001. Authenticity and sincerity in tourism. *Annals of Tourism Research*, 28(1), 7–26.

Turner, V. 1982. *From Ritual to Theatre: The Human Seriousness of Play*. New York: PAJ Publications.

Turner, V.W. 1986. Dewey, Dilthey, and drama: An essay in the anthropology of experience, in *The Anthropology of Experience*, edited by V.W. Turner and E.M. Bruner. Urbana and Chicago: University of Illinois Press, 33–44.

Turner, V. 1995. *The Ritual Process: Structure and Anti-Structure*. Hawthorn: Aldine de Gruyter.

Turner, V. and Turner, E. 1978. *Image and Pilgrimage in Christian Culture: Anthropological Perspectives*. New York: Columbia University Press.

van Gennep, A. (1960). *The Rites of Passage*. Chicago: University of Chicago Press.

Wang, N. 2000. *Tourism and Modernity: A Sociological Analysis*. Oxford: Pergamon.

White, N.R. and White, P.B. 2004. Travel as transition: Identity and place. *Annals of Tourism Research*, 31(1), 200–18.

White, N.R. and White, P.B. 2007. Home and away: Tourists in a connected world. *Annals of Tourism Research*, 34(1), 88–104.

Wilson, J. and Richards, G. 2008. Suspending reality: An exploration of enclaves and the backpacker experience. *Current Issues in Tourism*, 11(2), 187–202.

Chapter 11

Notes on Strategies for Leaving and Arriving Home

Sarah Rodigari

Dear Everyone

I am writing this in the hope that you will read this and decide to join me on my walk at some point.

On Saturday June 4, I will be leaving Melbourne and moving home to Sydney, on foot. I will walk four hours a day, more or less. It will take me two months, more or less. Most times I will camp, sometimes I will have to stay in a motel or if I'm lucky enough, someone, like you or a friend of yours will take me in for the night.

I will be following the train line so it is easy to meet me. You can walk for a day, you can stay the night, you can walk again the next day or longer if you wish. There is room in my tent but you're better off bringing your own, as well as food and please dress for the weather.[1]

Introduction

Travel evokes a sense of movement from one place to another, both literally and metaphorically. One could argue that in travel we search for what we cannot find at home. We travel to create distance and gain perspective. It is a space in which to find adventure and seek new horizons. Art, like travel, offers an alternative way to see and consider the world around us. Both offer a necessary distance for transformation to occur in which we leave our familiar environment to enter another. These notions are not without their problems. Is transformation inherent in the act of travel? In this chapter I address this question through my own experience of travel and transformation in the artwork *Strategies for Leaving and Arriving Home* in which I leave one home and return to another through long-distance walking. As an artist I consider physical, emotional and historical responses to making art as a way to investigate and articulate relations between the individual and the social world. Sitting within the genealogy of walking in art by artists such as Richard Long and Marina Abramović, *Strategies for Leaving and Arriving Home* was a six-week performative walk in which I relocated from Melbourne to Sydney (almost 1,000 kilometres) on foot. Throughout this time, the public were invited to participate by either walking with me or contributing to the project

---

1 *Strategies for Leaving and Arriving Home* blog: http://longestwaytoleave. wordpress.com/the-strategies [accessed: 10 August 2012].

blog.[2] In this chapter I investigate the transformative relationship between this artwork and its audience. I place particular focus on how the mediation of the audience changes the nature of the walk, the notion of travel and consequently this project. As this artwork takes place outside of the theatre, the 'audience' in this context is not considered in a traditional sense, as people seated in front of the stage; rather, they are referred to as 'participants' who, to various degrees, engage with the artwork by walking with me or through reading the blog. Art historian Claire Bishop (2006) describes participation in art as a *medium* that involves the audience as collaborators, co-producers and co-authors. Just as a painter uses pigment and canvas, the participatory artist uses participation to create an artwork. Inherent in this collaborative process, the participants and the artist transform the artwork and potentially themselves.

Beyond the literal movement of the action of walking from one place to another, the complexities of this project suggest how transformation might occur in the metaphysical space of 'sympathetic magic' (a form of empathy through which participants sometimes experience an artwork) found in the process of walking as a work of art. James Frazer (1922) first introduced the term 'sympathetic magic' in his classic anthropological text *The Golden Bough: A Study in Magic and Religion*. Frazer defines sympathetic magic as a performance of a symbolic object or an action in a ritual, with the hope of effecting change in a person or the course of an event. I argue that the conceptual premise of the artwork, the framework of participation and narratives of adventure, fear and nostalgia found by participants in the history of the surrounding landscape of my walk opened a space for sympathetic magic whereby the participants saw themselves in the artwork. As a result they experienced a metaphysical transformation as well as transformed the artwork, and in turn myself, without literally having to travel.

Concept

In 2011 I relocated 880 kilometres from Melbourne to Sydney in the middle of winter on foot. On my back I carried a tent, a sleeping bag and a four-day supply of food. As there was no designated walking route, I mapped out my own path, choosing to follow the train line as best I could. When this was not possible I followed the Hume Highway. It was not the most picturesque route, but it kept me close to food, water, safety and accommodation. I walked approximately 20 kilometres per day. There was no support vehicle; instead, I invited people to be my support by walking with me or joining me via the *Strategies for Leaving and Arriving Home* blog.

Walking in art can be traced back to dematerialised conceptual artworks developed in the late 1960s. These works marked a shift away from the institutional

2 *Strategies for Leaving and Arriving Home* blog: http://longestwaytoleave. wordpress.com [accessed: 10 August 2012].

art object housed in museums and galleries and out into public space.[3] The term 'dematerialisation', coined by art theorist Lucy Lippard in the early 1970s, referred to conceptual artworks that gave preference to the *idea* over the object (Lippard 1973). Dematerialisation emphasised a method of art making that shifted away from fixed or stable objective positions for both the spectator and the artwork, towards a renegotiation of this relationship. For example, Allan Kaprow's 'happenings' involved actions, games and everyday activities (such as brushing your teeth) in which both the performers and the audience (blurring the distinction between the two) performed the action. The structure of Kaprow's happenings allowed the audience to contribute to the artwork through participation. By focusing on the body and its relationship to space, art shifted its focus from product to process, from object to action, making the *relationship* between the artist and the audience paramount. Working within this tradition, *Strategies for Leaving and Arriving Home* invited participants to share in the making of an ephemeral artwork. This negotiated relationship offers a space in which the experience of travel is redefined through multiple perspectives. In turn, this creates a collective understanding of transformation as something that happens *in relation to others*.

In 1995, Suzanne Lacy coined the term 'New Genre Public Art' to describe dematerialised public art. Rather than using the term to denote large steel or concrete sculptures installed in urban places, Lacy challenged artists to think of *communicative actions in public* as a new form of art. She writes, 'what exists in the space between the words public and art is an unknown relationship that may itself be the artwork' (Lacy 1995: 20). Lacy proposes that public artwork is not only situated in the visual and physical qualities of a site (in this case, the Hume Highway), it is also situated in the relationship developed between the artist and the participant during the making of the artwork (relationships formed while walking, or reading and commenting on the blog). The communicative, public nature of this walk created an artwork that was never fixed in a particular place or to a specific definition. Instead it continued to evolve as participants brought their own perspectives to the walk. Participation in relation to this 'site' allows space for sympathetic magic between the artist, the artwork and those who engage with the walk. Dematerialised public art sees the participants actively transform the walk and their relationship to it through what they do and how they respond. By inviting them to contribute to making the artwork, the walk and the notion of travel and transformation become a shared experience.

---

3 *Strategies for Leaving and Arriving Home* was supported by the independent art collective Field Theory (http://www.fieldtheory.com.au) and presented as part of the *Walk* programme curated by Performance Space (http://www.performancespace.com. au) in Sydney.

The Structure of the Walk

The blog was a public framing device for the walk in which I invited others to join me, to share advice, opinions and knowledge. It created a collective space through which others could become involved. It also recorded my progress so participants could join me or track my whereabouts, allowing people to participate virtually, from a distance. Those who walked with me or contributed to the blog could change the nature of the walk by advising an alternative route, or projecting their own stories and opinions onto the walk. The blog was also a tactical public cry for help. I hoped that through the blog people would engage in the walk and, in turn, me. I was genuinely afraid of the journey that lay ahead and from the outset never imagined I would complete the walk. From the start I felt that the only way I would be able to actually do this walk was if people participated in it and created a supportive community around me. My first blog post, seen at the beginning of this chapter, was a public announcement inviting people across all walks of life to join me on this adventure.

Over six weeks, 20 people joined me. On average each person walked with me for two to three days. I camped, stayed with strangers I met along the way, friends of friends, council representatives, and extended family. I also slept in pubs, motels and a bed and breakfast; some were nice, others were horrible. In accordance with the rules that I set myself, I never asked for lifts; however if offered, I could accept them – but only to the next town.[4] I assigned myself the following rather whimsical guidelines as my framework:

- Find the longest way to leave.
- Announce your dramatic departure to be sure there's no turning back.
- Sell everything you've spent the last 10 years collecting on eBay so that you can afford ultra-light, warm, waterproof hiking equipment that you will only use this once.
- Source redundant road maps, scaled 1:2,500 and pin them to the wall across from your bed.
- Spend hours planning the flattest and most direct route, and then acknowledge that it's probably best to just follow the train line.
- Romanticise solitude and anticipate loneliness, invite everyone to join you.[5]

The project blog also included a 'Rules to live by' page, in which I set out four initial guidelines for myself as a means to keep focused and committed to the act of walking. These were:

---

4   *Strategies for Leaving and Arriving Home* blog: http://longestwaytoleave. wordpress.com/about [accessed: 10 August 2012].

5   *Strategies for Leaving and Arriving Home* blog: http://longestwaytoleave. wordpress.com/the-strategies [accessed: 10 August 2012].

1. If someone offers me a lift, I can take it but only to the next town.
2. If it's a matter of safety, which means no place to camp or no road to walk, I can take a train to the next town.
3. If someone offers to carry my pack for me, it's kind, friendly and OK.
4. If I find a puppy, I must keep it.[6]

In addition to these rules displayed on the blog, participants made suggestions such as 'make a point of contact in every town' or 'allocate a rest day once a week'. Following the advice of participants, I took safety precautions by contacting police, local councils, media and walking groups well in advance of my arrival at each destination. I kept a GPS tracking device on me at all times; it did not always work.

Seven million people fly between Melbourne and Sydney each year. This equates to one-third of the Australian population, placing this flight corridor amongst the top five busiest routes in the world. To fly takes an hour. Alternatively you could drive the 880 kilometres between the two cities (over 10 hours along the Hume Highway) or take an 11-hour train ride. To walk this distance is absurd in light of the speed, comfort and accessibility that is now so readily available through discounted airfares. Furthermore the dramatic shift in relation to how we perceive space and time, brought about through the industrialisation of transport, now positions long-distance walking in the realm of leisure activities such as hiking or bushwalking. However, *Strategies for Leaving and Arriving Home* was not a leisure activity and there was no walking trail or guidebooks to follow. The fact that transport between the two cities is a cheap, efficient daily occurrence for many people immediately situates this walk outside of a conventional holiday walking adventure, which begs the question: why would I choose to do such a thing in the first place?

Walking in Art

Walking, as an art experience, can be understood as a symbolic act of territorial transformation, which combines notions of geography, human agency and politics. Two notable artworks that address transformation through walking in art are *A Line Made by Walking* (1967) by conceptual artist Richard Long and *The Great Wall Walk* by performance artists Marina Abramović and Ulay. Richard Long creates sculptural actions by walking through nature. For example, in *A Line Made by Walking* (1967), Long walked back and forth along a straight line in the grass in the English countryside, leaving a track created by his footprints, which he then photographed in black and white. About his artwork, Long states:

---

6 *Strategies for Leaving and Arriving Home* blog: http://longestwaytoleave.wordpress.com/about [accessed: 10 August 2012].

> A walk expresses space and freedom and the knowledge of it can live in the
> memory of anyone ... A walk traces the surface of the land, it follows an idea, it
> follows the day and the night. A road is the site of many journeys. The place of
> a walk is there before a walk and after it. (Long 1980)

Like Kaprow's 'Happenings', Long's process of making art outside the gallery addressed the notion of the artwork as temporary, non-material and performative. As Long suggests, the pedestrian and embodied nature of walking potentially allows for a more diverse audience. Walking is something we can all identify with, and for this reason walking was my chosen form of travel. It was important to me that all people, not just the art community, could relate and engage with the artwork through walking. Transformation in *A Line Made by Walking* is subtle, derived from everyday activity. It is small-scale and could be carried out by anyone. In contrast to this, there is also a dramatic element to my walk that resonates with Abramović and Ulay's *The Great Wall Walk*. Starting from opposite ends of the Great Wall of China, these two artists walked towards each other, meeting in the middle. Their meeting marked the end of the artwork, their collaboration and their personal relationship. Abramović (1995) called this work a spiritual journey in which she reconsidered her relationship to nature. The scale of *The Great Wall Walk* is vast, marking transformation as a psychological and emotional change, brought about through physical action. *Strategies for Leaving and Arriving Home* is both conceptual like Long's walk, and (in hindsight) personal like Abramović and Ulay's.

Through the invitation to participate in my own artwork, I wanted the public to be more focused on their relationship to the walk, and less focused on myself as a 'performance artist'. This meant that during the walk I made little reference to my personal reasons for undertaking such a project, simply stating that the walk was about relocation, and that I wanted to take time to acknowledge and embody this change. Conceptually, the walk would, as Long suggests, remain open for conversation and interpretation in the spaces before and after the literal walk takes place. However, whilst anyone could participate in *Strategies for Leaving and Arriving Home,* I was the only person who walked from start to finish. Therefore, despite my best efforts to draw attention away from my personal reasons for walking, the continuity of my walking meant that like Abramović and Ulay I became a spectacle as I carried out the journey, whilst participants projected their narratives onto me. Borrowing from Long, and resonating with Abramović and Ulay, *Strategies for Leaving and Arriving Home* became a symbolic act of how both the participant and myself define ourselves, and the space around us through this walk.

Transformation

The structure of the walk, the actions, the rules, the letter of invitation, all framed and shared through the blog, suggested that transformation was both desired and feared in the conceptual premise of the artwork. Feeling stifled by my working life in Melbourne, I wanted change – hence the move to Sydney – and yet at the same time I did not want to leave my friends and the lifestyle I loved so much in Melbourne. The underlying question the artwork asked is this: 'Through this action what will become of me? Will I change? If so, how?' The structure of the artwork invited participants to also consider these questions. Their actions and responses to the artwork are implicit in the walk and, as participants began to invest in the artwork, its meaning changed. As I took on their suggestions, I also changed. The relationships between the participants and myself was a connection that moved back and forth as together we explored our own experiences of transformation through the artwork. This is significant when considering sympathetic magic and the role of transformation in travel.

> Thank the heavens you are nearly there Sarah ... what an adventure eh? I want to also say thank you for lifting the spirits of one stuck in an office in 'CBD' Melbourne – when i would have liked nothing more than traipsing the highway with you. You are to be admired for the courage involved and envied for all that you have seen ... you go girl!![7]

This comment was posted by Betty at the end of my walk. Betty followed and contributed to the project via the blog the entire way. This dialogue through the blog is one example of how participants invested and projected themselves into the artwork from a virtual distance. Without literally travelling, she was with me on the walk, projecting her own courage, sense of adventure and narrative of the Hume Highway onto me via the blog. In turn, I was her conduit, walking and enacting her sympathetic experience. It is this image that she has of us *walking the highway together* that propels me along.

Allan Kaprow (1993: 33) suggests that it is necessary to have a relationship between the internal and external motivations in an artwork: 'It's not only the transformation of the public consciousness that we are interested in; it is our own transformation that is important.' During the project, I spent a lot of time questioning my decision to walk. *Strategies for Leaving and Arriving Home* was not solely about inviting people to walk with me, it was also about processing my own difficult decision to move cities. I did not want to leave Melbourne because I loved my daily life there. However, I felt it was time, my parents were getting older, my sister had small children whose lives I wanted to be a part of, and career-wise I thought it best to move to Sydney. In this current globalised economy,

---

7 *Strategies for Leaving and Arriving Home* blog: http://longestwaytoleave. wordpress.com/maps-and-stats/#comment-52 [accessed: 25 June 2013].

moving between cities is common for many people; however, I chose to walk because I wanted to acknowledge my decision and my fears. Walking was a slow form of travel that allowed me to embody my decision, and the distance between the two cities. The walk allowed me space to let go of my past and prepare for my future. Travelling by foot was an opportunity to consider the relationship between my art practice, my life and my sense of place in the world. With every step I hoped to let go of my past, acknowledging the failure and successes and move towards my future. Walking slowly moved me from a point of departure to a point of arrival as I separated from one city and connected to another. Change wasn't immediate; it was slow, and barely noticeable. On a personal level, I romanticised this walk; again resonating with Abramović and Ulay's *The Great Wall Walk*, I put my heart into the walk, believing it was the best solution for coming to terms with the end of my time in Melbourne.

Figure 11.1 From Wagga Wagga to Wantabadgery
Source: Adeo Esplago 2011.

Transformation happens for individual participants as they recognise themselves in *Strategies for Leaving and Arriving Home*. Rebecca Solnit (2000) suggests in her book, *Wonderlust: A History of Walking*, that the universal act of walking becomes significant based on how we invest it with meaning. For example, for me this walk was an act of relocation and a personal quest; however, Liang Luscombe (2011), who followed the blog from Melbourne, noted that 'the rules of the project turned walking into a means of survival, so that performance and life becomes indistinguishable'. Michael-Snape, who didn't walk with me but heard about the walk, felt that 'each literal step was metaphorically suturing the wound between Sydney and Melbourne'.[8]

Narrative

Emerging through conversations conducted during and after the walk, with people I met in person and through online participation, the walk came to embody three major narratives. The first narrative was the 'reality' of a woman walking between Australia's two largest cities, solo in the middle of winter, in a desolate and sometimes dangerous landscape. The second was the dystopian image of the Australian landscape often represented in Australian gothic film narratives – brought about by the brutal history of white settlement, bushrangers and serial killers that accompany the highway. The third narrative was of a nostalgic past that carried family holidays and road trips with friends along the old Hume Highway.[9]

An example of dystopian narrative experienced through participation is found in the week I spent with travelling companion Adeo. Adeo was convinced that the harsh sublime beauty of the landscape just outside of Wagga Wagga in New South Wales was a precursor to a sick fate we were about to meet. Adeo, who during his time with me slept with a knife in his hand, was a film buff and had spent time researching for the walk by watching classic Australian horror films. In the face of the harsh Australian landscape, these films mark the struggle for a white Australian identity in a landscape that is so foreign to a European history. The simple fact that the landscape in Australia is referred to as 'bushland' as opposed to countryside implies a certain encumbrance to it, which is not quite suited to the idea of a romantic European stroll. As a parting gift Adeo gave me his trusty knife.

Violence entered the psyche of the audience and again myself as I approached the outskirts of Sydney, site of the 'Backpacker Murders'. In 1992, the bodies of seven travellers were found buried in the Belanglo State Forest in the Southern Highlands of NSW, just off the Hume Highway, 100 kilometres south of Sydney. The murders were traced to Ivan Milat, a road worker who picked up his victims as they hitch-hiked south along the highway. These murders resonate with the image of desolate towns and an Australian gothic film narrative 'involving inexperienced metropolitan travellers who find themselves stranded in remote and often deranged locations' (Rayner 2001: 28). The eerie abandon of a deserted highway town,

---

8 Taken from a conversation with Agatha Gothe-Snape during the walk, July 2011.

9 I acknowledge the deeply embedded and culturally important significance of Aboriginal history along this stretch of road, and the impact that white Australia's aggressive treatment of Aboriginal Australians has had on the perception of this landscape. However, as this was not directly discussed within this project, and the lack of an Aboriginal narrative in this work is a complex topic better served in a future essay and as such will not be discussed here.

combined with Australia's violent colonial history, adds to the image of a horrific Australian landscape exemplified in Australian gothic films such as *Picnic at Hanging Rock*, *Wake in Fright*, *Patrick*, *Mad Max* and *Wolf Creek*. Film historian Jonathan Rayner suggests that 'the Australian landscape is often depicted as a place of entrapment, where the town is portrayed as a repository for warped or degenerate tendencies ... a place defined by exaggerated violence, aggressive masculinity, misogyny, xenophobia, and corruption' (Rayner 2001: 28). The Australian bush as a harsh and desolate landscape has burnt into the retina of an Australian metropolitan psyche and this is what many people frequently reminded me about (and warned me of) as I walked.

These narratives are also indicative of the varied perspectives of the walk and how the individual relationship to landscape plays a major role in the type of metaphysical experiences conjured via sympathetic magic, especially for those familiar with the route. My action, as the only person walking from start to finish, became a conduit through which the participants began to project their own narratives, definitions and understanding of what the walk was – and in turn transformed their relationship to travel in this walk.

Sympathetic Magic

James Frazer divides the functioning of sympathetic magic into two categories. The first is 'imitation', in which like produces like, or the effect resembles cause, and can be found through the use of objects such as effigies, amulets and voodoo dolls. The second is 'contagion', in which a person is transformed after coming into contact with the object or the action (Frazer 1922: 11). According to Frazer, the most common example of contagion is the relationship between a person and their (detached) body parts: their hair and nails. No matter how far away these parts travel, the person who has them is able to effect change in the person they originally belonged to (Frazer 1922: 11). Both imitation and contagion assume that 'things' act on each other at a distance through a secret sympathy.

Participants 'travelled' in *Strategies for Leaving and Arriving Home* through sympathetic magic. This was experienced as 'imitation' for the primary participants, such as Adeo, who walked with me. They do not literally imitate me – rather they *perform the same action* as me, by walking as well. Sympathetic magic is also experienced as 'contagion' by secondary participants who engaged with the walk from a distance, via the blog. The following quote is an example of such contagion. Harvey was a man who came into contact with the walk by chance, when he met me on a road in Victoria. After he gave me a lift, he continued to stay in touch via the blog:

> Hi Sarah, trust you survived your night in Benalla and today [Friday] have a
> clear, milder day for the walk to Glenrowan. As stated yesterday the section
> from Wangaratta to Wodonga is pretty boring although you have Springhurst
> and Chlitern – birth place of '?' [*sic*]. Enjoyed the conversation yesterday and

look forward to reading all about it! I do recommend detouring at Wang. and going through Beechworth and Yackandandah – both have camping grounds, a little longer but you will come out at Wodonga. Best wishes ...[10]

Through contagion, the secondary participant engages with, is affected by and in turn affects the walk from a distance, without physically walking with me. As a result of Harvey's post, I followed his advice and walked through Beechworth. The participant and the space in which I walked acted on each other: I followed his advice and instructions, and his perceptions of the walk shifted as I continued to move.

Extending on James Frazer's argument for symbolic representation, art historian Jan Verwoert (2011) suggests that sympathetic magic moves *beyond* representation. It creates a deeper understanding of the artwork by the audience. For Verwoert, sympathetic magic is the identification with specific qualities within the artwork that connect with our own sense of self, resulting in a merging of our self and the artwork. In *Strategies for Leaving and Arriving Home*, sympathetic magic is a third space between the actual walk carried out by myself, and the imagined walk projected onto the artwork by the participants. Individuals are able to connect with the work because they identify with the same essential qualities such as adventure, fear and nostalgia, in the three major narratives, which emerged from the walk. Sympathetic magic occurs when the 'art object' acts as a medium through which these qualities (adventure, fear and nostalgia) are channelled. In turn, these qualities define and transform the artwork and its collective environment (the participants). At the tourist information centre in Bundanoon, in the Southern Highlands of New South Wales, I met an older woman who likened my walk to the pilgrimage of the *Camino de Santiago* in Spain. She thought it was a much better idea to undertake a spiritual trip in the country you live in than somewhere else. It was her perspective of the walk that forced me to consider the project as a pilgrimage, which until that point had not crossed my mind. The term pilgrimage acknowledged the walk as a quest for others and myself. It addressed the desire for change, that I kept denying, and the hope that it would come once I reached my final destination.

I liken sympathetic magic[11] to the philosophical notion of empathy, particularly the German term '*einfühlun*', which literally means 'feeling-into'. Empathy implies an emotional or psychological projection of one's self into another. Philosopher Robert Vischer (1872) used the term *einfühlun* in the late nineteenth-century to

---

10   *Strategies for Leaving and Arriving Home* blog: http://longestwaytoleave. wordpress.com/maps-and-stats/#comment-43 [accessed: 25 June 2013].

11   Sympathetic magic, where a person is transformed through the walk and placed in position of the person walking is not to be mistaken for sympathy in this chapter. Sympathy involves feeling 'for or with' as opposed to feeling 'like' or 'into' which is the case of sympathetic magic and einfühlun. For more detail on this see http://oxforddictionaries.com/ definition/english/sympathy?q=sympathy [accessed: 5 May 2013].

describe aesthetic sympathy as an experience or embodied response to an image, object or spatial environment, in particular that of a work of art. Art historian Juliet Koss notes that:

> Einfühlun offered a forum for abstract discussion of the active perceptual experience of the individual spectator ... it provided a potentially uncomfortable destabilisation of identity along the viewer's perceptual borders – a sensation at once physical, psychological and emotional. (2006: 139)

Like *einfühlun*, sympathetic magic is an experience of transformation, as individuals find themselves merging into the work of art without needing to be literally present in the place where the work happens. Both of these terms engage with how we recognise our sense of self and our feelings of comfort or unease in response to places we inhabit. For example, when I passed through small towns of Glenrowan and Gundagai, lost childhood holidays and interstate stopovers at these former tourist destinations leapt to the mind of participants reading the blog. My walking and presence in these dusty and almost forgotten places again created a space for sympathetic magic. For an older generation of participants, a nostalgic folklore for an iconic country Australia came to mind. Bakeries, pubs and vibrant fishing spots were once visited before twenty-first century highway technology paved the way to a faster era, leaving these towns behind.

Concepts such as sympathetic magic and *einfühlun* are significant when we think of travel as a virtual experience that transcends place, bridging different subject positions as well as geographical locations. The space of sympathetic magic happens in the distance between the artwork and the participant – both the actual distance and the metaphysical distance that is created through the artistic structure. This distance is essential when considering alternative modes of transformation in which sympathetic magic as a form of travel and transformation bridges different subject positions (through participation) as well as geographical location (through the blog).

Arrival and Hindsight

I arrived in Sydney with no injuries, no blisters, no aches or pains, no near-death experiences, no harrowing stories to tell, nor any discernible difference in how I felt or looked. The walk I had just undertaken confused me. I had had lofty ambitions of personal transformation on my 'pilgrimage'. I expected to develop a calm and responsive yogic mind, an appreciation for the great outdoors. And yet the creation of a new self through a personal quest was far from the reality of my experience. In truth, there was no sense of nineteenth-century wanderlust, where I would be safely roaming the countryside on groomed paths – the narratives, which emerged along the highway, and the pragmatic path I chose never really allowed for this. I did not sever myself from Melbourne and emerge a new person in Sydney. The dramatic life-changing transformation brought about through travel for Abramović and Ulay in *The Great Wall Walk* did not happen for me in my walk – at least not in a way I thought it would. Transformation happened through the open and shared conceptual structure of the walk, one that allowed participants to create personal narratives along the highway and in turn multiple perspectives of the same artwork. The complexity of this relationship created a metaphysical space for sympathetic magic, redefining the walk without participants literally having to travel.

As participants projected their own narratives of the walk onto me, their conduit for sympathetic magic, travel and transformation in this artwork was revealed to me as a series of small movements through which we define ourselves between the landscape and each other. Implied in the title *Strategies for Leaving And Arriving Home*, from the outset this project suggested a vulnerability in travel, which rather than connoting passivity or uncertainty, allowed for movement and change that could only happen in relation to others. By stepping into the work and inviting others to join me and share this consideration, the walk literally and slowly developed strategies for letting go of one home, of one notion of ourselves, and returning to another, which was not grandiose, rather it was difficult to detect through its intersubjectivity.

References

Abramović, M. 1995. *Marina Abromovic: Objects Performance, Video, Sound*, edited by C. Iles. Oxford: Museum of Modern Art Oxford.

Bishop, C. 2006. Viewers as producers, in *Participation*, edited by C. Bishop. London: Whitechapel, 10–16.

Frazer, J.S. 1922. *The Golden Bough: A Study in Magic and Religion*. New York: Macmillan.

Kaprow, A. 1993. *Essays on the Blurring of Art and Life*, edited by J. Kelley. Berkeley: University of California Press.

Koss, J. 2006. On the limits of empathy. *The Art Bulletin*, 88(1), 139–57.

Lacy, S. 1995. Cultural pilgrimages and metaphoric journeys, in *Mapping the Terrain*, edited by S. Lacy. Seattle: Bay Press, 19–47.

Lippard, L. 1973. *Six Years: The Dematerialization of the Art Object from 1966 to 1972*. New York: Praeger.

Luscombe, L. 2011. Walking is not a medium it's an attitude, *Un Magazine*, 5(2), 6–13.

Rayner, J. 2001. Gothic definitions: The new Australian cinema of horrors. *Antipodes*, 25(1), 91–7.

Solnit, R. 2000. *Wonderlust: A History of Walking*. London: Penguin.

Vischer, R. 1872. *On the Optical Sense of Form: A Contribution to Aesthetics*. Leipzig: Credener.

Film and Video References

Mad Max (dir. George Miller, 1979).
Patrick (dir. Richard Franklin, 1978).
Picnic at Hanging Rock (dir. Peter Wier, 1975).
Wake in Fright (dir. Ted Kotcheff, 1971).
Wolf Creek (dir. Greg Mclean, 2005).
Verwoert, J. 2011. *The Devils in the Thing Talk to the Devils out There: Sculpture, Manufacture, Juju-Magic.* Paper given at Portrait of Space Dublin, 9–11 September 2011 [Online]. Available at: http://www.youtube.com/user/GillespieTeresa/featured [accessed: 25 February 2012].

Artwork and Performance References

Abramović, M. and Ulay. 1988. *The Great Wall Walk.* A Performance. China.
Long, R. 1967. *A Line Made by Walking.* A Sculpture Made by Walking in the Landscape. England.
Long, R. 1980. *Five, Six, Pick Up Sticks, Seven, Eight, Lay Them Straight.* Offset lithograph on paper. London.

PART IV
Marking Transformation

Chapter 12

Facebook and Facelifts: Communities of Cosmetic Surgery Tourists

Meredith Jones, David Bell, Ruth Holliday, Elspeth Probyn and
Jacqueline Sanchez Taylor

Introduction

Cosmetic surgery has risen in developing and overdeveloped parts of the world and has steadily become a notable part of mainstream cultures (Haiken 1997). In the last decade, parts of the cosmetic surgery industry have become globalised and somewhat borderless: surgeons train and work in multiple countries, patients travel to undertake operations, diasporic healthcare communities establish, and associated tourism industries flourish (Bell et al. 2011). Cosmetic surgery *tourism* comes under the umbrella of medical tourism, which can be broadly characterised as 'a growing transnational circulation of patients, capital, and biomedical objects and knowledge' (Ackerman 2010: 404). Medical tourism is surrounded by questions about relationships between wealth and access to healthcare, equity and exploitation in developing economies, flows of labour, and patient safety (see Connell 2011).

This chapter focuses on data collected as part of an international multi-site and multi-disciplinary collaborative project exploring cosmetic surgery tourism, *Sun, Sea, Sand and Silicone*.[1] We explore how cosmetic surgery tourists use social media to conduct research and then to navigate, document and narrate their experiences. Our approach builds on feminist work around cosmetic surgery that Victoria Pitts-Taylor has called 'post-essentialist' (2009, see also Fraser 2003, Jones 2008). A post-essentialist approach refuses 'to valorise an authentic, natural female body or a proper female subjectivity' while insisting that 'we must think of the meanings of bodily practices like cosmetic surgery as neither solely internal nor external but rather as intersubjective' (Pitts-Taylor 2009: 122). Post-essentialist analyses of cosmetic surgery see it as a practice that is formed through interknit actors, including: technologies, media, patients, discourses, surgeons and narratives.

---

1   This project runs from 2011 to 2014 and is funded by the Economic and Social Research Council (UK). See http://www.gender-studies.leeds.ac.uk/research/cosmetic-cultures/aesthetic-surgery-tourism.php. It focuses on Australians who travel to undergo cosmetic surgery in Thailand and Malaysia, Chinese who travel to South Korea and Britons who visit Spain, Poland, Tunisia and the Czech Republic.

Crucially, this mode of analysis does not seek to find reasons for cosmetic surgery in the psyches of individuals but rather to examine the complex medical, cultural and economic networks in which cosmetic surgery unfolds. It posits a nexus between materialities (of bodies and spaces) and communications that together create the cosmetic surgery tourism experience. We propose a reversal of John Urry's (2003) notion of 'meetingness' to argue that the experience of cosmetic surgery, a corporeal process, is enhanced and even co-created by digital communications. The body is not only surgically shaped into existence, but also called forth via new media that provide platforms for 'little narratives' (Poster 2001: 621). In this way the identity-making that cosmetic surgery tourists enact happens physically and discursively, with their transformations happening at home, abroad and online.

Cosmetic Surgery and Narrative

Cosmetic surgery tourism has grown hand-in-hand with online media, through which patients contact agents,[2] seek surgical information, view the qualifications and experience of medical professionals, book flights and accommodation, and see pictures of hospitals and locations (Holliday et al. 2013). Indeed, it is argued that cosmetic surgery tourism, and medical tourism more broadly, could not exist without the Internet (Cormany and Baloglu 2011). Since the arrival of Web 2.0, the ubiquity of social networking sites like Facebook and YouTube means that online media now also provide accessible space for peer-to-peer networking, planning, community building and storytelling between cosmetic surgery tourists. At once paralleling the rise of 'virtual tourism' and of online health-related networks, cosmetic surgery tourism is a densely mediated phenomenon even as it is profoundly embodied (for discussion of online patient communities see for example Radin 2006).

Rebecca Huss-Ashmore analysed conversations between cosmetic surgery patients, cosmetic surgeons and associated practitioners, and found that for most patients cosmetic surgery is a positive experience described in terms of 'transformation' and 'healing' (2000: 29). Importantly, she suggested that transformation and healing do not come about because of surgery alone, but also through narrative. She noted that language in the clinic is paramount and listened to how narratives were created, recreated and performed by patients and medical practitioners before and after surgeries. Huss-Ashmore insisted that discursive and corporeal aspects of the surgical process are intertwined and that cosmetic surgery successes therefore occur:

---

2   Cosmetic surgery tourism agents, or consultants, sell and facilitate packages for travellers that can include fares, accommodation, surgeries, spa treatments, shopping trips and resort-stays.

through the creation and acting out of a therapeutic narrative, a lived story in which the 'me I want to be' or the 'me I really am' is brought into being through the linguistic, emotional, and physical experience of surgery and recovery. (2000: 32)

This language/surgery overlap in cosmetic surgery has also been examined by Carole Spitzack, who describes the surgeon–patient relationship as one where physical 'imperfection is "cured" through complex and overlapping mechanisms of confession and surveillance' (1988: 38; see also Gimlin 2013: 104). While Spitzack and Huss-Ashmore concentrate on practitioner–patient interactions, we are interested in the ways that cosmetic surgery tourists tell their stories to each other and to a wider, sometimes public, audience, specifically through social media. We discuss how cosmetic surgery tourists interact through and deploy social media before, during and after travel, and show how social media are part of the network or assemblage that creates both cosmetic surgery tourism and cosmetic surgery-altered bodies. In our discussion we take a temporal approach, using the familiar time-slices of before, during and after that structure many cosmetic surgery and tourism narratives.

Before Cosmetic Surgery Tourism

Research and Responsibility

We have shown in related research that cosmetic surgery tourism industries exist through and within online spaces, and indeed that the rise of cosmetic surgery tourism cannot be separated from the growth of the Internet (Holliday et al. 2013, also see Cormany and Baloglu 2011). Without digital modes of communication, contemporary cosmetic surgery tourism would not exist; interviewees told us these media were central to finding out about procedures and places. Nearly all spoke about beginning their cosmetic surgery tourism experience online, looking at the websites of surgeons, hospitals and agents: 'Well, everyone goes online, right, so I started online' (Bianca, Australia to Thailand).

As they make the decision to move away from national health schemes and beyond home-country regulations (and as there are still very few regulations or laws about provision of cosmetic surgery to non-nationals), patients take on the burden of responsibility for their choices of destination, surgeon, agent, recovery, etc. Most cosmetic surgery tourists have researched procedures and places thoroughly, many have taken years: 'it's something you need to research, you can't just go "oh yeah that's cheap I'll have that". You know, you've gotta look into it' (Sam, Australia to Thailand). So, before embarking on cosmetic surgery tourism, prospective patients become online researchers, picking their way through different sources of information and advice.

We are not concerned here with making claims for how cosmetic surgery tourists *should* do their research or whether they are qualified to conduct such research. Rather, we note that many patients feel an imperative to do the best research they can: 'I looked up Bumrungrad and it's like the second best hospital in the world or something ... I looked up all the surgeons, couldn't find a bad word about them, absolutely researched everything' (Anna, Australia to Thailand). Most were confident about the amount of information and knowledge they had developed prior to surgery and travel, and some strongly defended the adequacy of their own investigations: 'everyone always thinks the worst and then you hear the horror stories but they haven't realised how much I've looked into it and researched' (Sam, Australia to Thailand).

There are crucial differences between websites – such as those maintained by hospitals – and social media. Websites are reasonably stable, looking much the same from week to week, with content that has been previously determined by their producers. If reader comment is invited, it can be moderated, removed or edited. Websites therefore tend to be non-interactive and static. They are sources for information and knowledge that have been curated by professionals. They also, of course, act as advertisements, and so can be seen as somewhat untrustworthy (on tourism websites and trust, see Wilson and Suraya 2004; for a discourse analysis of official tourism websites, see Hallett and Kaplan-Weinger 2010). Social media pages, in contrast, change from day to day as individuals contribute and comment. Most social media platforms moderate or remove only comments that are illegal or that violate rules about racism or vilification and the majority of content in social media is user/consumer generated (Hjorth 2007). Our interviewees were almost uniformly aware of differences between social and more traditional online media, and tended to use both 'static' websites and Facebook or forums in their pre-surgery research:

> I thought 'well I'm not stupid, I wouldn't jump into something' so I thought I would research other companies as well. I compared, I looked at before and after photos of that doctor and researched his work and then I looked at other surgeons as well ... I'd researched the implants which were meant to be the best. I knew that the way he does things, he's very precise, I'd read lots of testimonials, not just from [the agent's] website but on forums. (Monique, Australia to Thailand)

Monique's research, using a mix of websites and social media, is typical. She saw these two forms of Internet-based research as working in tandem with neither having more authority than the other. We found that for most cosmetic surgery tourists, patient testimonials were very important. One interviewee noted that social media can provide things that are lacking on more formal websites, especially in terms of reassurance and emotional support:

> the fact that there are so many questions on a lot of these message boards and a lot of confusion and anxiety it just goes to show that there must be loads of

surgeons that aren't really providing people with the reassurance with what is normal, what is not normal and what we should be looking out for and all that kind of thing because that information just doesn't seem to be there. (Louise, UK to Belgium)

This 'word of mouse' (Yeoh et al. 2013) mirrors the offline 'word of mouth' routinely identified as a key decision-making resource for cosmetic surgery patients, including tourists; it is also a building block for forms of affinity and community, as we discuss below.

Armchair Travellers

Andre Jansson (2002) argues that consumer-generated media allow tourists to travel emotionally and cognitively without actually travelling in space. In this way they can be informed 'armchair travellers', 'experiencing' places before travelling. This is perhaps more important for cosmetic surgery tourists than others. For them, armchair travelling facilitates familiarity and reduces the strain of the unknown. Many scrutinised photos or videos of previous patients:

there was a lady on [Facebook] that had a tummy tuck and I thought, yeah, that's what I want. I knew I wanted a tummy tuck but that particular picture of that particular lady made me say, yeah, I'm going with [this agent] because that result was brilliant. (Neil, UK to Czech Republic and Poland)

There are some mainlanders posted something like interview videos about the procedures of plastic surgery. They posted online to let others to see if they think the surgery outcome is ok. I found it by accident and later found the link to browse the hospital's website. Then I called to make inquiries. Then everything went well. (Lun, China to Korea)

In cosmetic surgery tourism, it is the stories told by previous recipients that are often of most value to those in the anticipatory phases of their journeys. Engaging with others online, chatting or sharing images, helps to remove the element of surprise, so that people feel they are travelling to a more familiar place, for a procedure that is also becoming familiar via online discussion. Megan, visiting Thailand from Australia, told us about watching a previous patient's video diaries:

She put her whole experience on YouTube, the whole thing from start to finish. Even her crappy days. It was there for you to see. She recently put up some more photos up of her trip and that got me excited because it had more of the hospital and the surgeons. It was very useful for me to see others' experiences, just that she was ok I guess, and that she liked the hospital and the care – the care was nothing like you'd probably get here – and the follow up as well. (Megan, Australia to Thailand)

Others gained advice from previous patients about how to prepare for surgery: 'there's one girl who has got a very good YouTube video, she tells you to bring button down tops, you need to bring from home your own medication' (Cindy, Australia to Thailand). Jansson notes that mediatisation 'creates a new potential for mobility in mediascapes, which also involves the naturalisation of images and fantasies of foreign landscapes and socioscapes' (2002: 441). And, writing about the importance of patient testimony for cosmetic surgery patients more generally, Adams notes that the 'warm expertise' shared between past and future patients helps to make surgery seem 'more familiar, less bizarre, and more understandable' (2010: 760). In other words, social media allow the strange to become familiar before it is experienced.

Buyer Beware

Cosmetic surgery tourism is a 'buyer beware' market where the client is increasingly seen as being responsible for their surgery: for knowing its risks, for making the 'right' decisions in relation to technologies, surgeons, hospitals, countries and products. This is of course problematic in terms of health, safety and risk. However, it also comes hand-in-hand with a sense of patient autonomy, and helps to bring about a re-balancing of the expert/subject surgeon–patient relationship.

While websites played an important role in research, many of our interviewees also emphasised the importance of contact with peers and previous patients via social media. Most participate in Facebook, forums or YouTube, or at least 'lurk'[3] on them. We note that cosmetic surgery tourists are generally not content with the singular authority figure of the surgeon, or the advertising of hospitals and clinics, and to augment these modes of information they rely on each other:

> really at some point I wanted some idea of his workmanship more than anything else, but everybody, I kept asking the girls, 'but how do I know?' so I would keep getting feedback everywhere and I would trawl online … and see 'suture work is impeccable', so since scarring is one of the things that I'm most worried about then it's a good thing, but you know. (Bianca, Australia to Thailand)

Many cosmetic surgery recipients, whether at-home or tourists, see cosmetic surgeons as skilled technicians rather than as aesthetic experts (Gimlin 2013, Holliday and Cairnie 2007). However, we have observed that communities of cosmetic surgery *tourists* often discuss surgical techniques and the results of particular surgeons as a matter of course in their pre-surgical research.

The fact that social media are often populated by communities of peers for the conversational sharing of information rather than made by professionals

---

3   Lurking is the practice of observing but not participating in online forums, and is often viewed negatively.

for pedagogical or promotion purposes also means that they are seen as more trustworthy. As one patient said:

> I would have shared my experience if it had gone bad because, at the end of the day ... it's a true experience. I wouldn't glamorise it because, at the end of the day, if I was in pain, I would have said I'm in pain because I wouldn't want people to think, 'oh, he's saying he's not in pain and I've been and I've had this and I'm in agony'. What would be the point? It's got to be the truth. It was a truthful account of my experience. If there were any bad experiences, I would have said it. But there wasn't. But if there were, I would have said it. (Neil, UK to Czech Republic and Poland)

Neil was not merely relaying his own experiences but actively contributing to a community of online peers that was seen as trustworthy because they are not selling anything.

John Urry's (2003) notion of 'meetingness' is useful here. He argues that online communications and real life meetings are mutually constitutive and that 'networked sociality' (made up of 'weak ties') is far more meaningful when combined at least occasionally with embodied 'co-presence' (Urry 2003: 170). Urry observes that face-to-face or eye-to-eye meetings help to imbue digital communications with trust. For Urry, it is in moments of corporeal co-presence that trust is solidified, and then carried back into networked communications: 'trust is an accomplishment of such meetings ... which facilitate disembedded network sociality sustained in between at-a-distance' (Urry 2003: 168–9).

Although it is clear that cosmetic surgery tourism is conducted within digital communications and in real life (face-to-face), for our purposes a *reversal* of meetingness makes sense. Trust is built up in the online world, with people the cosmetic surgery tourist is never likely to meet. It is this physically disembodied trustfulness that facilitates the corporeal meetings between patient and surgeon, scalpel and flesh, not the other way around. Cosmetic surgery, an utterly spatial and bodily process, is here augmented by digital communications. Trust is vital where surgery and recovery are concerned; it plays a large part in patient satisfaction and in whether operations are seen as successful or not. Trustfulness in cosmetic surgery tourism is partly designed by industry players such as agents, surgeons and hospitals, but is also significantly created in online patient-to-patient communications. Although physically separated from each other, cosmetic surgery tourists often share bodily experiences and images online; analysing YouTube videos, Patricia Lange (2009) writes about the role of the body in producing 'affinity' between video-poster and audience: modes of performing embodiment online are used to 'interpellate' viewers into a shared social relationship. Lange gathers many different YouTube videos under her banner 'videos of affinity', and cosmetic surgery tourists' YouTube clips certainly work in this way. By narrating and sharing bodily experiences, a sense of commonality or community is produced.

With the availability of new portable media, previous tourists have input into the planning as well as the actual experiences of future tourists in ways that were previously restricted to agents, guides, experts, etc. Gayle Jennings and Betty Weiler (2006) have noted that tourists interact with each other in order to formulate, understand and mediate their own experiences, and, in turn, to facilitate the experiences of others. This is deliberately performed in cosmetic surgery tourism, with patients like Neil, quoted above, actively documenting their experiences in order to help others. Expectations, fears and hopes are negotiated with peers using narratives and scripts based around information-sharing and 'truthfulness'. The pre-surgical research of cosmetic surgery tourists is a mutual endeavour.

Another patient told us of following, via Facebook, a group of cosmetic surgery tourists' surgery and recovery in the weeks leading up to her own trip:

> It's been really helpful. Some have been having a bad time, they've been in more
> pain than they expected, whereas some of them are out on the back of elephants,
> so it's good to see how everybody is different but it's not all … and one girl got,
> like, an infection, you know. So it's not showing only the good side of the story. I
> hope none of this happens [to me]. I'm very excited. (Sue, Australia to Thailand)

For Sue, seeing people miserable with infections alongside those well enough to take post-surgical elephant rides gave her confidence. While she hoped she would have a good experience, she was able to moderate that against the possibility that she might not. It was access to others' stories that allowed her to negotiate the various possibilities of cosmetic surgery tourism in ways that were more accessible, and arguably more useful, than the online advice provided by surgeons or hospitals.

Finally, before their operations, we found that some patients used social media to perform a devil-may-care attitude and to make light of the surgery while also acknowledging it as a mode of identity-making and a consumable item: 'before I left I was like "oh, getting my last swims in before I get my new flotation devices installed", so everyone knew' (Kellie, Australia to Thailand). With this Facebook status update Kellie was celebrating and performing – with her peers – the surgical experience before it had happened, anticipating and foreshadowing a successful, happy result.

During Cosmetic Surgery Tourism

Alone but Connected

In her fascinating paper about recovery clinics (retreats) for cosmetic surgery tourism in Costa Rica, Sara Ackerman writes that:

Some travellers arrive with companions, but many travel alone, and retreats offer a temporary surrogate family. Guests (particularly women) find camaraderie with each other, and many people told me that these friendships were critical to their personal, spiritual, and corporeal recovery. (2010: 418)

While some of our interviewees travelled in groups or with family and friends, or met up with people while they were away, many were solo travellers. For them, social media was a way to access the camaraderie that Ackerman mentions. In the case of the travellers that Ackerman describes, the cosmetic surgery tourism experience is partly built through collective interchange. For many of our interviewees this shared making of stories was conducted in social media: in this way they were alone but connected. Neil found a community on the Facebook page of his agent:

> you got all this support from all these people that are on Facebook … that are commenting, that's making you feel you're not completely alone. It is nice. It's a lovely thing that … although I couldn't speak to anybody because there was nobody really out and about that spoke English, it was nice being able to go on Facebook and being able to just make comments. (Neil, patient, UK to Czech Republic and Poland)

In addition to providing pre-surgical information, social networking sites are used for ongoing peer-to-peer networking, community building and storytelling while patients are away. Travellers upload pre- and post-surgery images of themselves, write in detail about their experiences, and share 'videos of affinity'. Social media saturated the experience of many of our interviewees while abroad and were integral to their experience, helping them to connect with home, check on other patients, narrate surgical stories, and make sense of unfamiliar surroundings. Without portable devices and social software, many of the people we interviewed would have had a significantly different experience: '[social media] was a big part of it really and you kind of felt that you weren't doing it all alone. You felt like there were people along for your journey' (Neil, UK to Czech Republic and Poland).

Others used social media to celebrate their surgeries. Immediately after her surgery one patient posted a Facebook status update that read 'Got boobs? Yeah I do now!' (Kellie, Australia to Thailand). Posting on Facebook was not only a way to let friends and family know that she had made the right decision, but also a way to communicate a positive outcome with the rest of the cosmetic surgery tourism community.

Managing Heightened Moments

All tourism is about the experience of risk and difference within limits: with cosmetic surgery tourism, those limits must be extremely carefully managed. Nelson Graburn suggested in 1989 that the tourist experience follows a temporal arc from ordinary to heightened and back to ordinary. Heightened moments may be adventurous, unexpected or even frightening, and while they are desirable for many tourist experiences, they are less welcome for the cosmetic surgery tourist. While some of our interviewees certainly went looking for exciting moments, for example visiting ping pong strip shows in Bangkok, drinking heavily, or going to wildlife parks, none wished for 'heightened' moments to be part of their surgical experience. Communications in social media helped people to manage the temporal arc so that unexpected heightened moments were less likely to occur. A patient told us happily that there had been 'no surprises' on her trip, and attributed this to the way she was in constant communication with a friend at home and with her agent: 'no negatives … [there were no surprises] because my girlfriend had watched me the whole way and I was sending emails to [the agent] left, right and centre' (Cindy, Australia to Thailand).

Some patients used social media to actively manage the future temporal arcs of others. For example, Neil posted Facebook updates throughout his journey:

> I kind of put pictures through my journey, if you will. So it's like I showed my loose skin and then I had the operation and then pictures through the various stages through the week. I even took pictures of my apartment and the view. I put them on, you know, so people could see what to expect when you go as well.
> (Neil, UK to Czech Republic and Poland)

Neil's intention was to help others. By showing them 'what to expect' in terms of both his body and the countries visited, he was managing the heightened moments of future patients. In these ways cosmetic surgery tourism narratives serve to construct identity in relation to surgery and to place, and – crucially – to lay foundations for others to do the same; each narrative becomes a script or template upon which others can build their own stories. Neil was also in a sense 'authenticating' the site and process of cosmetic surgery tourism by making a recording of it. This makes sense when we consider Dean MacCannell's (1999: 48) and later Nick Couldry's (2005) arguments that tourist sites only become 'authentic' once the first copy has been made – in other words, once the first tourist has been there, taken photos, made drawings, or 'Facebooked'. In this way Neil was acting as a pioneer. By creating the 'first copy' he was making cosmetic surgery tourism available for others. His representations of experience online helped to authenticate his new sense of self but also served to make the surgery 'real' for future travellers.

While away, cosmetic surgery tourists use social media to construct complex and overlapping experiences of place, of identity, and of surgery. They create online spaces where 'virtual' meetingness happens, and in these spaces they share knowledge, work out what is realistic in terms of pain and recovery, celebrate decisions and results, and pave the way for new tourists.

After Surgery

The Beginning of the Rest of my Life

Cosmetic surgery tourists use blogs and sites like Facebook and YouTube to tell stories of their experiences after surgery, often summing up the entire process from preliminary enquiries to coming back home, under headings like *The Beginning of the Rest of my Life* (All Wrapped Up 2012) and *Cosmetic Surgery Thailand – Actual Post Breast Augmentation Testimonial* (Cosmeticsurgerythai 2011). Post-surgical stories might be posted immediately after surgery and can be updated for years afterwards (see *Boobie Mumma* 2011–). One breast augmentation patient on YouTube (Australia to Thailand) had uploaded 28 videos at the time of writing (TheMrsForman 2012), and a gynecomasty patient (UK to Poland) offers his video in a stand-up-comic style (Anonymous 2011). Online communities created around cosmetic surgery tourism, then, can continue beyond the immediate parameters of before/during/after. How long they might last, and whether relationships built up during cosmetic surgery tourism continue, is something only a longitudinal study would be able to answer.

Immediately after surgery, patients often share and compare their transformations and recoveries on social media, helping to contextualise experiences of pain, complications and healing:

> I feel really good. A lot of ladies like, cos I have a facebook page and a lot of people have like video blogged it and stuff and a lot of the ladies are like you know 'I've been bed-ridden' … it takes to people really differently and I've taken to it really well. Like I wasn't really … I wasn't really in agony, I was just in like you know like a bit of pain and the hardest thing was probably trying to get up out of the bed. (Sam, Australia to Thailand)

Even though it was hard for her to 'get up out of the bed', Sam insisted that she wasn't 'bed-ridden' like others. We suggest that being able to contextualise one's pain in this way is important as far as being able to decide what is normal or acceptable – without social media Sam may have perceived her pain as abnormal or unacceptable. Because of social media her pain was not experienced in isolation but in a shared context, and was perhaps therefore more tolerable.

When Things Go Wrong

Given the intimacy shared by cosmetic surgery tourists on social media, it makes sense that these forums are also used to communicate when things go wrong. Some patients who had suffered complications from their surgeries were able to support each other online:

> I just felt, although my story was different to Jane, I wanted to support her a little
> bit because I know how I felt, although she was ten times worse than me, I didn't
> know what was going on, I just wanted to let her know that she wasn't alone.
> (Tracy, UK to Poland)

Louise, who travelled from the UK to Belgium, found that an American forum was
the most useful for support:

> I have found [the forums an] absolute godsend. I mean there are a few, there is
> this American one … which is really active and it has just been amazing support
> because I ended up in A&E the day after I got back, because I was just in so
> much pain. (Louise, UK to Belgium)

Tracy, like Neil, was keen to provide support to someone she had never met.
Louise felt rescued from her pain by the NHS but equally by a forum that was not
even on her own continent. In this way, again, it is clear that spaces of trust and
'meetingness' in cosmetic surgery tourism are likely to be found online.

In addition to surgical complications, sometimes destinations failed to live
up to expectations. There was great disappointment when the material realities
of place did not match what had been represented (usually on hospital or agent
websites). This is what Jansson calls 'decapsulation', a state where disjuncture
between the represented and the real occurs and upsets the tourist experience:
'decapsulation is most often produced through the interplay between material
and symbolic processes' (2007: 9, see also Couldry 2005). There can be profound
dismay when expectations that have been built up via online interactions do not
match with actuality. Angie, visiting Tunisia from the UK, found that the guide she
had been expecting, Ben, had left months earlier:

> Had I known Ben wasn't there and had I known that the language barrier would
> have been a huge problem I would have still gone and had the surgery because
> I went for surgery, I didn't go for conversation, so I would have still gone but I
> would have been aware, I would have been prepared … I still would have gone,
> had they informed me more I would have still gone, but I would have gone
> slightly differently, I would have gone with a different outlook, I would have
> done things slightly differently. (Angie, UK to Tunisia)

Interestingly, when things had gone wrong patients did not tell us that they
regretted their decisions to have cosmetic surgery abroad, rather that they had
been disappointed by what they generally characterised as a lack of information.
And notably, if Angie had been able to have contact with other patients who were
already in Tunisia, she would have 'been aware … been prepared'. We suggest
that it is the lack of social media in this case that caused the unpleasant feeling
of decapsulation.

Little Narratives and Community

Narratives create experience and memory as much as they tell of pre-existing conditions; they also reflect the ideals and desires of the cultures in which they are made (McNay 2002). Accordingly, most cosmetic surgery recipients narrate their surgeries using 'scripts' that fit in with cultural expectations, and deploy different narratives in order to be heard (see Ancheta 2002, Frost 1999, Gimlin 2002, 2013). The narratives we have examined here are not grand or transcendent but rather personal, largely unedited stories facilitated through social media that is 'cheap, flexible, readily available, quick' and therefore not exclusive (Poster 2001: 621). Lois McNay writes that identity itself is constructed through narrative and that because all narratives are intertwined it follows that identity-making is an intersubjective and communal process: 'the idea of narrative is also explicitly relational, that is, it draws attention to the irredeemably intersubjective nature of identity' (McNay 2002: 83). In line with this we suggest that the identity- and body-making that cosmetic surgery tourists conduct happens both corporeally and discursively, and that social media play a large role in the discursive/representational elements of transformation.

Pitts-Taylor (2009) notes that cosmetic surgery discourses are unstable, changing according to mode, speaker and context. Despite this flux, cosmetic surgery patients are 'expected to employ methods of description that make sense to others, thus complying with already scripted codes of meaning that are set out before [them]' (Pitts-Taylor 2009: 127). We suggest that part of being a recipient of cosmetic surgery is being able to identify and then position oneself 'correctly' in relation to whichever discourse is appropriate.[4] Amongst many other possible subject positions, a cosmetic surgery tourist might discursively represent him or herself as adventurer (like Kellie), as pioneer and truth-teller (like Neil) or as caring stranger (like Tracy). All positions make it clear that cosmetic surgery tourism identity is constructed through narrative, and is not confined to individuals, but formed in conjunction with myriad others. The ongoing narrating of cosmetic surgery tourism experiences, in common with other tourist narratives, moves from anticipation to memory, and forms the basis for continued sharing, bonding and 'mattering' – in short, for making community (Heimtun 2007).

Cosmetic surgery tourists thus use 'symbolic-material structures' to make what Jansson calls 'textures of travel' (2007: 6), by mixing online and real-life interactions, and in doing so they in fact render this distinction obsolete. Their online communities, with shared vocabularies and discourses, are intricately connected to the very corporeal aspects of actual surgeries. In this way a nexus between

---

4   Several feminist scholars have looked at narrative and discourse in relation to cosmetic surgery, especially Brooks (2004), Fraser (2003), Gimlin (2010), Holliday and Cairnie (2007) and Huss-Ashmore (2000). Debra Gimlin (2013) summarises that 'stories about cosmetic surgery and the surgical process itself are fully interwined and interdependent' (2013: 64).

material space – of the body and of place – and forms of communication create the cosmetic surgery tourism experience and validate the subsequent transformation.

In turn, this means that cosmetic surgery tourists have something that is different to their stay-at-home counterparts – they have more of a sense of being part of a community. The fact that their corporeal experiences happen offshore and away from what they know encourages them to connect with strangers, to make community. As one Australian agent told us: 'It's just about connecting, it really is about connecting' (Yvonne).

Conclusion

Ackerman writes of her Costa Rica clinic that 'the labors of local caretakers and social interactions among patients operate on the embodied subjectivities of guests and staff and act as an adjunct to the cuts and sutures performed by surgeons' (2010: 405). Similarly, we note that social media networking augments the work of the scalpel for the people we interviewed.

The practices of cosmetic surgery tourists are complex and detailed. As Pitts-Taylor writes about her own cosmetic surgery, it is 'a very personal experience, but it is also incredibly social, public, and semantically unstable, one that is not static but unfolds through various processes of imbuing the body and self with symbolic meaning' (2009: 122). It is not adequate to think of cosmetic surgery tourists as individuals who travel simply because they cannot afford surgery at home. They make up communities, with patterns of behaviour, modes of being, and unique ways of bonding and identity-making.

In the instances of transformation that we are examining in relation to cosmetic surgery tourism, change comes about through a collective rather than through individual subjects. Collectives cannot exist without communication technologies – in this instance social media. So transformation of the self or of many selves is actually *brought about* by and through media. Here, communicative technologies are far more than conduits for information; they are portals for identities, through which bodies and selves can be refashioned.

References

Ackerman, S.L. 2010. Plastic paradise: Transforming bodies and selves in Costa Rica's cosmetic surgery tourism industry. *Medical Anthropology: Cross-Cultural Studies in Health and Illness*, 29(4), 403–23.
Adams, J. 2010. Motivational narratives and assessments of the body after cosmetic surgery. *Qualitative Health Research*, 20(6), 755–67.
All Wrapped Up 2012. [Online]. Available at: http://wrapperharris.wordpress.com/2012/04/19/the-beggining-of-the-rest-of-my-life [accessed: 20 June 2013].

Ancheta, R.W. 2002. Discourse of rules: Women talk about cosmetic surgery, in *Women's Health: Power, Technology, Inequality and Conflict in a Gendered World*, edited by K. Strother. Boston: Allyn & Bacon, 143–9.

Anonymous 2011. *Gynecomasty Surgery in Poland – Patient Testimonial* [Online: Secret Surgery, YouTube]. Available at: http://www.youtube.com/watch?v=S7yaPPd4Dfk [accessed: 20 June 2013].

Bell, D., Holliday, R., Jones, M., Probyn, E. and Sanchez Taylor, J. 2011. Bikinis and bandages: An itinerary for cosmetic surgery tourism. *Tourist Studies*, 11(2), 137–53.

Boobie Mumma 2011– [Online]. Available at: http://www.youtube.com/user/CinnamonSpank [accessed: 20 June 2013].

Brooks, A. 2004. 'Under the knife and proud of it': An analysis of the normalization of cosmetic surgery. *Critical Sociology*, 30(2), 207–39.

Connell, J. 2011. *Medical Tourism*. Wallingford: CABI.

Cormany, D. and Baloglu, S. 2011. Medical traveller facilitator websites: An exploratory study of web page contents and services offered to the prospective medical tourist. *Tourism Management*, 32(6), 709–16.

Cosmeticsurgerythai 2011 [Online]. Available at: http://www.youtube.com/watch?v=uBA40eq5x88 [accessed: 20 Feburary 2014].

Couldry, N. 2005. On the actual street, in *The Media and the Tourist Imagination: Converging Cultures*, edited by D. Crouch, R. Jackson and F. Thompson. Routledge: London, 60–75.

Fraser, S. 2003. *Cosmetic Surgery, Gender and Culture*. New York: Palgrave Macmillan.

Frost, L. 1999. Doing looks: Women, appearance and mental health, in *Women's Bodies: Discipline and Transgression*, edited by J. Arthurs and J. Grimshaw. London: Cassell, 117–36.

Gimlin, D. 2002. *Body Work: Beauty and Self-Image in American Culture*. Berkeley: University of California Press.

Gimlin, D. 2010. The 'Other' of aesthetic plastic surgery. *Body and Society*, 16(4), 57–76.

Gimlin, D. 2013. *Cosmetic Surgery Narratives: A Cross-National Comparison of Women's Accounts*. Basingstoke: Palgrave Macmillan.

Graburn, N. 1989. Tourism: The sacred journey, in *Hosts and Guests: The Anthropology of Tourism*, edited by V. Smith. Philadelphia: University of Pennsylvania, 21–36.

Haiken, E. 1997. *Venus Envy: A History of Cosmetic Surgery*. Baltimore: The Johns Hopkins University Press.

Hallett, R. and Kaplan-Weinger, J. 2010. *Official Tourism Websites: A Discourse Analysis Perspective*. Bristol: Channel View Press.

Heimtun, B. 2007. Depathologizing the tourism syndrome: Tourism as social capital production. *Tourist Studies*, 7(3), 271–93.

Hjorth, L. 2007. Domesticating new media: A discussion on locating mobile media, in *The New Media and Technocultures Reader*, edited by S. Giddings and M. Lister. New York: Routledge, 437–48.

Holliday, R. and Cairnie, A. 2007. Man made plastic. *Journal of Consumer Culture*, 7(1), 57–78.

Holliday, R., Bell, D., Hardy, K., Hunter, E., Jones, M., Probyn, E. and Sanchez-Taylor, J. 2013. Beautiful face, beautiful place: Relational geographies and gender in cosmetic surgery tourism websites. *Gender, Place and Culture*, (ahead-of-print), 1–17.

Huss-Ashmore, R. 2000. 'The real me': Therapeutic narrative in cosmetic surgery. *Expedition*, 42(3), 26–38.

Jansson, A. 2002. Spatial phantasmorgia: The mediatisation of tourism experience. *European Journal of Communication*, 17(4), 429–43.

Jansson, A. 2007. A sense of tourism: New media and the dialectic of encapsulation/decapsulation. *Tourist Studies*, 7(1), 5–24.

Jennings, G. and Weiler, B. 2006. Mediating meaning: Perspectives on brokering quality tourist experiences, in *Quality Tourism Experiences*, edited by G. Jennings and N. Polovitz Nickerson. Amsterdam: Elsevier, 57–78.

Jones, M. 2008. *Skintight: An Anatomy of Cosmetic Surgery*. Oxford: Berg.

Lange, P. 2009. Videos of affinity on YouTube, in *The YouTube Reader*, edited by P. Snickers and P. Vonderau. Stockholm: National Library of Sweden, 70–88.

MacCannell, D. 1999. *The Tourist: A New Theory of the Leisure Class*. Berkeley: University of California Press.

McNay, L. 2002. Communitarians and feminists: The case of narrative Identity. *Literature & Theology*, 16(1), 81–95.

Pitts-Taylor, V. 2009. Becoming/being a cosmetic surgery patient: Semantic instability and the intersubjective self. *Studies in Gender and Sexuality*, 10(3), 119–28.

Poster, M. 2001. Postmodern virtualities, in *Media and Cultural Studies Keyworks*, edited by M.G. Durham and D.M. Kellner. Blackwell: Massachusetts, 611–25.

Radin, P. 2006. 'To me, it's my life': Medical communication, trust, and activism in cyberspace. *Social Science & Medicine*, 62(3), 591–601.

Spitzack, C. 1988. The confession mirror: Plastic images for surgery. *Canadian Journal of Political Studies*, 18(40), 27–44.

TheMrsForman 2012. [Online]. Available at: http://www.youtube.com/user/TheMrsforman?feature=watch [accessed: 20 June 2013].

Urry, J. 2003. Social networks, travel and talk. *British Journal of Sociology*, 54(2), 155–75.

Wilson, T. and Suraya, R. 2004. The tourist gaze goes on-line: Rojak (hybrid) reception theory structures of ludic looking at/from Malaysia. *Tourist Studies*, 4(1), 69–92.

Yeoh, E., Othman, K. and Ahmad, H. 2013. Understanding medical tourists: Word-of-mouth and viral marketing as potent marketing tools. *Tourism Management*, 34(2), 196–201.

Chapter 13

Material Transformations: Place, Process and the Capacity of Tourist Souvenirs in the Home

Kimberley Peters

Introduction

Recreational travel is often a transformative process. Touristic travel necessarily involves making a transition through space, whereby the traveller transforms as they encounter a world removed from their own. This movement between the spaces of 'home' and 'away' have framed tourist studies, yet they are increasingly unravelling with recognition that dualisms do not reflect the realities of our lives, and the line between categories such as 'home' and 'away' are often blurred and uncertain (Larsen 2008), overlapping (Soja 1996) and enfolded (Whatmore 2001). In this chapter, through an exploration of the material culture of souvenirs, I contend that travel is an open-ended process, one which cannot be divided neatly between the 'home' and 'away', with the 'away' being the space of travel, the 'home' the space of stasis (see Larsen 2008). Rather, I adopt a fluid ontology (Latour 2005) for thinking about the *relations* between 'home' and 'away', illustrating how they often collapse into one another as these seemingly discrete spatialities and realms of experience are ever connected and folded into one another through the merging of disparate spaces and times.

In doing so, I pay attention to the 'home', an often neglected category in tourist studies (although see some recent exceptions: Larsen 2008, Lean 2012, Peters 2011). Indeed, the 'home' is often regarded as the uninteresting, banal, everyday realm of experience compared with the category of the 'away' which typifies tourist experience. Yet the home is a key space of transformation in the *process* of travel. As Lean writes, 'there are innumerable elements encountered at *home* that may stimulate recollection of moments and facilitate continued performances' (2012: 278, emphasis added). Indeed, conceiving of travel and tourism as open, fluid, processual and relational brings the site of 'home' more firmly into focus as a connected and networked space in these experiences – a space which foregrounds experience prior to travel (for example being a site of anticipation, excitement, planning and so on) – and a site to which the traveller returns 'inwardly transformed and outwardly changed' (Turner 1977: 36).

In order to reveal this processual nature of travel and transformation that merges and transcends the 'home' and 'away', I focus on the material culture of tourism: souvenirs. Souvenirs provide a useful vehicle for exploring these connections as they, like tourists, move across spaces and times, from the space of the 'extraordinary' to the 'ordinary', and in these items, elements of tourist experience, personal feelings and attachments, and memories, are ascribed (Hoskins 1998). Literature on tourist souvenirs has grown in recent years (see for example: Morgan and Pritchard 2005, Peters 2011, Ramsey 2009) with a renewed interest in materiality and matter in critical social science and geography (Bennett 2004, Jackson 2000) and through theoretical frames which focus on the biography of objects (Gosden and Marshall 1999, Hoskins 1998, Kopytoff 1988), the vibrancy of matter (Bennett 2010) and object fetishisation (Marx 2010), enchantment (Bennett 2001) and resultant affects (Thrift 2004). However, in spite of such advances, the significance of travel, and its transformative capacity, has yet to fully *materialise*. As well as arguing that travel cannot be confined to discrete spatialities and particular temporal moments – the 'home' and 'away', the 'then' and 'now' – this chapter advocates engaging with the agencies of commodity cultures to explore questions central to enquiries in tourism studies.

This chapter begins by introducing the theoretical framework for exploring the ways in which transformation is processual across the times and sites of the 'home' and 'away' via the souvenir. Here I provide a background to souvenir studies before examining conceptually the abilities of objects to hold 'biographies' and elicit 'affects'. I then draw on empirical research (in the form of in-depth interviews) from a research project that considered the impacts of the material culture of tourism on home spaces. Drawing on this data I illustrate how 'transformation' or 'change' transcends the space of travel alone, connecting the experience of being at 'home' and being 'away'. I firstly trace the ways in which the home is a space transformed through travel, as souvenirs from 'afar' are embedded into the 'everyday' place of 'home', making this familiar space somehow 'strange'. This discussion is then taken a stage further, exploring the ways in which material culture (individual souvenirs) are transformed through their placement in the home, as the 'biographies of objects' move into another life stage in this setting. This chapter thus considers the broader transformative process of travel, exploring the space of the home as one of transformation *post-travel*, and the sites of 'home' and 'away' as intimately related.

Objectifying Tourist Studies

Within tourism and leisure studies, the souvenir has long been an object of study and continues to shape the agenda in these subject areas (see Gordon 1986, Healey 1994, Hume 2008, Kim and Littrell 2001, Love and Kohn 2001, Love and Sheldon 1998, Swanson and Horridge 2006, Wilkins 2011). This reflects the importance of souvenirs in tourist culture. As Wilkins (2011: 239) notes, the purchase of mementos and souvenirs is an established behaviour associated with many activities, including travel and other leisure activities. Few people will take a vacation without acquiring some form of evidence to tangibilise the experiences gained. Indeed, souvenirs are best described as the tangible, physical objects that mark tourist travel, which have a retrograde function as 'reminders' of extraordinary journeys, in the past, when they are engaged with in the present (Gordon 1986: 135). There are many motivations for souvenir purchase. Primarily they function as tangible reminders of something intangible and fleeting – experience (Gordon 1986), which in turn allows the traveller to 'prove' they have been elsewhere (Wilkins 2011: 239). They may, however, also be purchased as gifts for others (Wilkins 2011: 243). Importantly, people often have differing values when they purchase souvenirs, for themselves or as presents (Swanson and Horridge 2006). They may value the apparent 'authenticity' of the item in terms of its connection to a particular place visited (MacCannell 1999), they may value its uniqueness (compared to 'everyday' items), and even value how useful it will be upon returning home (Swanson and Horridge 2006: 674).

It is widely acknowledged, then, that souvenirs have a spatial and temporal component – they come to represent, andmoreover contain, particular times and places (whether or not they are actually produced in the places they are bought, with global commodity chains and trade shaping the material culture bought and sold in the industry, see Nicolson 2007). It is also acknowledged that souvenirs have a role both in practices of tourist consumption whilst 'away' (see Goss 2005) but also have saliences in the space of the home (Love and Kohn 2001). However, work in tourism and leisure studies has focused mostly on the type and function of souvenirs and motivations for purchase (see Gordon 1986, Wilkins 2011), their aesthetics, origins and price (Swanson and Horridge 2006) and their economic importance in the tourist trade (Healey 1994). Only more recently has a plethora of work examined the cultural significance of souvenirs and the qualitative narratives contained within, and spun forth, from these objects (Collins-Kreiner and Zins 2011, Hume 2008, Lean 2012, Morgan and Pritchard 2005, Peters 2011, Ramsey 2009).

These latter studies demonstrate the ways in which objects are geographical, in that they move (Watts 1999: 309), and it is this movement that makes souvenirs a useful vehicle for exploring transformation, a process of mobilisation and change. This is because objects come to represent the memories of transformation of the owner, working as 'shorthand message(s) about the place or time they come from' (Gordon 1986: 142). Yet objects too, transform and change. They have qualities that make them mutable and malleable, depending on their spatial and temporal context. One useful way of thinking seriously about the cultural significance of objects and their changing connections to people and places is through the concept of biography (see Kopytoff 1988). Kopytoff advocates that the significance of objects is not static. Rather it changes over the lifecourse of theitem. As Gosden and Marshall write, 'objects are continually picking up new significances, connections and meanings' (1999: 170).

A biographical approach to the object asks the same questions of objects as you might of a person (Kopytoff 1988: 66), because objects are like people, 'they are born, they live and they die' (Jones 2002: 83). Biography allows us to trace the intricate life of objects and their influences, but these influences are forged in relation to the people and places connected to the lifecourse of the object (Gosden and Marshall 1999). In other words, objects gain meanings at differing stages of their life through their enmeshment in personal relationships (Miller 1998) and the shifting spatial and temporal contexts they occupy. On the one hand, then, objects can tell us about individuals and societies and how these are transformed (Hoskins 1998). On the other hand, objects themselves have their own stories to tell, and are transformative. Additionally, the web of relations to people, places, past and present, embodied by the object, reflects the ways in which separations between 'here' and 'there', both spatially and temporally, are unproductive, as objects cause such boundaries to dissolve and categories to coalesce.

However, the idea that objects themselves have a transformative capacity is currently shaping social science and the (re)turn of interest in material culture (Bennett 2001, 2004, 2010). While objects are engaged in a meshwork of relations with people and places, scholars have argued that the significance and agency of objects cannot be wholly attributed to humans placing that significance and agency on them (see Whatmore 2006). Rather, contemporary debates have demonstrated a growing interest in 'more than human' materialities and the 'vibrancy of matter' (Bennett 2010). This is not to say that objects exist independently of humans (after all, humans produce objects in the first instance), but rather that 'things' can have power quite unexplained, when bound up with 'the intimate fabric of corporeality' (Whatmore 2006: 602). In other words, 'there is an existence peculiar to a thing that is irreducible to the thing's imbrications with human subjectivity' (Bennett 2004: 348). Things, then, are *more than* human; they have an intrinsic agency or 'force' 'which is not specifically human' but has an impact on the human. As Whatmore (2006) states, the more than human 'turn' in cultural geography is concerned not with a material world 'out there' but, rather, with how the more than human is enjoined with human *being* (2006: 602). Things can enchant us (Bennett 2001) as we are 'struck and shaken', 'transfixed in wonder and transported by sense' due to the inherent agency or power of the 'thing' itself (Bennett 2001: 4–5).

Indeed, objects can be seen to elicit affects when they come into contact with people and places. Affect refers to a 'transpersonal' capacity; an ethereal force not contained within objects or bodies, but a sparked outcome that 'surfaces ... in-between' when these elements touch (Adey 2008: 439). Affect, then, is the outcome of more than human and human engagements, as these two material surfaces meet in moments of encounter (Tolia-Kelly 2013: 154). Such affects are instantaneous, spontaneous and pre-cognitive (as opposed to feelings or emotions, which are *representations* of affects) (Pile 2010). Affect, as Thrift (2004: 59) notes, 'has no stable definition', but it is largely associated with the capacity of the body to respond *in relation to* other bodies and more than human things.

Such affects are explored by Love and Kohn (2001) who demonstrate how, as the biography of the souvenir develops over time and across space, such objects touch their new contexts in significant ways. When the surfaces of the object, home and individual coalesce, affects arise. They explore the 'fraught possibilities' of the souvenir, as, when tied in a relation with the 'foreign mileu' they 'make our home spaces strange and lively' (2001: 48). The idea that objects can elicit reactions and responses demonstrates the potential of souvenirs to explore the transformative capabilities of tourism and travel; affects emerging from the coming together of various states: here, now, past, present, home and away, ordinary and extraordinary.

In what follows, I draw on a series of in-depth interviews with souvenir owners, conducted in their own homes, between 2007 and 2010.[1] I pursue the partial biographies of souvenirs once they have returned home with tourists, exploring the ways in which, firstly, these objects have the capacity to transform the home as they touch this new spatial and temporal context via the particular and peculiar spatial and temporal biographies contained within these souvenir objects. I thus show how the home and away can be thought of less as separate but rather as combined through the affective agency of the object to bring the 'far' to the 'near' resulting in an intermingling of 'here' and 'there'. I then demonstrate the ways in which objects do not remain static within their home setting. Rather, they themselves develop further biographies, transforming in this new spatial setting, acquiring (or losing) parts of their affective agency through the passage of time.

Transforming the Materiality of Home

For Nisha, souvenirs facilitate the evocation of times past and distant geographies. As she told me:

> From the Maldives ... from the beach, we picked up some sand and put it in a container ... and now we want to do that from any beach we go to, we want to collect that, so we have sand from different places (because) I touch it and I think of the Maldives! I'm close to it! ... I think, wow, we walked on that sand, in the Maldives, its bringing that little bit back with you. I think that sand means more to us than any of the souvenirs we bought because it is a part of the place you've brought back with you. (Interview 2008)

Beverly Gordon's pivotal work on souvenir culture outlines differing souvenir 'types' (1986). To be classed as a souvenir, an object needs only to 'remind' and 'freeze in time, a fleeting, transitory experience' (Gordon 1986: 135). Some souvenirs are 'natural', such as Nisha's sand. Others are 'commercially produced,

---

1   Where these interviews are used, pseudonyms are employed to protect the anonymity of those who participated. This is in line with the ethical guidelines of the Economic and Social Research Council (ESRC).

purchased objects' (Gordon 1986: 135). These can be grouped into those which are locally produced 'craft' items or those which are mass produced items. Such mass produced items are often aesthetically linked to the destination where they are sold. For example, a miniature model of the Eiffel Tower connotes meanings associated with Paris (Gordon 1986: 142). Other souvenirs may simply have 'markers' on them and 'no reference to a particular place or event, but are ascribed with words which locate them in a place or time', for example, a t-shirt or tea towel, inscribed with words or pictures from a tourist location (Gordon 1986: 142).

The sand collected and transported from the Maldives to London 'invades' Nisha's home space (Love and Kohn 2001), as the 'lingering' materiality (Lean 2012) of another time and place becomes embedded into the home space; bringing two separate and disparate spheres into collision with one another. As Nisha notes, the sand is actually a very real material 'bit' of another place, displaced and emplaced in a new setting, transforming that new setting with 'a huge amount of meaning' (Interview 2008). The fact it is an actual piece of the distant 'other' 'extraordinary' space of tourism heightens its agency in the home. As another interviewee, Laura, reflected, souvenirs are 'more so you can have a little piece of that place back home' (Interview 2007). The idea of one place (a holiday destination) simultaneously occupying another place (the home) disrupts both geographically ordered and mapped perceptions of space, demonstrating how multiple places can exist in just one mapped location (following Massey 1997) as place is an assemblage of fragments of other places which coalesce in a particular locale. Notably, these constellations of geographically and temporally disparate 'things' in a new setting sparks affects. In this case, the agency of the matter (the sand) evokes a series of feelings for Nisha of being closer to the far away (Thrift 2004); a closeness to memories of a past which is at once as distant as the Maldives themselves. As Lean notes, 'memories and moments often linger in the objects that were carried with a traveller, or those acquired and/or created while travelling' (Lean 2012).

Kathryn also felt that souvenir objects changed and transformed the home. Reflecting on her collection of glassware from Gozo, she told me:

> These souvenirs [looks to the side where the Gozo glass is on display] are special because it's a special place to me – it's a very peaceful and lovely place that I am extraordinarily fond of. All the things we that we have brought back from there – and many of the items are glass – remind me of [pause] a very sunny, warm, happy place where the pace of life is very different from the pace of life here ... Um, they (the glass objects) are very beautiful, many are made to remind you of the sea and of the landscape. So, so the colours and the way that they look actually does do that – they are particularly provocative and very special. (Interview 2007)

In this instance, although the souvenir is not an actual physical part of the distant place, brought into contact with the home (like the sand), the locally produced glassware is both a traditional craft item associated with the island culture, and, for Kathryn, it reflects the features and colour of the place of purchase: the landscape and the sea. Bundled up within the objects' biographies are a set of temporalities and spatialities which make them 'special' (Miller 1998). For Kathryn, the transformative capacity of these objects on her home space is profound. She told me how when she sees the glassware, 'I stop and think ... and it will make me feel happy, and um, more relaxed and more peaceful' (Interview 2007). These objects create effects of happiness and calm; feelings of being 'away' whichoverlap and envelope the sphere of the 'everyday', making this space 'strange' (Love and Kohn 2001: 48) and 'extraordinary', whilst at once ordinary.

For both Nisha and Kathryn, however, these affects and the coalescing of home and away are only sparked when recognition is given to the souvenir. In other words, the presence of a souvenir in the home does not automatically serve to 'remind' (Gordon 1986) or 'transfix' (Bennett 2001) the owner; its position in one sphere does not involuntarily evoke other places, times and associated memories. As Nisha stated, 'all souvenirs are pretty silly really because it ... just sits on your desk or in your living room', so, as Kate noted 'sometimes I have to stop and make myself think ... consciously focus on something' (Interviews 2007, 2008). As another participant, Clara, explained:

> If I look at something I think 'oh yeah' that was from wherever and we did this and that! But if it is not there to prompt you – then I wouldn't think about it ... it does help, it does prompt you. (Interview 2007)

In other words, the coming together of home and away, past and present, through the affects evoked from the combining of souvenir objects and people in the ordinary everyday setting, occurs in transitory moments, most often when the souvenir object is brought into consciousness; when we are 'prompted' to reflect.[2] Here preconscious reactions are sparked as affects such as peace or relaxation or happiness are felt and home space temporally transforms through sensations of the 'other' in the space of the familiar.

This temporary coalescing of spatialities and temporalities can be a consequence of the position of tourist souvenirs in the home (Peters 2011). For example, Francesca kept her collection of souvenir bookmarks quite separate from other, everyday objects in her home. They were stored in a small wooden storage box with drawers. On a day-to-day basis, the home is not transformed through travel, the bookmarks, stowed out of sight and recognition. However, as Francesca reflected:

---

2   Interestingly, the research process worked as one such 'prompt', as Francesca noted, 'this interview has really made me think and want to rejuvenate my (bookmark) collection' (Francesca, Interview 2007). As such, the process of research was one of evoking the 'away' in the 'home' transforming this space for the duration of the conversation.

> I kind of forgot I had it (the box). It's strange. I did look once for a way of displaying it (the bookmark collection) but it's so big and I wanted to find like a wood cabinet with glass on top to put them underneath, but then I thought, what would I do with it? And I think by having it in the box and just getting it out occasionally, I mean, if I had it out all the time I don't think I'd look at it, I'd pass by it or like, it would just sit there and I wouldn't notice it. But by having it in a box and getting it out … It makes it more special and the memories more [pause]. (Interview 2007)

In some senses, then, the home is transformed temporarily but also repeatedly. Each time the bookmark collection is viewed, places and times collide as memories are sparked through the affective capacity of the souvenirs. Often owners of tourist objects can manage the salience of their souvenirs through their placement in the home. As Laura told me 'if I had something tucked away in a draw somewhere and only (got) it out on special occasions it would probably hold the memory better' (Interview 2007). In other words, the ability of souvenirs to transform the home, bringing the experience of tourism beyond the usual borders of travel, depends on maintaining the significance or 'place' of the souvenir (Peters 2011), a significance which can be protected through sacralisation.

That is not to say that hiding souvenirs away so that they are soon 'covered in a layer of dust' (Blanche, Interview 2009), is the only way to ensure a sacralisation that maintains the affective capacities of souvenirs to shape home spaces and the experiences within the everyday setting. For Bill, his souvenir display of drinks miniatures in the living room invaded the everyday space of home with fragments of the 'away' – 'Tenerife, Fuerteventura, Jersey, Greece, Egypt, Cyprus' (Interview 2007). Bill's miniatures are instantly recognisable in the room, collected together in a cabinet. As Bill's wife Jennie remarked 'you want to make a feature of it. I mean, I might bring a tea towel back but I would use it' (Interview 2007). Whilst Bill's miniatures are on display and Francesca's bookmarks hidden, what both have in common is the separation of these items from everyday items, and the decision to not use such items (as Francesca noted, 'I used one once and it really annoyed me because it started to get worn down, so I put it back in the collection', Interview 2007). Rather, the affects sparked from interactions with these objects result from the status or protected biography of the object, as something from 'afar'. Although making the home 'strange and lively' (Love and Kohn 2001: 48), this liveliness is only possible by, paradoxically, maintaining a binary between 'home' and 'away' – with the objects as 'exotic' and 'other'. As such, whilst the presence (temporary or more persistent, as is the case with Bill's miniatures) brings disparate spaces and times in touch– intermingling in a moment of recognition – such coalescing relies on the discrete separation of home and away, and preserving a sense of an object's distinct 'otherness' to usual household items. Such sustaining, through object placement, ensures its affective quality and transformative capacity.

Transforming the Materiality of Souvenirs

When the home and away merge through the material culture of souvenirs, sometimes souvenirs themselves are enveloped into the home setting and then themselves transform. Here the home is not made strange and lively, as the object loses its strangeness and liveliness (Love and Kohn 2001) and its 'vibrancy' fades (Bennett 2010). Arguably this occurs when the biography of the souvenir traces a path whereby its use renders it insignificant (Peters 2011). Although souvenirs are objects that 'signify physical travel', those meanings and memories contained within can diminish as they transform into everyday, banal objects, merging into the everydayness of home. The transformation of tourist objects occurred most frequently when the object had an alternative function to that of a souvenir (to remind).

Paula often bought fridge magnets for her children when on holiday, as a memento of time away. Whilst these magnets can at first act as a reminder (for both her, and her children) of past times and distant places, they soon merged into the fabric of the home. Preston notes that all objects have an intended 'use function' (2006: 15). The intended function of a souvenir is to 'remind' (Gordon 1986: 135), yet many of these items resemble everyday items (Peters 2011: 237); they are merely 'marked' as souvenirs with place names or destination images (Gordon 1986: 142). As such, some souvenirs have a function alternative to that of 'memory triggers' (Sarah, Interview 2008). For Paula, the magnets, once significant in reminding her of family holidays, soon became nothing more than objects which held school letters to the fridge. As she told me, 'it is just something that sits on the fridge … it's just there to hold the school letters and if it broke you would just get another one!' (Interview 2007). Paula demonstrates how, when not kept distinct or 'apart' in the home, as an item from 'afar', together with a changed 'use function', the magnet transforms into something banal, generic and replaceable. Rather than being a treasured memento, its biography develops and with it some of the sacredness of the object is lost. For Blanche, souvenir tea towels likewise lose their significance when they are used. She told me how a tea towel from Chesil Beach in Dorset was 'a rag – just look how well used it is! It's just become a tea towel' (Interview 2009). The statement, 'it's just become a tea towel', suggests it was, at one stage of its life, something else. Thus objects are rarely static, they transform through their temporal and spatial lifecourse (Hoskins 1998, Jones 2002). Paula too, confirmed that tea towels would often lose their special connotations, 'tea towels get used, and eventually they get worn out, don't they?' (Interview 2007).

Paula's observations of how the tea towel transforms also recognises that objects may lose some of the significance of the place of purchase, embedded with them, if they are 'worn out'. This suggests that memories can literally erode away (hence Franscesca's decision to not use one of her bookmarks when 'it started to get worn down', Interview 2007). Arguably preservation of objects enables the maintenance of their cultural meaning. As DeSilvey notes, 'the erosion of physical integrity is associated with a parallel loss of cultural information' (2006: 318).

214   Travel and Transformation

When objects are used, worn or changed through deterioration or breakage, something of the places and times ascribed to them are also lost. Items lose their significance and transform into objects which can then be readily disposed of, no longer treasured objects from 'afar'. As Andy told me, 'yeah, I mean, you buy a keyring then you use it – so obviously in time it gets broken and falls apart and you throw it in the bin' (Andy, Interview 2008). Paula also reflected how, '[t]he magnets, they do tend to get a bit broken with the children, so they just sit on the side, but if they are really broken they will end up in the bin' (Paula, Interview 2007). As such, for Bill and Francesca, who separate their souvenirs from other household items, the passage of time is arrested and the object life is suspended, keeping this object tied firmly to its place of purchase.

However, the transformation of souvenirs – their 'birth, life and death' (Jones 2002: 83) – is part of a cyclical process of accumulation and replacement. For Andy, it is inevitable that memories will fade, and new memories will layer on top of existing ones; that old souvenirs will get damaged and break and new souvenirs will take pride of place. As Andy stated, new objects enter the home, displacing the old:

> I mean, some things are there for a few years and then I dunno, you put them in a box somewhere – out of sight – you know? And you replace it with something else … You still have the memories, (but) once a holiday has gone by, it's in the past, so over the years, with things (souvenirs) you just replace them with something else. So whether it's a holiday or a gig, a trip to the coast in this country [pause] things always get replaced. (Andy, Interview 2008)

This is not to say that the 'old' disappears entirely. As Andy reflects, 'you still have the memories'. Consequently, transformation is not a singular event that occurs when an object enters the home (transforming this space) or when an object transforms (from exceptional to ordinary). Rather, transformation is a complex, multifaceted *process* post-travel. Moreover, use does not always lead to the loss of cultural meaning, but can heighten and cement meaning through incorporation into everyday life. As Kathryn told me:

> I do have other souvenirs of Gozo (aside from glass) – silly little things like calendars and bookmarks which I don't display but are there and used – so everything really is used or displayed so that it is part of my life and my world. (Interview 2007)

Accordingly, the transformation of objects, and the transformation of the home, is always in process, the home and souvenirs being ever remade in relation to each other, and in relation to times and places in the past, present and future.

Indeed, Sarah explained how souvenirs may not only transform in shedding their cultural significance, but take on additional memories and meanings in the home setting. A necklace purchased on holiday and a jumper bought during a weekend away at a music festival picked up additional fragments of other places and spaces where they were worn, assembling within these items a complex mix of various distant locations and times past. As she told me:

> Like – I dunno – it reminds me of other times I've worn it. Other places I've had it on – like special times I've had it on. It's the same with the hoody – I wore it a lot in the first year [of university] and it reminds me of sitting in our rooms in the evening, watching TV and playing guitar and it really reminds me of Claire and Dave and all sitting in my room and playing guitar and generally arsing about until four in the morning! And we used to have a car and go out and drive for miles and miles in the evening and it reminds me of things like that. So it reminds me of the Reading Festival but also reminds me of other times. (Interview, 2008)

Souvenir lives and their affective capacities may therefore follow new routes post-travel that bring together multiple constellations of 'near' and 'far', 'past' and 'present' into a significant object assemblage which, whilst founded on a binary, continually blurs and transcends the home/away division.

Transcendental Transformations

Transcending the home/away binary is essential to understanding the transformative nature of travel. Transformation is itself a processual condition which involves crossing borders and boundaries between 'then' and 'now', 'before' and 'after' (Turner 1977), and as such transformation is not simply a socio-cultural condition which can be linked to travel alone, but also extends and crosses borders into the home. Transformation, then, is as an open-ended *process* (one which does not finish when travel does nor one which can be linked only to being 'away'). The site of home, therefore, is a key space of transformation in the process of travel, when experiences from 'afar' are brought into the sphere of the 'near', combining these spatialities and temporalities in often multiple, complex and shifting constellations. In this chapter, following Larsen (2008) and Lean (2012), I have thus contended that the home is an important site that tourist studies and geography must engage with, given that experiences of travel are fluid and cannot be compressed within the discrete bounded experiences of being 'away'.

In occupying the home space of returned tourists, I have demonstrated how the home and away fold into one another through the material culture of souvenirs. I have thus also contended that a further way to unpack the transformative capacity of travel is to follow recent debates in the social sciences which look beyond the human world and consider this human world as co-composed with the material, more-than-human world of materiality (see Whatmore 2006). Objects have biographies which stretch back into the past and to distant places, and extend into the future. They represent and contain fragments of other times and destinations that they carry with them into new settings, which they lose over the passage of time, or which they replace with new accumulated memories. They both elicit transformative affects in owners, or such affects lessen through a loss of cultural significance in a new setting. Souvenirs, then, are a useful vehicle for exploring the transformative nature of travel and the combining, blurring and merging of 'home' and 'away'. Indeed, souvenir items are vessels which contain, encompass and embody stories of transformation – the 'here' and 'there' – as they transform and are transformed when they enter the spatiality of the home.

References

Adey, P. 2008. Airports, mobility and the calculative architecture of affective control. *Geoforum*, 39(1), 438–51.

Bennett, J. 2001. *The Enchantment of Modern Life: Attachments, Crossings and Ethics*. Princeton: Princeton University Press.

Bennett, J. 2004. The force of things: Steps towards an ecology of matter. *Political Theory*, 32(3), 347–72.

Bennett, J. 2010. *Vibrant Matter: A Political Ecology of Things*. Durham, NC: Duke University Press.

Collins-Kreiner, N. and Zins, Y. 2011. Tourists and souvenirs: Changes through time, space and meaning. *Journal of Heritage Tourism*, 6(1), 17–27.

DeSilvey, C. 2006. Observed decay: Telling stories with mutable things. *Journal of Material Culture*, 11(3), 318–38.

Gordon, B. 1986. The souvenir: Messenger of the extraordinary. *Journal of Popular Culture*, 20(3), 135–46.

Gosden, C. and Marshall, Y. 1999. The cultural biography of objects. *World Archaeology*, 31(2), 169–78.

Goss, J. 2005. The souvenir and sacrifice in the tourist mode of consumption, in *Seductions of Place: Geographical Perspectives on Globalisation and Touristed Landscapes*, edited by C. Cartier and A.A. Lew. Abingdon: Routledge, 56–71.

Healey, R.G. 1994. Tourist merchandise as a means of generating local benefits from ecotourism. *Journal of Sustainable Tourism*, 2(3), 137–51.

Hoskins, J. 1998. *Biographical Objects: How Things Tell the Stories of People's Lives*. London: Routledge.

Hume, D.L. 2008. The development of tourist art and souvenirs – the arc of the boomerang: From hunting, fighting and ceremony to tourist souvenir. *International Journal of Tourism Research*, 11(1), 55–70.

Jackson, P. 2000. Rematerializing social and cultural geography. *Social and Cultural Geography*, 1(1), 9–14.

Jones, A. 2002. *Archaeological Theory and Scientific Practice*. Cambridge: Cambridge University Press.

Kim, S. and Littrell, M.A. 2001. Souvenir buying intentions for self versus others. *Annals of Tourism Research*, 28(3), 638–57.

Kopytoff, I. 1988. The cultural biography of things: commoditization as process, in *The Social Life of Things: Commodities in Cultural Perspective*, edited by A. Appadurai. Cambridge: Cambridge University Press, 64–91.

Larsen, J. 2008. De-exoticising tourist travel: Everyday life and sociality on the move. *Leisure Studies*, 27(1), 21–34.

Latour, B. 2005. *Reassembling the Social: An Introduction to Actor-network Theory*. Oxford: Oxford University Press.

Lean, G. 2012. The lingering moment, in *The Cultural Moment in Tourism*, edited by L. Smith, E. Waterton and S. Watson. London: Routledge, 274–90.

Love, L.L. and Kohn, N. 2001. This, that and the other: Fraught possibilities of the souvenir. *Text and Performance Quarterly*, 21(1), 47–63.

Love, L.L. and Sheldon, P.S. 1998. Souvenirs: Messengers of meaning. *Advances in Consumer Research*, 25, 170–75.

MacCannell, D. 1999. *The Tourist: A New Theory of the Leisure Class*. Berkeley: University of California Press.

Marx, K. 2010. *Capital: Volume 1: Section 4: The Fetishism of Commodities and the Secret Thereof*. [Online]. Available at: www.marxists.org/archive/,arex/works/1867-ul/chol.htm#54 [accessed: 10 September 2010].

Massey, D. 1997. A global sense of place, in *Reading Human Geography: The Poetics and Politics of Enquiry*, edited by D. Gregory and T. Barnes. London: Arnold, 315–23.

Miller, D. 1998. *A Theory of Shopping*. Oxford: Polity Press.

Morgan, N. and Pritchard, A. 2005. On souvenirs and metonymy: Narratives of memory, metaphor and materiality. *Tourist Studies*, 5(1), 29–53.

Nicolson, A. 2007. War on tat. *The Daily Telegraph, Travel Supplement*, 23 June, 1–2.

Peters, K. 2011. Negotiating the 'place' and 'placement' of banal tourist souvenirs in the home. *Tourism Geographies*, 13(2), 234–56.

Pile, S. 2010. Emotions and affect in recent human geography. *Transactions of the Institute of British Geographers*, 35(1), 5–20.

Preston, B. 2006. The case of the recalcitrant prototype, in *Doing Things with Things: The Design and Use of Everyday Objects*, edited by A. Costall and O. Dreier. Aldershot: Ashgate, 15–28.

Ramsay, N. 2009. Taking-place: refracted enchantment and the habitual spaces of the tourist souvenir. *Social and Cultural Geography*, 10(2), 197–217.

Soja, E. 1996. *Thirdspace: Journeys to Los Angeles and Other Real-and-Imagined Places*. Oxford: Blackwell.

Swanson, K.K. and Horridge, P.E. 2006. Travel motivations as souvenir purchase indicators. *Tourism Management*, 27(4), 671–83.

Thrift, N. 2004. Intensities of feeling: Towards a politics of affect. *Geografiska Annaler B*, 86(1), 57–78.

Tolia-Kelly, D. 2013. The geographies of cultural geography III: Material geographies, vibrant matters and risking surface geographies. *Progress in Human Geography*, 37(1), 153–60.

Turner, V. 1977. Variations on a theme of liminality, in *Secular Ritual*, edited by S.F. Moore and B.G Myerhoff. Amsterdam: Van Forcum Assen, 36–52.

Watts, M. 1999. Commodities, in *Introducing Human Geographies*, edited by P. Cloke, P. Crang and M. Goodwin. London: Arnold, 114–21.

Whatmore, S. 2001. *Hybrid Geographies: Natures, Cultures, Spaces*. London: SAGE.

Whatmore, S. 2006. Materialist returns: Practising cultural geography in and for a more-than-human world. *Cultural Geographies*, 13(4), 600–9.

Wilkins, H. 2011. Souvenirs: What and why we buy. *Journal of Travel Research*, 50(3), 239–47.

Conclusions

Conclusions

Chapter 14
Lasting Impressions

Garth Lean, Russell Staiff and Emma Waterton

Three Stories of Travel and Transformation

Entwinement (Garth's Reflection)

It's hard to know who I'd be without travel. It has come to pervade my life. Not a day seems to pass that I don't think about it, reflect upon it, read about it, write about it, talk about it or 'see' it. It is an interesting irony, then, that my interest in travel is so great that I now spend more time thinking and writing about it than physically 'doing it'. I wasn't always so captivated by travel, however. There was a time when I had no interest in it at all – well, at least, not in 'performing' it. This began to change in 2002 when I found myself studying tourism, with no real ambition, at the University of Western Sydney. I had only gained access to university through an early admissions programme that didn't consider final examination results; this place ended up being my only option as, after losing interest in my final year of secondary school, I didn't have the marks to apply for anything else through the regular entrance pathways. I deferred university in the hope that I could forge a career that wouldn't require further study. After several months of unemployment, I spent the remainder of my travel-less gap-year working in the medical records room of a Sydney hospital.

I was in a dark place when, as a last resort, I finally turned up to university. After a month of looking for ways to escape, something clicked. The subject matter was interesting, the lecturers kind, inspiring, engaging and supportive and a deep-seated, yet temporarily submerged, fixation with the geographical melded well with the themes explored in the environmental management and tourism degree. I read widely and studied a variety of media related to the themes explored, including conscientiously watching travel programmes. The degree was my first fling with travel, albeit a theoretical one.

The next key moment was a final year project that I completed in 2004 for a local government in Sydney's northwest. They were interested in developing a relationship with East Timor – at that time, the 'newest nation' on Earth. I researched and wrote a report on the possibility of aiding sustainable tourism development within the country and this ignited a personal interest in the concept of 'poverty alleviation through tourism', which was emerging as a popular theme in tourism scholarship at the time. As such, in 2005, I decided to make this a focus of my year-long honours undergraduate research project. This topic quickly changed, however, as I noticed that, in relation to traveller activities, the literature had a preoccupation with the moment of travel itself, with little about how tourists/travellers could 'alleviate poverty' upon their return. This got me thinking about how tourism could be used as a tool for changing attitudes and behaviours in line with sustainability ideals and I spent the next few months using a purpose built website and email interviews to collect accounts of people who had been 'transformed by travel'. With little thought, but with tremendous benefit for the project, I had chosen to use the word 'travel' instead of 'tourism', and to provide a separate data form to capture all changes/transformations, in addition to those related to sustainability. As a consequence, I received an overwhelming collection of accounts from 61 individuals who had travelled to all corners of the Earth and who had been moved by travel in all manner of ways. At the same time, after a year of full-time work and study, I found myself again spiralling into a dark place. Worried by how low I may go this time, and with the powerful stories of my participants' transformations through travel reverberating in my head, I knew I only had one choice. In a brief moment of brightness, I booked my ticket to fly to East Timor in a week's time.

Aside from the extreme anxiety faced leading up to leaving, and in the first few hours of what was both my first solo travel and first trip to a developing country (let alone the poorest country in Asia), the journey was an amazing one in which I discovered a contentment unlike any previously experienced. I knew I had to continue my investigation of transformative travel as a PhD and, above all, I knew I had to continue travelling. And so over the course of the next few years I found myself traversing Thailand, Cambodia, Laos, Vietnam, France, Niger, Benin, Togo, Burkina Faso, Mali, Cote d'Ivoire, England, Germany and Vanuatu in a quest to understand the complexities of transformation through travel.

* * *

When people find out about my project, they're often curious to know if I've been transformed by travel myself. This question had, however, always sat uneasily. As much as I had been affected by my travels, I had never felt any lasting changes or association with something as strong as 'transformation'. While I believed a few changes of thinking and behaviour had clung upon my return, for the most part they seemed to fall by the wayside as more pertinent concerns came to the fore. It wasn't until penning the conclusion to my PhD thesis that I could see that I had indeed been changed by travel, but not necessarily as it is most commonly conceptualised as physical movement from one location to another. My personal transformations have come through study, social interactions, various roles, performances and engagement with representations and media. Corporeal travel has been directly and indirectly entwined in all of these journeys. My travels to 'exotic' locales had changed the way I saw myself, my ambitions, relationships, conversations, life narrative, work and the way I marked the spaces I inhabited upon my return. It seemed problematic, however, to disentangle these changes from the plethora of other travels/mobilities that had contributed, not only to these shifts, but to every aspect of my being.

Not Always a Happy Ending (Russell's Reflection)

Transformations are rarely straightforward except, perhaps, in retrospect; and they are inevitably complex and sometimes ambiguous in meaning and effect. The story of Kye, a young graduate from the north of the Lao People's Democratic Republic, embodies this ambiguity. I first met Kye (not his real name) in an antique shop in Luang Prabang, the former royal capital of Laos and now a World Heritage site. He explained to me the significance of the wooden Buddha sculptures he was selling. I was intrigued, but somewhat sceptical about the tale of 're-discovered' antique Buddhas found in nearby caves (see Staiff and Bushell 2013). From this initial conversation our paths crossed many times and eventually my research colleague and I employed him for translation and research assistance on a project we were conducting in Luang Prabang. Kye's story is one of profound transformation through travel.

Kye grew up in a very poor village in the northern province of Bakeo, the youngest of seven children. After finishing high school he was sent by his family to Luang Prabang (a two-day boat trip down the Mekong) to teachers' college to become a high school English teacher. As he tells it, Luang Prabang, a town of about 24,000 people, was a revelation to him. He had never experienced any urban centre of this size and certainly no town that had 32 monasteries and a population of 1,000 monks and novices. The excitement and the range of possibilities offered by this bustling urban settlement, with its ever-growing number of international visitors, was an eye-opening, challenging and emotional experience for him, particularly after the quiet and hard farming life in his small rural village. His studies and part-time work in Luang Prabang (in the tourism industry) permanently extended his outlook and his contact with international, mostly Western, tourists, along with his mobile phone and the Internet, connected him to his home village and his family and, significantly, to other parts of the world.

I took Kye to Bangkok for a medical test. It was an intense and memorable journey for us both: for Kye, his first trip outside of Laos and for me the experience of observing Kye. He had never flown in a plane. He had never seen a plane bigger than a twin-propeller ATR-72. He had never seen a building the size of Bangkok's Suvarnabhumi Airport. He had never seen or experienced an escalator or a lift. He had never seen a super highway, let alone motorways rising high above the city-streets below, with multiple lanes and only cars and bigger vehicles and no motorbikes. The tall, densely clustered buildings in the Sukhumvit area of Bangkok left him awe-struck. Hotel doors with no keys but a card that one tapped on the door to open it and a room where the lights came on automatically on entry seemed impossible feats. Bangkok's sky-train public transport system, the scale and density of the city, the opulent display of wealth, the vast shopping malls like Siam Paragon with its internal lakes, gardens and soaring atriums, the experience of going to a cinema for the first time, a book shop with thousands of volumes, go-go bars and strip joints, these were all completely new and quite astonishing to Kye. The hospital we attended was vast and more in keeping with a four-star hotel (the medical clinics in Luang Prabang are extremely poorly resourced and, in comparison, quite Dickensian). Often I would catch him, day and night, sitting cross-legged on the carpet staring out the ceiling-to-floor windows of the sixteenth-floor hotel room with its panoramic views of the city. He would say quietly, 'this is amazing'. He frenetically photographed everything as though it may all disappear.

Later I asked him about his trip to Bangkok and he said it was both a life-changing unveiling and it was disturbing, so big, so fast, so crowded, so impersonal and maybe too exciting. It also made him sad, he said, because it seemed to offer something his country could not, Laos being so poor. He was also deeply affected by the restlessness the trip had provoked in him, knowing there was such a different world just across the border. For the first time in his life he doubted his ambition to be a high school teacher 'locked away' in a remote rural community earning a pittance. He became confused about his direction in life. And this led him to seek other opportunities in Luang Prabang. Kye became involved with the management of the Luang Prabang International Film Festival that, in turn, won him a scholarship to Germany to attend the Berlin Film Festival and attend a film festival management workshop for people from developing countries. It was his first trip to the West and in the depths of winter. And it was another powerful life-enhancing experience.

Kye is now deeply ambiguous about his experiences. He cannot, he said, go back and live a contented life in a village in northern Laos as a schoolteacher. He does not want to leave Luang Prabang because there are opportunities there, but to remain means he's separated from his family and in Luang Prabang his future is riven with unknowns. There's no longer a clear path forward. He is restless and distracted. The job and lifestyle that match his experiences elsewhere increasingly seem unattainable to him. The transformations instigated by intersecting travel itineraries (the Westerners he meets who travel to Luang Prabang, the ex-pat community living in Luang Prabang with its global connections and Kye's travels outside Laos) are both exalting and enlightening but equally they have left changes that cannot be easily erased. Today, Kye is unlike the confident and idealistic young man I first met; he is now plagued with doubts and feels caught between desire and reality.

A Professional Life, Set in Motion (Emma's Reflection)

Putting together an academic call for papers about travel and transformation is one thing; reflecting on the way those two words can affect a life – my life – is quite another. I seemed to stumble at the first hurdle, stalled because I couldn't fathom a way to claim 'transformation' by travel when I can't remember myself without it. I first went 'overseas' at the age of two; a year later, my family moved across the world, from England to Hong Kong. In the 30-odd years since then,

I have travelled domestically and internationally numerous times a year. It has almost become a habit; rarely have I felt unsettled by travel as a consequence. Of course, there have been some shocking times along the way – moments punctuated by outrageous humour, pleasure, unexpected trauma, boredom and so on. For example, as an eight-year-old I was shaken rather badly when a man stubbed his cigarette out on my shoulder. Deliberately. He did it in the hopes that my cries of pain would distract my mother long enough for him to mug her. My memories of Nairobi (where we were at the time), my taste for Wimpy's burgers (we were strolling towards the restaurant near Nairobi Central when it happened), and my impressions of my father (as I saw him lift himself out of his everyday 'self' and sprint after the mugger) were all transformed directly by that event. Even my skin was transformed; literally. I wear a permanent scar on my shoulder, a reminder in the form of a raised bump that periodically catches my eye in the mirror. Such moments can certainly knock us about, but for the most part we take the hit and settle back as quickly as we can into our everyday lives.

But we can often find transformation in less cataclysmic contexts, too. We might find it in seemingly skittish moments which turn out to have a slow-burning intensity, one that murmurs away for years, labouring and working away at our 'selves' just beneath the surface. Maybe we can all find those moments of change, transformation, if pressed into thinking about such things more carefully. Perhaps, if we scrutinise the various memories of our travels, we can spot those moments, pressure points we might call them, during which time certain things came together and set us in motion. Their significance may not lie in any immediate alterations or altercations but in their silent energy, which subtly affects the way we think or do things: loose recollections of a certain place, taste, smell, museum collection, postcard, landscape or conversation with a stranger. For anybody else, those moments might quickly be forgotten; but for us, for you or for me, they tangle together in a way that is far heavier and more compelling, sliding across and through our surfaces for so long that they, quite simply, endure.

I scanned my own personal pockets of memory many times while working on this volume. Each time, my mind's eye seemed always to shift and settle on a trip I took to Kobe, Japan, in 1999 to compete in a karate tournament. I was there for two weeks. In addition to competing, I travelled leisurely from Kyoto to Hiroshima (and back) as a tourist with a small group of Australians and British. I remember a great deal about that trip but one particular 'scene' has gathered itself together and hardened into something that for me has a power that reaches far beyond that of most of my other travel stories. I've replayed that scene endlessly to myself ever since, especially in recent years. Each time I wait for some kind of satisfying ending; it is yet to come because there is something about that memory that I have never managed to shake off. Yet, while it never ends the memory always begins in the same way: our group, standing excitedly on a busy train heading into Hiroshima. Our first stop that day was the Hiroshima Peace Memorial Park, specifically the Hiroshima Peace Memorial Museum housed within it. In years to come, heritage and museums would become a firm fixture in my professional life, but at that time I was a very recent graduate from the University of Queensland with quite an eclectic Bachelor of Arts degree. As such, I entered the museum freed from the academic baggage I now carry with me. I also entered it, I'm ashamed to say, with very little thought for what I might find inside. And so I remember quite clearly walking through the first few exhibitions within the museum, one of which revolved around an illuminated map. I was equipped with only the flimsiest will to learn, to know, and I remember strolling (so casually) past different displays, my eyes roaming lazily from one interpretation board to the next.

I then remember seeing a small section of a wall and two adjoining steps. Both bore battle scars, but impressed into their fabric there was something else: a smudge, a smear, a shadow. In a rush I realised that those markings were all that were left of a man who had been sitting on those steps as the heat of an atomic bomb engulfed the city around him. The room came to a complete stop in that moment – for me, at least. I remember taking a few moments, to blink, to register, to digest, to catch up: what I was seeing? Where was everyone else? Who could possibly explain this to me? And it wasn't only my mind that raced. My body was interrupted, too, in ways I hesitate – still – to put into words, other than to say that my body filled and roiled with a haze of sensations. I must have looked quite wild in those moments, realisation and disbelief chasing their way across my face. I turned then and left: shocked and without an ending.

Writing this now, I know that something happened in that museum: something about that visit got under my skin on a very personal level. I'm not sure if it continues to affect my travelling companions like it continues to affect me, but I'm certain I sensed it radiating from them at the time. Ever since then, something about that visit has followed me around in my professional life, too. And once those memories had dug their way in they stuck, assembling themselves over and over again in various academic contexts, charging my interest in dissonant histories and their contemporary affects. In 1999, when I had just finished my undergraduate degree, I didn't have the vocabulary to name what I was experiencing. All I knew was that the day had not unfolded as I expected it to. Only more recently have I begun to really recognise that moment, to see it more clearly as a pressure point that moved me to react, to change and head towards a career I had never, not for one moment, seen coming.

Future Directions

We chose to start this closing chapter with our own personal vignettes, written independently and without discussion. Our hope was that three distinctly positioned reflections would emerge; yes, we anticipated a small amount of overlap, but given our different backgrounds and stages in life we felt certain that their differences would be far more pronounced than their similarities. Reading over them as a collective, however, we were struck by one significant commonality: all three of us had struggled to really name 'that' moment, that precise point of change. There remains something tantalisingly unsayable about the process of transformation. Perhaps that is because those moments are simply too difficult to put into words; they take shape easily enough in our bodies and minds, but click like peppermints against our teeth when we try to reshape them into words and get them out. While this may at first seem like an oddly defeatist observation to close a volume focused on transformation with, we are by contrast firmly optimistic about it. Indeed, re-reading each contribution to this volume has allowed us to take better stock of the academic landscape; and what this has revealed is that there is still a great deal of richness to pursue in the area, a richness that will undoubtedly advance debate on broader theorisations of transformation, not only within tourism studies, but geography, sociology, heritage studies, literary studies, history, philosophy and cultural studies, too.

This optimism, however, does not preclude some editorial attempts to draw out key themes and point to what we see as clear future directions in terms of continued research. It is with these particular challenges in mind that we have taken an opportunity here to lay down our thoughts on where these elusory intimations might take us theoretically. As was the case in an earlier volume we edited together, *Travel and Imagination*, also in this book series (Lean et al. 2014), our first instinct is to point to any significant holes that remain in the overarching literature. Then, as now, we argue that there is an ongoing need for scholarship that considers travel from perspectives that extend beyond the 'Western' lens with which we are currently more familiar. In this regard, Tim Winter's (2007, 2009a, 2009b) work on heritage and tourism in Asia continues to be a strong influence, especially his persistent calls for the academy to find ways to engage with non-English language scholarship and thus account for a more nuanced understanding of tourism practices and industry. Though Winter's own work deals primarily with tourism in Asia, his broader purpose is to extend his call much further beyond the Western academy to include those working in other regions outside of the West, such as the Middle East, Latin America and the African continent. While such a task would undoubtedly be a disparate and challenging one, encumbered with the need to speak, read and write in multiple different languages (thus pushing us far beyond the parameters of this particular project), it would do much to pad out the still patchy understanding we have of the ways people are moved to transform through, and be affected by, travel.

In *Travel and Imagination* we also argued that research, writing and thinking needs to recognise a variety of different collectives (including differently gendered, classed, religiously-inclined, cultural and minority groups), especially those whose voices are not always well represented, if at all. The same holds true for those of us researching the transformation of individuals, societies and cultures brought about by corporeal travel. This volume has made a great deal of progress in this respect, with Sazzad (Chapter 6) and Walsh (Chapter 7) considering Palestinian and African perspectives respectively, and Mannik (Chapter 9) looking at refugees and migrants. All three chapters bring into focus a range of social and cultural groups often neglected in the literature. But, that said, there still remains a vital need for more scholarship that allows for a greater diversity of people to express their own viewpoints, with their own voices – irrespective of the power imbalances that currently do not work in their favour.

Closely tied to this is the need to look at a wide variety of physical mobilities that extend beyond leisure travel and, most importantly, the intersections of these travels, rather than studying them as separate entities. In this regard, the current volume has done well, as in it are reflected the perspectives of 'tourists' (Baker (Prelude) and Peters (Chapter 13)), backpackers (Allon and Koleth (Chapter 4) and Matthews (Chapter 10)), lifestyle travellers (Anderson and Erskine (Chapter 2)), spiritual travellers/pilgrims (Leggett (Chapter 5), Dawney (Chapter 8)), migrants/refugees (Walsh (Chapter 7) and Mannik (Chapter 9), medical tourists/travellers (Jones et al. (Chapter 12), walkers (Dawney (Chapter 8) and Rodigari (Chapter 11)), returnees (Walsh (Chapter 7) and Peters (Chapter 13)), an exile (Sazzad (Chapter 6)) a homeless/inner-city nomad (Walsh (Chapter 7)) and a performance artist (Rodigari (Chapter 11)). All of these divergent, yet related, forms of physical mobility have in some way been brought into conversation. Despite the diversity presented here, of course, there still remain many other forms of physical mobility that can, and should, be incorporated within any continuing discussions of transformation. For example, we are mindful that our own volume failed to capture reflections on transformation triggered by travelling as part of the military or a sporting team, working abroad or as a consequence of slavery and human trafficking, as well as the more mundane forces of change associated with our ordinary lives, such as daily commutes to and from work. This is a list that, given half a chance, could become unwieldy in a matter of moments.

Processes of transformation are at work not only when we travel physically, as many of our contributors have been at pains to suggest, but when we are moved in more metaphorical senses, too, and find ourselves in circumstances animated by less tangible forms of composition. Opening things up beyond *literal* movement means that there is simultaneously a need to more carefully observe the intersections of non-physical travels (and resultant transformations) and their relationships to physical journeys and transformation. While these are directly and indirectly touched upon throughout all of the chapters in this book (it is impossible not to given that they are so intimately tied to corporeal mobility), we are nonetheless compelled to suggest that greater attention, still, needs to be paid to communicative, virtual and imaginative mobilities, along with the movement of objects, ideas, concepts, discourses and so forth.

It has probably not escaped notice to this point that we have seemingly been at pains to avoid using the term 'tourism' – ours is a book about transformative *travel*, after all. At this juncture, then, it seems important to address this head on and outline what we see as a concerning trend within commentaries and scholarship observing transformation through travel. While this may seem like a concern we have already passed judgement on and now wear metaphorically on the 'sleeve' of this book, we remain acutely concerned by this continuing dialectic. Indeed, it seems to us that 'travel' has come to be privileged over 'tourism', with the former defined as a niche of tourism. A significant consequence has been the associated figure of the 'true traveller', who is seen as an individual that engages with people, avoids big hotels, eats local food and does not travel on package tours. Those independent experiences, or so the assumption goes, lend themselves to greater engagements with the 'unfamiliar' and thus a heightened opportunity of transformation. The endgame of these sorts of assumptions is the proposition that forms of travel that are qualitatively *not* like that, such as 'mass tourism' and 'business tourism', will fail to bring about transformation (see Reisinger 2013: 29). We see these kinds of hierarchical distinctions as ultimately constraining and thus unhelpful for broad explorations of transformation through travel, not to mention the problematic, and outdated, nature of a typology-centred analysis (see Franklin 2007, Franklin and Crang 2001, Robinson and Jamal 2009, among others, for a critique of this approach to the study of tourism and travel).

Our decision to prioritise the term 'travel', then, has rather less to do with any misconceived ideas about the relative worth of either term in a comparative sense and more to do with the pragmatics of scope. Travel is the broader concept, quite simply. When casting its net at its widest, it refers to movement from one point to another, with tourism imagined as only one small component of the more fulsome travel spectrum (Lean 2012). And we believe that all forms of travel ought to be granted attention in the investigation of travel and transformation. Importantly, as shown by Sazzad (Chapter 6), Walsh (Chapter 7) and Mannik (Chapter 9), travel is not always leisurely, or strictly voluntary: forced, involuntary and non-leisurely journeys may be some of the most transformative. In addition, while there may indeed be elements that lead to a greater likelihood of transformation, these are unique for every 'traveller' and we argue that any form of mobility (physical or otherwise) is potentially transformative for individuals, social and cultural groupings, places, spaces and/or landscapes. Transformation through travel is complex and unpredictable, and innumerable elements 'before', 'during' and 'after' travel may influence, or not, a traveller for a wide variety of reasons. Albeit to varying degrees, these elements (such as social relationships, roles, routines, performances, multi-sensory experiences, imaginings and random happenings, to name only a few) that relate to transformation are present within all forms of travel (regardless of destination, purpose/intention and whether international, domestic or in daily routines) (see Lean 2012 for an extended exploration of these factors). What is more, even in the most 'unfamiliar' of places, familiarity can be present: familiar travel companions, conversations, performances, food, drink, hierarchical/colonial/power interactions/relations, the clothing and objects that we carry and, at the very least, our mind and its conscious, and sub-conscious, memories, thoughts and imaginings. As Alain de Botton quips in *The Art of Travel* (2002: n.p.), 'it seems that our suitcases are not the only baggage we're fated to bring with us'. And, of course, on the flipside, courtesy of inhabiting a mobile world, it is increasingly possible to encounter the 'unfamiliar' within the 'familiar'.

And so we shift our attention to the notion of 'transformation'. No matter how the term transformation is used, whether as personal experience, whether idealistic, hopeful or the effect/affect of a disastrous turn of events, whether deliberately sought and purposely plotted or whether an act of circumstance, of happenstance, there remains one overriding spectre that haunts the whole discourse about travel and transformation: why is the very *idea* of transformation conjured at all? While we speculated about a deep affinity with modernism/ postmodernism in the Introduction by illustrating how profoundly various (Western) modernism(s) informed the analytic of the writers represented in this volume, and while we have intimated that there are cultural resonances and tropes with long histories and numerous re-articulations and re-workings that provide the description under which we live/understand, there remains the question of why 'transformation' has currency, why it seems to do the analytical work we desire, why it seems to capture the imagination as an analytical possibility, as a way of thinking travel.

Why couldn't the chapters in this volume exist under the rubric of 'movement' or 'mobility' or 'change'? For the writers, and for us, these words are somehow inadequate; they fail to capture some essential ingredient, some profundity that we all feel works its way into particular travel scenarios. Why this lack in commonplace words like 'movement', 'change' and 'mobility'? What does this perceived lack of profundity encapsulate? Fear? Hope? Is it the desire to re-invent our lives and our worlds; is it the need for autonomy, individuality, personal freedom and a sense of being in control (or its opposite, of giving ourselves to what our forebears would have called fate)? Is it seeking answers? Is it the desire for something called 'wholeness' in a fractured, discordant and disenchanted world of splintered identities? No matter how we phrase this belief/observation that travel is not just movement or mobility or change, the modernist/modernism inescapably erupts into the space we have created by the question. We are both intrigued by this and, at the same time, vaguely concerned that we cannot seem to escape from the discourses within which our project is conceived and pursued. Look at the language of the opening pages of the Introduction: self, quest, migrate, explore, learn, enlighten, alter, discover, seeking the novel and so on.

While 'travel and transformation' is of our time and ensnared, necessarily, in discourses with which we are familiar, is there any legible horizon of where this thinking might now go? Two possibilities immediately present themselves. One is *desire* itself, a contemporary theoretical analytic, and another is *metamorphoses*, a more historically and spatially defined project. As Derrida might have argued, desire is travel/transformation's blind spot, essential to *thinking* it and *knowing* it, deep in its conceptual DNA, but often not interrogated as crucial, stated but not as a central analytic (Derrida 1982). In relation to theory, Lacan wrote that 'it is at the level of desire that we will be able to find the answer' (Lacan 1986: 160). While we are not so optimistic, we do believe that desire offers a means of invigorating the travel/transformation linkage. This is work to be done and psychoanalytic theory, beginning with Lacan (1986), and discourse theory, beginning with Derrida (1982, 1987), offer a variety of avenues for this task (see Fuery 1995). For Lacan, desire, that inexpressible something that was best represented in a terms like *jouissance*, famously without an adequate translation in English, was modal in nature and could be understood in four modal interconnections: subjectivity, signification, cultural production and in the analytic processes themselves. Lacan's subject driven by desire, subject inseparable from desire, is compelled towards the 'other' via the 'symbolic' (the social world of language and culture). It is in these folds that we perceive the travel/transformation entwining that is not just 'merely' movement or change. Desire for Lacan is foundational to being. Derrida goes further. Desire cannot, by definition, be satisfied; it is always marked by non-arrival (and Derrida is most eloquent about this quality in his study of postcards) (Derrida 1987). Desire is the great activator and the great anticipator, but what it activates and what it anticipates is perpetually deferred. Importantly, the hope we have noted under the sign of many of the travel/transformation renderings is not privileged at all in this calculus. Marginalisation, transgression, instability, abjection, and so on, all figure in these elucidations (Fuery 1995). In relation to travel/transformation it is perhaps worth concluding with the observations Deleuze and Guattari make about desire:

> For it is a matter of flows, of stocks, of breaks and fluctuations of flows; desire is present wherever something flows and runs, carrying along with it interested subjects – but also drunken or slumbering subjects – towards lethal destinations. It is a problem of desire, and desire is part of the infrastructure. (Deleuze and Guattari 2004: 115)

By using the word 'metamorphosis' instead of transformation we conjure something that is historical, cultural and geographical in ways 'transformation' does not. The recent interest in Ovid's *Metamorphosis* is the clue (Hardie 2006). The Roman epic has a long history of influence in Western culture and is highly suggestive in its intricate workings of myth, religion, history and its concerns with love, violence, art, power and of course mutability. The opening lines of the epic poem announce the subject: 'I intend to speak of forms changed into new entities' (Ovid, Book 1, lines 1–2). By evoking the Ovid epic we are gesturing to deep cultural resonances in the notion of transformation and raising the possibility of its symbolic power born of intertextuality, performance/ritual, spirituality and the geography of cultural roots/routes. Ovid immediately locates us within and expresses Western thought and imagery. Christianity expresses the most profound of transformations – transubstantiation – in its Roman Catholic and Orthodox rites. Hinduism and Buddhism in their own different ways express it too. Travel and transformation does not come from nowhere. It is deeply laced with the symbolic and powerfully operates in the sign-ordered economy. But as we have suggested elsewhere, there are cultural geographies involved. Thus it seems that a historical, cultural and spatial project may be another way to unlock the analytic possibilities of the travel and transformation dyad.

232 *Travel and Transformation*

References

de Botton, A. 2002. *The Art of Travel*. London: Hamish Hamilton.
Deleuze, G. and Guattari, F. 2004. *Anti-Oedipus*. Originally published in 1984. Translated by R. Hurley, M. Seem and H. Lane. London: Continuum.
Derrida, J. 1982. *Margins of Philosophy*. Translated by A. Bass. Chicago: Chicago University Press.
Derrida, J. 1987. *The Post Card: From Socrates to Freud and Beyond*. Translated by A. Bass. Chicago: Chicago University Press.
Franklin, A. 2007. The problem with tourism theory, in *The Critical Turn in Tourism Studies: Innovative Research Methodologies*, edited by I. Ateljevic, A. Pritchard and N. Morgan. Oxford: Elsevier, 131–48.
Franklin, A. and Crang, M. 2001. The trouble with tourism and travel theory. *Tourist Studies*, 1(1), 5–22.
Fuery, P. 1995. *Theories of Desire*. Melbourne: Melbourne University Press.
Hardie, P. (ed.) 2006. *The Cambridge Companion to Ovid*. Cambridge: Cambridge University Press.
Lacan, J. 1986. *The Four Fundamental Concepts of Psycho-Analysis*. Translated by A. Sheridan. Penguin: Harmondsworth.
Lean, G.L. 2012. Transformative travel: A mobiliities perspective. *Tourist Studies*, 12(2), 151–72.
Lean, G., Staiff, R. and Waterton, E. (eds) 2014. *Travel and Imagination*. Farnham: Ashgate.
Ovid. 2004. *Metamorphoses*. Translated by D. Raeburn. London: Penguin.
Reisinger, Y. (ed.) 2013. *Transformational Tourism: Tourist Perspectives*. Wallingford: CABI.
Robinson, M. and Jamal, T. 2009. Conclusions: Tourism studies – past omissions, emergent challenges, in *The Sage Handbook of Tourism Studies*, edited by T. Jamal and M. Robinson. London: SAGE, 693–701.
Staiff, R. and Bushell, R. 2013. Souvenirs at the margin? Place, commodities, transformations and the symbolic in Buddha sculptures from Luang Prabang, Laos, in *Tourism and Souvenirs: Glocal Perspectives from the Margins*, edited by J. Cave, L. Jolliffe and T. Baum. Bristol: Channel View Publications, 82–97.
Winter, T. 2007. *Post-Conflict Heritage, Postcolonial Tourism: Tourism, Politics and Development at Angkor*. Abingdon: Routledge.
Winter, T. 2009a. Asian tourism and the retreat of Anglo-Western centrism in tourism theory. *Current Issues in Tourism*, 12(1), 21–31.
Winter, T. 2009b. The modernities of heritage and tourism: interpretations of an Asian future. *Journal of Heritage Tourism*, 4(2), 105–15.

Documentary References

The Art of Travel (dir. Neil Crombie, 2005).

Index

For Product Safety Concerns and Information please contact our
EU representative GPSR@taylorandfrancis.com
Taylor & Francis
Verlag GmbH, Kaufingerstraße 24, 80331 München, Germany